The New French Philosophy

In memory of Ann and Alan Deyermond

The New French Philosophy

Ian James

polity

First published in 2012 by Polity Press

Polity Press
65 Bridge Street
Cambridge CB2 1UR, UK

Polity Press
350 Main Street
Malden, MA 02148, USA

ISBN-13: 978-0-7456-4805-7
ISBN-13: 978-0-7456-4806-4(pb)

A catalogue record for this book is available from the British Library.

Typeset in 10.5 on 12 pt Times Ten
by Toppan Best-set Premedia Limited
Printed and bound in Great Britain by MPG Books Group Limited

For further information on Polity, visit our website: www.politybooks.com

Contents

Acknowledgements

I would like to offer my warm thanks to all those who have helped with the production of this work, in particular Sarah Lambert at Polity Press. Special thanks are also due to John Thompson, who commissioned this project and to the three anonymous readers of the manuscript whose comments were of enormous help in the production of the final draft. For the various ways in which they have helped, supported or inspired, I would like to thank Martin Crowley, Barry Everitt, Gail Ferguson, Alison Finch, Peter Hallward, Leslie Hill, Michael Holland, Christina Howells, Jonathan Miles, Gerald Moore, John Mullarkey, Hannes Opelz, Dan Smith, Chris Watkin, James Williams and Emma Wilson. In particular, I would like to extend special thanks to Andrew Benjamin, Adriana Cavarero, Griselda Pollock, Max Silverman and Samuel Weber for helping me to formulate some key issues at a decisive moment in the completion of this work. I am also very grateful to the University of Cambridge and to Downing College for the period of research leave which allowed me to complete this book. I would like to express my infinite gratitude to Ruth Deyermond, without whose support, both intellectual and personal, it would not have been possible to research and complete this project. Lastly, I would like to dedicate this book to the memory of Ann and Alan Deyermond, whose generosity, warmth and kindness are greatly missed.

Introduction: The Demands of Thought

To speak of the 'New French Philosophy' is to make the claim that thought may have decisively transformed or renewed itself. It affirms a discontinuity or rupture, a break between a thinking which came before and one which comes after. Such a claim immediately raises a number of different questions which are themselves philosophical: questions relating to the very possibility of novelty itself, to causality and determinism, or to the nature of transformation or change.[1] It also raises questions relating to the distinctiveness or identity of a specifically French, rather than, say, a broader European, philosophy and to the possibility of aligning a diverse range of thinkers according to a shared logic or paradigm of renewal.

To complicate matters further the question of the 'new' has also been one of the central preoccupations of French philosophy itself since at least the 1960s.[2] As the American philosopher Dan Smith has shown, the conditions or the production of the 'new' is a key concern of Gilles Deleuze's philosophy of difference and, as Deleuze himself suggested on a number of occasions, one of the fundamental questions posed more generally by his contemporaries (Smith 2007: 1, 19 n. 2). This is easily borne out with reference to the other major figures of French philosophy who rose to prominence in the 1960s and then came to dominate French thought in the decades which followed; figures such as, for example, Jean-François Lyotard, Jacques Derrida and Michel Foucault.

Lyotard, for instance, conceived the 'event' as that which contests received modes of discourse and requires that existing ways of thinking be transformed. His conception of the event has been described as 'the founding moment of any postmodernism' (Malpas 2003: 99).

Likewise, in one of Lyotard's most important works, *The Differend*, the 'differend' itself is understood as an instability of language and discourse which, if we give it its due, will institute 'new addressees, new addressors, new significations and new referents' and will admit into language 'new phrase families and new genres of discourse' (Lyotard 1988: 13). Similarly, in Derrida's *Spectres of Marx*, the motifs of the messianic, of the undecidable and of the incalculable are all orientated towards the possibility of incorporating 'in advance, beyond any possible programming, new knowledge, new techniques, new political givens' (Derrida 1994: 13). This major late text of Derridean philosophy demonstrates clearly that one of the central concerns of deconstruction is 'to produce events, new effective forms of action, practice' (Derrida 1994: 89). At different times and in different works, Deleuze, Lyotard and Derrida will all use the term 'event' in order to designate the emergence of the radically new into the field of thought, practice or historical becoming. The 'event' is also a term used by Foucault in his archaeology of knowledge and his thinking of epistemic breaks developed in *The Order of Things* (Foucault 2002). For Foucault, the question of the new is posed in terms of discontinuity, or the way in which 'within the space of a few years, a culture sometimes ceases to think as it had been thinking up till then, and begins to think other things in a new way' (Foucault 2002: 56). The key question he poses is that of 'how is it that thought has a place in the space of the world, that it has its origin there, and that it never ceases to begin anew?' (Foucault 2002: 56).

Foucault's question is one which frames this book and the specific formulation of its title, *The New French Philosophy*. It is also a question that continues to be posed in an insistent and sometimes urgent manner by all the thinkers who are discussed here: Jean-Luc Marion, Jean-Luc Nancy, Bernard Stiegler, Catherine Malabou, Jacques Rancière, Alain Badiou and François Laruelle. In different ways, all these philosophers continue to be preoccupied with the question of how something new might enter the world. They are concerned with questions of transformation and change, with the emergence of the unexpected, the unforeseeable or the uncategorizable. They are concerned with the possibility of contesting existing forms in the name of invention and creation, of reformation and renewal. Posing the question of how thought may have its place and origin in the space of the world, and yet nevertheless may never cease to begin anew, Foucault suggests that the process of renewal 'probably begins with an erosion from the outside, from a space which is, for thought, on the other side but in which it has never ceased to think from the very beginning' (Foucault 2002: 56). In their different ways, each of the philosophers discussed here seek to rethink the relation of thought both to worldly existence or appearance and to what might be termed 'the outside'. In each case, albeit it still in different ways, the emergence of the 'new' or the possibility of change or transformation can be understood as an 'erosion from the outside', as an exposure to an instance of excess, an excess over the finite limits of conceptual or categorial determination.

Insofar as all the philosophers discussed here can be seen to continue the preoccupation with the new which is so central to the work of Deleuze, Lyotard, Derrida and Foucault, the title of this book could be considered something of a misnomer. The question of the new and its advent is itself far from new. By the same token, five out of the seven figures discussed here began to establish their careers in the 1970s and are not 'new' in the sense of being a young generation beginning to write in the first decade of the twenty-first century. Badiou and Laruelle were both born in 1937, Nancy and Rancière in 1940, and Marion in 1946. All of these five are still alive and publishing works today but all of them are, to varying degrees, in the latter part of their careers as philosophers (and mostly retired from their university positions). Only Stiegler (b. 1952) and Malabou (b. 1959) are of a younger generation and, although well established, can be placed in 'mid career'. Perhaps most importantly for the purposes of this book and its potential readership, all these figures have become more widely known in the anglophone academic community over the past ten to fifteen years and their work has, over the past ten years, been more widely available in English translation.

Despite the strong sense of continuity with the generation of philosophers that can be associated with the names Deleuze, Lyotard, Derrida and Foucault and, very broadly, with the problematic labels 'post-structuralism' and 'postmodernism', all of the thinkers discussed here can be viewed as a successor generation. This might not always be the case in strict age terms; Badiou, after all, was born only seven years after Derrida. Nevertheless, even on these terms, Deleuze, Foucault and Lyotard (born 1925, 1926 and 1924 respectively) are far more clearly of an earlier generation. What will become clear throughout this study is that the five older philosophers – Marion, Nancy, Rancière, Badiou and Laruelle – all begin to establish their distinctive positions in the 1970s and begin publishing their major works of philosophy in the 1980s and 1990s (and continue to do so today). The two younger philosophers, Stiegler and Malabou, begin publishing their major works in the 1990s and their philosophical projects are still very much ongoing. However helpful these indications may or may not be, it should be underlined that simple calculations of generational difference and age cannot be enough, in themselves, to establish a plausible argument about the renewal or transformation of French thought over the past three decades.

The argument of this book is that, beginning in the 1970s, the French philosophers discussed all, in different but decisive ways, making a break from the thought of the preceding generation. The difficulty in making such an argument is that attention to the difference and specificity of each thinker must be balanced with what they might, however loosely, share. The danger, of course, will be that quite divergent developments of thought will be assimilated to a unified paradigm which in fact blurs or misrepresents the specificity of each thinker. A very preliminary rehearsal of this book's argument might run as follows: in different and sometimes directly opposing ways, and beginning in the 1970s, the philosophers treated in this book explicitly distance themselves from the linguistic paradigm which informed much of what has gone under the name of structuralism and post-structuralism and which can be associated with diverse terms: with the order of signifiers, signifieds and of the symbolic, or with the categories of discourse, text, and writing (or arche-writing). They do so in the name of a systematic attempt to radically rethink questions of materiality and the concrete, together with questions of worldliness, shared embodied existence and sensible–intelligible experience. They can all be said to rethink the status of the 'real', of worldly appearance, or to re-engage in new and highly original ways with the question of ontology.

Before pursuing a rehearsal of this argument in anything but the cursory and preliminary manner just given, it may be useful to consider some of the broad surveys of contemporary French philosophy which have been published to date and some of the questions which are raised by them. John Mullarkey's *Post-Continental Philosophy: An Outline* (Mullarkey 2006) is without doubt the most ambitious and fully developed attempt that has been made to date to argue for a paradigm break within the development of contemporary French thought. *Post-Continental Philosophy* brings together four philosophers, two of whom are also discussed in this book. They are Gilles Deleuze, Michel Henry (1922–2002), Alain Badiou and François Laruelle. As Mullarkey himself points out at the very beginning of the introduction, his work does not address something that is, or which has already occurred, but rather something that 'is unfolding, an event in the making' (Mullarkey 2006: 1). More precisely, the book takes as its premise the claim that a certain moment in the ongoing development of French thought might be accorded the status of an 'event'. The moment he identifies is 1988, a year which sees the publication in French of important texts by each of the philosophers he discusses: Deleuze's *The Fold* (Deleuze 2006), Badiou's *Being and Event* (Badiou 1988; 2005b), Henry's *Voir l'invisible* [*Seeing the Invisible*] (Henry 2009), and an important discussion between Laruelle and Derrida on the possibility of a science of philosophy (Mullarkey 2006: 11). The event that he identifies is a change in philosophical thought which is centred on the question of immanence. More precisely this 'event' marks an attempt by philosophy to articulate 'an embrace of absolute immanence over transcendence . . . to make immanence supervene on transcendence' (Mullarkey 2006: 1). *Post-Continental Philosophy* argues, both persuasively and powerfully, that this attempted embrace of immanence leads to a realignment of French thought with naturalism and with the life sciences, with mathematics and with the reaffirmation of 'philosophy as a worldly and materialist thinking' (Mullarkey 2006: 2).

As will become clear, this book broadly reaffirms Mullarkey's arguments relating to the realignment of French thought with a non-reductive naturalism and the life sciences, with mathematics and with a worldly and materialist thinking.[3] Yet stark differences also present themselves and these relate to the question of the 'canon' of philosophers which have been chosen, to questions of periodization (i.e. the identification of 1988 as a key date), as well as to the adoption of immanence as the sole principle governing the realignment of French philosophy over the past thirty years. It certainly is true that nearly (but not) all of the thinkers here can be seen to affirm what might be called the immanence of material life and to this extent Mullarkey's argument is borne out well by many of the analyses offered here.[4] Whether it be Marion's thinking of givenness and the auto-affection of the flesh, Nancy's thinking of the 'trans-immanence' of sense, Malabou's conception of a material or metamorphic ontology, or, indeed, the different conceptions of immanence that can be found in Badiou and Laruelle, the question of immanence will be returned to throughout this study.[5]

This book differs from Mullarkey insofar as it takes the idea of a break from the linguistic, textual or discursive paradigm of (post-) structuralism as its initial premise and locates the beginnings of this break in the 1970s.[6] The broad shift towards a thinking of immanence is certainly a result of this, but not all the thinkers discussed here can easily be said to be thinkers of radical or absolute immanence (at least not to the same degree) and, as will become clear, a range of other important philosophical shifts can be seen to follow on from this break: a re-engagement with the question of ontology as has already been mentioned, but also a sustained renewal with the question of the subject and of subjectivity, with questions of community, politics and political change, and with questions relating to the aesthetic and aesthetics. Within the logic of the break from structuralism and/or post-structuralism, the thought of both Deleuze and Henry arguably offer indispensable resources to some of the thinkers treated here (e.g. the influence of Deleuze and Henry on Laruelle or of Henry in particular on Marion).[7] To this extent, it could be argued that they represent an important, and specifically French, trajectory of thought which can be traced from Bergson which is of decisive importance for the generation of thinkers treated here but that they do not belong to this generation (and have been excluded on these grounds).

It should be clear that the question of inclusion or exclusion is of central importance when it comes to constructing an argument relating to what may be contemporary or 'new' within a body of thought. A shorter account of this field has been given by Peter Hallward in his introduction to a special edition of the journal *Angelaki* published in 2003 and entitled 'The One and the Other: French Philosophy Today' (Hallward 2003b). Although shorter than Mullarkey's full-length work, Hallward's introduction is very inclusive and wide-ranging and takes in thinkers from across the span of the twentieth century, including well-known figures such as Bergson, Sartre, Deleuze, Henry and Levinas, and less well-known thinkers such as Henry Corbin (1903–1978). It also includes a number of thinkers who may be said to be of roughly the same generation as those treated here but who do not feature in this study, e.g. Clément Rosset (1939–), Christian Jambet (1949–) and Guy Lardreau (1947–2008). Rather than argue for a localized or specific 'event' within recent French thought (as does Mullarkey) or for a break or discontinuity with a preceding generation (as is the case here), Hallward suggests that much philosophy in the twentieth century is marked by an affirmation or privileging of the singular, of singularity, and of the creative principle of singular individuation or becoming: 'If anything holds the field together, if anything (beyond the contingency of languages and institutions) allows us to speak here of a field . . . then it is the continuous persistence of singularity as the strong polarizing principle of the field as a whole' (Hallward 2003b: 5).

However, taking Henry's thought as more or less paradigmatic of this privileging of singularity and creativity, Hallward goes on to argue that this field has consistently affirmed 'an immediate and non-relational process of individuation' and with that a 'radical refusal of mediation or representation' (Hallward 2003b: 9). This leads him to conclude that: 'Recent French philosophers came to embrace a singular conception of thought to the degree that they judged the world incapable of redemption' (Hallward 2003b: 22). On this basis, he suggests that French thought has developed a highly non-relational mode of thinking and has entirely lacked an account of worldly and mediated relationality. He therefore concludes that the task of those wishing to continue the tradition of French thought today will be to provide a 'relational alternative' (Hallward 2003b: 23). If there is to be a break or an event within thought then, for Hallward at least, this is one which thought must now *anticipate* and take up as a challenge in order to re-engage with the world and its possible transformation.

It is arguable that many, if not all, of the seven thinkers discussed in this study have sought to take up this demand of thought, that of re-engaging with the world and with the question of relationality, and have done so in various ways and at various key moments from the 1970s onwards.[8] More importantly, though, what this brief survey of Mullarkey's and Hallward's accounts shows is the extent to which any attempt to characterize 'French philosophy today' and to articulate what is or is not 'new' within this tradition is itself a philosophical argument which entails philosophical decisions and judgements. As was indicated at the beginning of this introduction, to speak of the 'New French Philosophy' is to raise questions which are themselves philosophical. To do so is also implicitly to stake out a position and make a series of philosophical arguments. As has been indicated, the principal argument of this book is that, despite their obvious differences from each other and despite the fact that this remains a field defined by major lines of conflict, argument and polemical opposition, all the thinkers treated have come to reaffirm what one might call the 'materiality of the real' in the wake of the preceding generation's focus on language and signification.

Yet any attempt to make such an argument or to characterize the field of contemporary French philosophy more generally will, of course, also define itself as much by those thinkers who have been excluded as by those who have been included. This study, for example, excludes a number of important philosophers who are all of the same, or similar, generation as those who have been included. Rosset, Jambet and Lardreau have already been mentioned but one could also offer a long list of other key figures, for example, Étienne Balibar (1942–), Jacques Bouveresse (1940–), Pierre Macherey (1938–), Michèle Ledoeff (1948–), Philippe Lacoue-Labarthe (1940–2007) and Monique David-Ménard (1947–).[9] Younger philosophers such as Quentin Meillassoux (1967–) who have more recently begun to publish significant work might be mentioned.[10] Important thinkers who have for some time been associated with the philosophy of science or with Science and Technology Studies are also key points of reference here and have, to date, been accorded varying degrees of recognition: Bruno Latour (1947–) would feature most prominently in this regard, as would Dominique Lecourt (1944–) and Michel Serres (1930–). What should be clear from such a long (and far from complete) list of exclusions is that the present study makes no attempt whatsoever to be exhaustive in its overview of contemporary French thought or, indeed, to give an account of the recent development of philosophy in France from an institutional or disciplinary perspective.[11]

What links all the thinkers who have been included here is a specific set of continuities and discontinuities with the work of the preceding generation of philosophers. It is on the basis of continuity (marks of influence, continued concerns, instances of repetition) and of discontinuity (specific gestures of critical distance, differentiation, and ruptures or breaks) with the generation of Foucault, Deleuze, Derrida and Lyotard that this study identifies something which could be called the 'New French Philosophy'. In this context, the innovations explored within this book can be assimilated to a broad and shared paradigm of renewal and innovation rather than to an emergence of radical novelty. By the same token, some of the thinkers treated here (e.g. Badiou and Laruelle) *do* seek to proclaim their radical novelty and these positions and their related claims are explored critically rather than being taken at face value.

Throughout the first four chapters, the figure of Derrida perhaps looms largest. Marion's engagement with, and distance from, Derrida is discussed at some length in chapter 1. Nancy, Stiegler and Malabou were very closely associated with Derrida, either as younger colleagues, collaborators or former students (or, indeed, all three). The relation of each to deconstruction is marked in the discussions of chapters 2, 3, and 4, as is their decisive self-distancing from key moments of Derridean thought. It is arguably on these key moments of distancing or divergence that they all build their own highly distinctive philosophical positions and come to sharply differentiate themselves from deconstructive or more broadly 'post-structuralist' concerns. In the final three chapters, a figure of great importance that has not yet been mentioned occupies a key position of influence. He is the structuralist-Marxist philosopher Louis Althusser (1918–1990).[12] Both Rancière and Badiou were closely associated with, and heavily influenced by, Althusser at the very beginning of their careers. In different ways and to different degrees each makes a break from Althusserianism in the 1970s, a break which, as will become clear, can also be framed as rejection of the linguistic paradigm that under-pinned its structuralist orientation. Laruelle is a slightly more diffi-cult figure to position in relation to the preceding generation. On the one hand, he is clearly marked and formed by philosophies of differ-ence, and in particular by Deleuzian philosophy and Deleuze's think-ing of radical immanence (but also, as mentioned earlier, by the thought of Henry). At the same time, he describes his thought as a 'non-Heideggerian deconstruction' and, from the 1980s onwards, develops his 'non-philosophy' as a radical break from the philoso-phies of difference (e.g. Deleuze, Derrida, Lyotard) of the preceding generation and, of course, from philosophy more generally. Then again, as is argued in chapter 7, Laruelle's conception of a 'science' of philosophy and of science more generally can be aligned with an Althusserian structural conception of science or theory.

It should be clear, then, that the continuities and discontinuities with which this study engages are both multiple and complex and, within the context of seven short chapters being devoted to seven individual philosophers, there is no claim to have given exhaustive treatment of these. However, the key discontinuity that has been already identified in preliminary fashion, that is to say, the break from the linguistic paradigm of (post-)structuralism, is articulated in dif-ferent, more or less explicit ways, by each of the philosophers dis-cussed. The argument is made in a polemical manner by Badiou in a seminar given originally in November 1977 and published in French in 1982 in *The Theory of the Subject* (Badiou 1982; 2009e). He identi-fies the anti-humanism of the 1960s generation (citing Foucault, Lacan and Althusser) with their privileging of the category of dis-course and their orientation according to a linguistic paradigm. He clearly identifies the structuralist attempt to think beyond the cate-gory of the human with its claim that language is the condition of possibility for the production of human subjectivity or experience per se (i.e. with the argument that the human as a category is an 'effect' of discourse). It is this privileging of the paradigm of language and discourse that Badiou directly and polemically challenges (Badiou 1982: 204; 2009e: 187–8). He suggests that this paradigm is a form of 'linguistic idealism' and states flatly: 'the world is discourse: this argu-ment in contemporary philosophy would deserve to be rebaptized "idealinguistery"' (Badiou 1982: 204; 2009e: 188). The linguistic ideal-ism of structuralist conceptions of discourse is challenged by Badiou in the name of materialism and the demand that thought re-engage with the material world: 'it is materialism that we must found anew with the renovated arsenal of our mental powers' (Badiou 1982: 198; 2009e: 182).[13] Arguably Badiou's mathematical turn, discussed in detail in chapter 6, is precisely the 'renovated arsenal' which he calls for in this 1977 seminar which so polemically demands a renewed materialism and a break from the linguistic idealism of structuralist discourse.

This break from the structuralist paradigm, effected in the name of a renewed materialist thought, is also an inaugural moment of Rancière's philosophy and is discussed at length in chapter 5 (in relation to his decisive rupture with Althusser). Rancière's break from Althusser and the Althusserian conception of ideology is, very much like Badiou's criticism of 1960s anti-humanists, framed in terms of a specific rejection of the category of discourse. This is made explicit in his 1974 work *Althusser's Lesson*: 'Ideology is not simply a collection of discourses or a system of representation' (Rancière 1974: 252–3; 2011c: 142). As chapter 5 argues, Rancière's subsequent conceptions of the 'distribution of the sensible', of historical and political agency or community, and his thinking about art and the aesthetic, all can be seen to follow on from this decisive break with Althusser and with the structuralist-linguistic paradigm.

Such a break can also be seen in key works of the 1970s written by Nancy and Laruelle, albeit with very different outcomes. In, for instance, *Ego Sum* (Nancy 1979), Nancy criticizes the return to a dominant position of the category of the subject and identifies this most prominently with the privileged status enjoyed in this period by Lacanian psychoanalysis.[14] However, this return of the subject is also identified more broadly with the structuralist paradigm, specifically with the instances of 'Structure, Text, or Process' (Nancy 1979: 11). It is identified also with the adoption by philosophy of the notion of the symbolic and its alignment with disciplines (anthropological, sociological) exterior to philosophy (Foucault is cited in this point; see Nancy 1979: 12 n. 2). *Ego Sum* has as its task the attempt to uncover beneath the 'anthropological profusion' of symbolic, textual, or structural subjects an instance that would be 'not a subject, nor the Subject, we will not name it, but this book would like it to name itself: *ego*' (Nancy 1979: 13). The instance that Nancy identifies in *Ego Sum* via a reading of Descartes's *cogito* is a singular and bodily site of enunciation and existence which is prior to, or in excess of, the symbolic order, and in excess of any possibility of theorization by (psychoanalytic) discourse (see James 2006: 58–62). Nancy's philosophical arguments relating to this bodily and ungrounded site of exteriority, excess or exposure open the way for all his later formulations around questions of community, embodiment, shared existence and his ontology of the singular plural (discussed in chapter 2).

By the same token a break from a linguistic or textualist paradigm is marked in the very title of Laruelle's 1977 work *Le Déclin de l'écriture* [*The Decline of Writing*] (Laruelle 1977b). Laruelle, like Badiou and Rancière, explicitly articulates the theoretical and philosophical aspiration of his work around a demand for a materialism (Laruelle 1977b: 8). Specifically, he aligns the motif of the 'decline of writing' with 'a materialist critique of textual and linguistic codes' (Laruelle 1977b: 14). The work as a whole could be characterized as a full-frontal attack on the very category of 'text' and the structuralist paradigm which privileges such a category. This is borne out in polemical statements such as: 'text must be stripped of the ontico-ontological primacy with which structuralist ideology and the majority of "textual" ideologues comfort themselves' (Laruelle 1977b: 222). From this demand, Laruelle takes as his task the attempt to think materiality as being in excess of theoretical or transcendent criteria, and therefore as 'material immanence', and as an exteriority or heteronomy 'more radical than that of the symbolic chain' (Laruelle 1977b: 43, 76). *Le Déclin de l'écriture* is still heavily marked by Laruelle's attachment to 1970s' libidinal philosophy and a machinic conception of desiring production (clearly demonstrating the influence of Deleuzian philosophy). His break from the philosophies of difference in the 1980s, his shift into the register of non-philosophy and his championing of the absolute immanence of the One is, however, clearly shaped by the anti-structuralism and anti-textualism of 1970s' works such as *Le Déclin de l'écriture* (as discussed in chapter 7).

The three other thinkers discussed here can also very clearly be seen to take a distance from the organizing paradigm of text or writing which form the objects of the 1970s' polemics of Badiou, Rancière, Nancy and Laruelle. This is most clearly marked in the title of a recent work by Malabou, *Plasticity at the Dusk of Writing* (Malabou 2005a; 2010b). Strongly echoing Laruelle's formulation relating to the 'decline' of writing, Malabou's book gives an overview of the development of her concept of plasticity from the 1990s onwards. The wider contemporary significance of the concept of plasticity, Malabou suggests, lies in the fact that 'writing' is no longer the key paradigm of our time (Malabou 2005a: 36; 2010b: 15). The figure of writing, she goes on to argue, found its legitimation in structuralism, but also more generally in the linguistics, cybernetics and genetics of the mid-twentieth century (Malabou 2005a: 108; 2010b: 58). The thinking of plasticity which is developed by Malabou is, once again, placed in the service of the demand to think a 'new materialism' (Malabou 2005a: 112; 2010b: 61) (as discussed in chapter 4). This sense of a shift away from the paradigm of text or writing is explored again in the work of both Marion and Stiegler. In chapter 1, it is located clearly in Marion's insistence that givenness is anterior to any economy of writing or difference (conceived in Derridean terms as *différance* and as an economy of arche-writing or the inscription of the trace).[15] In chapter 3, it is located in Stiegler's argument that technics and the specific memory traces embodied in tools and technical prosthetics more generally is a 'putting into actual play' of *différance* or of the Derridean trace (Stiegler 1994: 240; 1998: 234). In very different ways, therefore, Malabou's plasticity, Marion's unconditional givenness (in the auto-affection of flesh), and Stiegler's conception of the technological rooting of temporal experience all represent attempts to think a fundamental materiality of human life which is prior to or in excess of any economy of discourse, text, writing or of the symbolic.

The fact that an affirmation of materialism can be identified across all the thinkers discussed here and aligned in each instance with an unambiguous break with or distancing from a linguistic, structuralist, textualist or discursive paradigm is striking. What might be even more striking in relation to the polemics of Badiou, Rancière, Nancy and Laruelle in the 1970s is that the questions of materialism and materiality were, of course, already central to the (post-)structuralism they sought to repudiate. Whether it be the materiality of the signifier as championed by the Tel Quel group (see ffrench 1995: 110, 122, 138), the materiality of the word or of discourse posited by Lacan (Lacan 1988) or the material practices of ideology thought by Althusser (Sharma and Gupta 2006: 103), it cannot be said that the bodies of thought that can be associated with structuralism lacked a concern with the 'material'. Yet, as these indications clearly show, the concern for materiality in this context was often a concern for the materiality of *discourse*, of *language* and of the *symbolic* which might then form or inform material practices. Such a linguistic materialism is perceived by all the thinkers here to be unable to account for a more fundamental materiality: of givenness in the auto-affection of the flesh (Marion), of sense of and embodied existence (Nancy), of technical prosthetics and their constitution of a temporal world (Stiegler), of plasticity (Malabou), of the sensible and its distribution (Rancière), of immanent inconsistent multiplicity (Badiou) and, finally, of the absolute immanence of the One (Laruelle).

The call for a new materialism articulated in the thought of the seven philosophers treated in this book is developed in different ways by each. It leads to highly original attempts to rethink the question of ontology or of being (Nancy, Stiegler, Malabou, Badiou). It leads to the rethinking of the status of the immanent real as an instance which is in excess of ontology or any horizon of being whatsoever (Marion, Laruelle). The demand for a material worldly thinking also leads many of these philosophers to re-engage with the question of political relationality and community and to rethink these instances in new and original ways, whether it be Nancy's thinking of community and his ontology of the singular plural, Rancière's conception of sensible community, or Badiou's more recent thinking of the logic of worldly appearance (to name but three examples). The concern with the new, with transformation and change, is also, as was indicated at the beginning of this introduction, a key aspect of all the thinkers discussed here. Such a concern is most often expressed in terms of political change and an attempt, in the work of philosophy itself, to think the conditions of political transformation and to affirm, facilitate or bring about political change itself (this is true for all the philosophers discussed here with the exception, perhaps, of Marion and Laruelle).[16]

Linking many of these philosophical innovations is also a sustained attempt to re-engage with the question of the subject and to resituate something which might still be called subjectivity within a pre-symbolic/linguistic and material dimension. All of these philosophers can be said to engage in diverse ways with the question posed by Jean-Luc Nancy namely, 'Who comes after the subject?' (Nancy 1991f). After the destruction, deconstruction or dissolution of the traditional subject of metaphysics that has been the task of so much philosophy unfolding in the wake of Nietzsche, Heidegger and structuralism, how is thought to reconceptualize the reality of human agency and subjective consciousness? This question is posed in relation to the themes of embodiment and bodily existence (in Marion, Nancy, Malabou, Rancière, and in the later Badiou). It is posed also in relation to problems of political subjectivity or 'subjectivation', and to politically inflected arguments relating to individuation (in Stiegler, Malabou, Rancière and Badiou). Indeed, the question of the subject, rethought as an embodied, 'fleshy' instance, or as a material process of collective identification or differentiation, is posed in a manner which is inseparable from the wider demand for a material worldly thought to which these philosophers in their different ways respond.

From this, it can also be argued that the philosophers discussed here under the rubric of the 'New French Philosophy' are a long way from renouncing the political radicalism which is often associated with the 1960s generation of thinkers that preceded them.[17] Indeed, the re-engagement with the material and with the worldly can most often be framed within the context of a response to the situation of the contemporary world in the final decades of the twentieth century and first decade of the twenty-first. This is born out arguably in Nancy's thinking of community and of the political, Stiegler's critique of hyper-industrial society, Malabou's questioning of the 'neuronal' organization of contemporary capitalist culture, and both Rancière's and Badiou's quite similar conceptions of political subjectivation.

It could be argued that these philosophers do not just simply reject the ideological orthodoxies of what might more or less conventionally be called contemporary 'neo-liberal' capitalism and its accompanying political forms. They also reject the political ontology implicit in these orthodoxies. They reject, of course, the conception of the subject as an autonomous self-grounding instance (the subject of metaphysics so repeatedly deconstructed in the twentieth century). Such a conception of subjectivity could arguably be said to persist and to inform contemporary liberal thinking about rational agency, about 'choice', and about the exercise of economic and individual freedom. They reject also the ontological assumptions regarding worldly relationality implicit in any conception of the human as *homo economicus*. It is not, it should be stressed, that these philosophers are anti-democratic. If they address the question of democracy they most often argue that what we need is better or more fully evolved democratic thinking and democratic agency or forms (see, for example, Nancy 2008a; 2010c; Rancière 2005a; 2006b). It may be that, in their different ways, these thinkers understand that the ideological orthodoxies and implicit ontology of liberal capitalism are simply not philosophically sufficient or even plausible means to describe what fundamentally, really and actually, unfolds in human agency and shared relational existence.[18] It may also be that if, in the wake of the Cold War, the orthodoxies of liberal capitalism have enjoyed a significant degree of global hegemony, then our future crises (political, economic, environmental) are likely to be crises of these ideological and philosophical orthodoxies as well as of the political forms they represent.

In light of this, it could be said that the task of philosophical renewal taken up by the seven thinkers presented here is as much orientated towards the future as it is predicated on a logic of continuity and discontinuity with the past. They might all be united by a shared sense that the destruction or deconstruction of metaphysics, subjectivity, or traditional notions of being, truth and knowledge, is a necessary (and unfinished) but certainly not sufficient gesture to meet the demands of contemporary thinking. Instead, subjectivity, ontology, truth, epistemology, as well as questions of universality, ethics and politics, all must be thought anew in an affirmative and constructive, rather than deconstructive, manner.

Yet, in spite of all that these thinkers might arguably be said to share, their respective bodies of work are clearly marked by strong divergences, by incompatibilities, and by at times highly polemical forms of opposition. This is most clearly evident in the break that Badiou and those broadly aligned with him (such as Žižek, Meillassoux, Hallward) proclaim with respect to the legacy of phenomenology and philosophies of difference or finitude. It also manifests itself in Laruelle's attempt to identify an invariant structure of philosophy per se, to assimilate all forms of (post-)phenomenology or philosophies of difference to that structure, and to oppose to these his own conception of 'non-philosophy'. While this book accords a high degree of innovation and originality to all of the thinkers it discusses, such affirmations of radical novelty need to be treated with some caution and even with a degree of critical distance or philosophical scepticism. In the case of Badiou, this is because, by his own admission, his mathematical turn and its accompanying formalism can be placed within a continuous trajectory of French thought that would take in such figures as Jean Cavaillès, Jean-Toussaint Desanti and, more immediately, Lacan and Althusser (see chapter 6; in particular, Lacan's demand for a mathematical approach to the real as affirmed in his seminar of the 2 December 1971 is in direct continuity with Badiou's approach). At the same time, his claims relating to the emergence of radical novelty in contemporary philosophy need to be understood in the context of his thinking about the need to 'split' any given situation into two (again, see chapter 6). It is also true that many of Badiou's key concerns with, for instance, multiplicity, undecidability, excess and the advent or the 'event' of the radically new are also central preoccupations of the preceding generation of poststructuralist thinkers he ostensibly opposes. By the same token, his stark difference from, and polemical opposition to, a contemporary thinker such as Jean-Luc Nancy belies key similarities between the two philosophers: again a concern with multiplicity, but also an (albeit very differently inflected) return to the discourse of ontology and to the categories of, for instance, truth and universality (see Nancy 1990a: 13; 2003c: 5; 1993a: 25; 1997e: 12; 2002a: 69, 75; 2007c: 60, 62). Similar objections could be raised in relation to Laruelle's attempt to decisively oppose his non-philosophy to the work of his contemporaries and their immediate predecessors.

It should nevertheless become clear that each of these thinkers meets the demands of contemporary thought in very different ways. They are therefore treated separately in individual chapters and are presented broadly speaking on their own terms. The aim of each chapter is to give a critical-philosophical overview and interpretation of each on the basis of close reading of texts. In each case, the presentation will aim to highlight the strengths of each philosopher, the significance of their achievements and, in particular, their originality and the distinctiveness of their respective philosophical innovations. The discussion will also, however, indicate some of the problems or limitations associated with the distinctive positions of each thinker. The presentation aims to be accessible but, at the same time, to do some justice to the complexity of the thought under discussion.

As Peter Hallward has remarked, contemporary French philosophy has all too often been associated with an excess of unnecessary complexity, with 'a daunting if not arcane difficulty and sophistication which restricts access to insiders only' (Hallward 2003b: 1). What should become clear as these discussions unfold is that these philosophers seek to renew the way in which they think, to transform the manner in which they come to write philosophy itself. This attempt to renew the style, techniques and procedures of philosophical writing is itself intimately connected to the renewal and transformation of thought that each thinker pursues. The French philosophies presented here are highly ambitious in their attempt to renew the claims, possibilities and transformative power of philosophical thinking. The renewal of philosophical thinking, however, can only be achieved in the transformation of the techniques of thought itself.

1

Jean-Luc Marion: Appearing and Givenness

Jean-Luc Marion's philosophy of givennness stands as perhaps one of the most important recent and contemporary contributions to phenomenology in France. Along with the thought of Michel Henry (1922–2002), Marion's work has radicalized key aspects of Husserlian and post-Husserlian philosophy. It has also opened up new and original, albeit highly disputed, possibilities for phenomenology in the wake of structuralist and post-structuralist critiques of phenomenological thought. His publications since the 1970s can be divided into three separate but closely interrelated areas: besides the phenomenological work already mentioned, he is an important, and in France widely recognized, Descartes scholar, and he is also the author of a number of works of theology. In 2008, he was elected to a chair at the Académie Française. Outside of France, however, it was as a theologian that Marion first became widely known.[1] Until recently, his work on Descartes has been less recognized in the anglophone academic world and he has been best known as an important figure working at the intersection of phenomenology and theology.

Yet, as Christina Gschwandtner has persuasively argued, Marion's work on Descartes is of great importance for both his theological and phenomenological writing and shapes the concerns of both in decisive ways.[2] In this context, the overall scope of his philosophical output needs to be assessed in terms of his position both within a specifically French scholarly and philosophical tradition as well as within a broader French appropriation and transformation of German thought. Marion was schooled in philosophy under Jean Beaufret at the Lycée Condorcet,[3] he studied at the École Normale Supérieure, and then at Paris IV-Paris-Sorbonne under Ferdinand Alquié (1906–1985). Alquié was an important philosophical commentator on Descartes as well as a thinker who engaged with a wide range of modern philosophy. Marion's writings on Descartes are clearly influenced by Alquié, as they are by Étienne Gilson (1884–1978), another key French scholar of Descartes and of medieval and early modern thought more generally. At the same time, Marion's thinking emerges from within the context and milieu of French engagements with Nietzsche and Heidegger in the 1970s and, decisively, from his sustained engagement with Husserl.

Much of the more negative criticism of Marion's work to date has come either from theologians unhappy with the way in which his theology deviates from more orthodox strands of the discipline – deviations which arise largely from his philosophical engagements – or from phenomenologists who perceive his work in this area to be too contaminated by his theological concerns. Derrida also responded, directly but more indirectly as well, to aspects of Marion's theological and phenomenological writing.[4] Most prominently, Marion was one of a number of figures (including, amongst others, Michel Henry, Paul Ricoeur and Emmanuel Lévinas) accused by Dominique Janicaud of aligning phenomenology too closely with theology in a 'theological turn' which, Janicaud polemically asserted, threatened to undermine the true method and scope of phenomenological thought.[5]

While what follows will seek to relate the core of Marion's philosophical concerns to both his commentaries on Descartes and his theological writing, it will focus first and foremost on his phenomenological thought such as it emerges in three key works: *Reduction and Givenness* (Marion 1989; 1998), *Being Given* (Marion 1997; 2002c), and *In Excess* (Marion 2001; 2002a). It will argue that Marion's achievement and the originality of his transformation of phenomenology lie in the specific ways in which he assimilates the diverse anti-foundationalist critiques levelled at phenomenological thought by structuralism and post-structuralism. The critique of presence, of the phenomenological reduction and of the transcendental ego, for instance, are all accepted by Marion, but in rereading Husserlian thought as a thought of givenness, he aims to move phenomenology beyond its metaphysical foundations while at the same time widening the scope of what might be considered as a phenomenon per se. In redefining the scope of phenomenality itself, and in assimilating the aim of an 'overcoming' of metaphysics, Marion has in many ways helped redefine the terms of philosophical debate in France in the wake of deconstruction and the 'death of the subject'.

The overcoming of metaphysics

Marion's concern to situate his thought within what one might broadly term a post-Heideggerian and post-Nietzschean overcoming of metaphysics can be traced back to his earliest publications of the 1970s, most notably his first major commentary on Descartes, *Sur l'ontologie grise de Descartes* [*On Descartes's Grey Ontology*] (Marion 1975), and his first important work of theology, *The Idol and Distance* (Marion 1977; 2001b).

Heidegger's conception of metaphysics as a history of ontotheology and Nietzsche's framing of the philosophical tradition as a history of Christian-Platonism are of decisive importance for Marion in this period. In each case, what is at stake is the tendency of the tradition of metaphysics to think first and foremost of being in general in terms of the totality of beings, and then to view those beings in terms of foundations, grounding, or causal principles (timeless essences or identities, notions of foundational substance, of a grounding subject of knowledge, a priori conditions of possibility, or, perhaps most importantly for Marion, the idea of God as the Supreme Being who would act as the first cause and creator of all beings).

In the earlier text, Marion uncovers, with considerable patience and scholarly attention, Descartes's debt to, and close engagement with, the philosophy of Aristotle in the *Regulations for the Direction of the Mind*. What he discovers is that the seemingly epistemological concerns of Cartesian thought conceal an ontology. Descartes appears to reject the Aristotelian category of substance (thought as an ontological ground, or as the being of beings) in favour of the ego that knows things through the criteria of evidence and certainty. This epistemological gesture in fact dissimulates an ontology, since the being of beings now finds itself grounded in that ego, and, in a rather equivocal gesture, the solidity and identity of that ego also finds itself grounded, according to Marion's reading of Descartes, in the existence of God. Descartes's ontology is therefore 'grey', because concealed, and ambivalent or equivocal because it relies on a twofold metaphysical foundation of the ego and of the traditional notion of God as Creator and Supreme Being (Marion 1971: 186–90).

This concern with ontology and metaphysical grounding is developed further in Marion's slightly later theological text. *The Idol and Distance* argues that when we think of God in terms of a fixed identity or presence or as an entity or Supreme Being, then we are caught up within a metaphysical mode of thinking par excellence, and firmly inscribe ourselves within an ontotheological framework (as described by Heidegger). Indeed, viewing God in this way, we only view an all-too-human image; we create an idol of God, refuse the distance and withdrawal of the divine, and fall into idolatry or, indeed, blasphemy.[6] The work then stages an opposition between a metaphysical notion of God as Being, substance or presence, and a notion of God as infinite distance, separation and withdrawal from, or excess over, Being. The former moment is framed in our gaze upon God conceived as an idol, which fixes divine presence, the latter in our contemplation of what Marion terms the 'icon'. The icon, for Marion, is an image which internalizes within itself the separation, absolute distance and non-being of the divine (Marion 1977: 25; 2001b: 8). Not surprisingly, *The Idol and Distance* contains a detailed engagement with the tradition of negative theology (in the figure of Pseudo-Dionysius the Areopagite whose works were written in the late fifth and early sixth century CE). Perhaps more unexpectedly for a work of theology, it also contains a sustained reading of the Nietzschean motif of the Death of God. Here, Marion argues that Nietzsche announces only the death of the God of metaphysics (the God of being, substance, etc.), and that the Nietzschean twilight and demise of idols leaves open a space of absence which, in its very absence and withdrawal, can all the more properly be called divine. This persistence of the divine in Nietzschean thought is marked most clearly, according to Marion, in the way in which it is haunted by Christ and Christ-like figures: the Anti-Christ, Dionysus, Zarathustra and so on.

Both these early works open up philosophical concerns and lines of argument which will prove to be decisive for Marion's later phenomenology of givenness. His critique of Descartes allows him to delineate very clearly an understanding of metaphysics and ontotheology as a logic of the foundation of beings and their grounding in causal principles. His theology of distance allows him to pose the question of a conception of the divine which would situate itself beyond any horizon of being (Marion 1977: 294; 2001b: 233). In this respect, his thinking at this point quite closely aligns itself with the philosophical concerns of both Jacques Derrida and Emmanuel Lévinas (Marion 1977: 286, 226; 2001b: 298, 237). Perhaps most significantly, *The Idol and Distance* allows Marion, like Derrida and Lévinas, to pose the problem of exactly how thought might extricate itself from, or think beyond, the horizon of being, to think in excess of ontotheology, or otherwise than being. Marion suggests the following: 'There remains therefore only one path: to travel through ontotheology itself all along its limits, its marches. . . . To take ontotheology tangentially, from the angle of its lines of defence, and thus to expose oneself to what already no longer belongs to it' (Marion 1977: 37–8; 2001b: 19). This way or path of thought arguably defines the philosophical strategy that informs Marion's reading of Husserl and Heidegger in his later more strictly phenomenological work.

Phenomenology and givenness

Reduction and Givenness begins, perhaps surprisingly, by aligning the beginnings of Husserlian phenomenology with the final accomplishments of Nietzsche's philosophical thought. In late 1887, just as Husserl gives his inaugural lecture at the University of Halle ('The Goals and Tasks of Metaphysics'), so Nietzsche embarks on the final period of his writing, marked by works such as *On the Genealogy of Morals*, *Twilight of the Idols*, and *Ecce Homo*. As Nietzsche dies after a decade of paralysis in 1900, so Husserl publishes the first volume of the *Logical Investigations* (Marion 1989: 7; 1998: 1). What the two share, Marion claims, is a question posed in relation to phenomenal appearance and the possibility of thinking the presence of phenomena in the absence of any hidden supra-reality of essences or grounding principles: 'Can the givenness in presence of each thing be realized without any condition or restriction? This question marks Nietzsche's last advance and Husserl's first point of arrival' (Marion 1989: 7; 1998: 1). Nietzsche's affirmation in *The Gay Science* that there is appearance only and 'nothing more' could be cited in this regard, as could his assertion in *Twilight of the Idols* that the opposition between the Platonic 'true' world of ideal essences and the world of 'false' appearances has been abolished (Nietzsche 1974: 116; 1990: 51). Husserlian phenomenology, for its part, is concerned to describe the character of consciousness in the most clear and systematic way and addresses that which appears to consciousness in lived experience alone. The existence of a supra-phenomenal realm of 'real' entities existing independently of our consciousness of them is not posed, nor, indeed, is it thought to be a viable philosophical question. In each case and in different ways, Marion underlines, both Nietzsche and Husserl seek to liberate thought from metaphysical prejudices by affirming a field of appearance which is to be thought outside of any reference to a hidden or higher realm of reality.

This alignment of Husserl with Nietzsche, however surprising it may be, is decisive for the way in which the arguments of *Reduction and Givenness* unfold. According to Marion the philosophical break-through made by Husserlian phenomenology lies in its reduction of lived experience to that which manifests itself in the immanent realm of consciousness alone. It is only that which is given immanently in sensible intuition or perception that will be described by the phe-nomenologist, with all else being 'bracketed off'. As Marion puts it: 'the phenomenological breakthrough is accomplished by leading back to intuition everything that claims to be constituted as a phe-nomenon' (Marion 1989: 17; 1998: 8). In describing the character of phenomenal appearance as given to consciousness, the phenomenol-ogist refers, first and foremost, not to any form of a priori category, nor to any notion of sensible experience or reality which would tran-scend that which is given immanently in intuition, nor, indeed, to any other form of presupposition of any kind. Nor, Marion insists still further, can intuition itself be seen in this context as a founding prin-ciple: 'Intuition itself cannot be understood as a last presupposition, since it is neither presupposed nor posited, nor given, but originally giving' (Marion 1989: 19; 1998: 9). In what will become a central premise of all of Marion's phenomenology after *Reduction and Givenness*, he insists on the primacy of givenness over all the other key instances which underpin Husserlian phenomenological thought. The intentional directedness of consciousness towards the perceived phenomenon, the act of sense constitution, the phenomenological or transcendental ego, and even the immanent intuitions and percep-tions of consciousness itself all, without exception, are posterior to, or result from, an originary giving. If intuition is 'originally giving', if it gives the world of phenomena to us, that is only because something *is given*, in and to intuition: 'Intuition results from givenness without exception' (Marion 1989: 27; 1998: 15).

It is this anteriority of givenness or giving which allows Marion to read Husserl as liberating phenomenal presence from any anterior condition or grounding principle. This is because the givenness or the giving of phenomena to the immanence of sensory intuition does not found or ground anything; it simply makes manifest that which is given and does so in the absence of any prior principle. It is this asser-tion of the absolute unconditionality of phenomenological givenness that allows Marion to claim that Husserl's wider project can and must be viewed as a post-Nietzschean liberation from the tradition of metaphysics. Indeed, this is the key point with which *Reduction and Givenness* begins and which is pursued throughout the work as a whole: 'In undertaking to free presence from any condition or pre-condition for receiving what gives itself as it gives itself, phenomenol-ogy therefore seeks to complete metaphysics and, indissolubly, to bring it to an end' (Marion 1989: 8; 1998: 1). And yet, as will become clear, Marion's position relies on a very specific reading of Husserl, a reading which is perhaps as disputable as it is both forceful and original.

As the title of *Reduction and Givenness* plainly suggests, it is, for Marion, the phenomenological reduction itself which plays a key role in the unfolding of his argument. For the phenomenologist, the 'bracketing off' of the empirical referent (and the concomitant isolation of the phenomenon in the immanence of consciousness alone) allows for its appearance to be rigorously described and circumscribed according to the key instances alluded to above: the presentation of the phenomenon in sensible intuition, the directedness of intentional consciousness towards it, and, as a result of both intuition and intention, the constitution of the meaningfulness or signification of the phenomenon. In this context, Marion's argument unfolds as a radicalization of Husserl's thought in the most proper sense, that is to say, as a return to what is perceived to be the root or most fundamental moment of phenomenology: givenness itself. Marion radicalizes the Husserlian reduction by showing that all the instances which inform its operation *except givenness alone* can themselves be reduced or bracketed off. Central to this argument is a double meaning of the term 'givenness' (*donation* in French): the term refers to the fact that something is given and to the act of giving and therefore has both a substantive and verbal meaning. In relation to phenomenal appearance, *donation* articulates a strict correlation or identity between the giving (appearing) and the given (that which appears). Husserl is directly cited on this point: that which is given is so in an act of appearing which gives the given (Marion 1989: 52; 1998: 32). This correlation between the appearing and that which appears, between the giving and the given, confirms for Marion the primacy of givenness over the categories of sensible intuition, intentionality, and signification or sense constitution. The breakthrough of Husserlian phenomenology lies in the way in which it insists that givenness precedes, and is not conditioned by, all other instances (Marion 1989, 53; 1998: 32). Without the giving of that which is given, none of the other instances would function as such: intuition would be empty of content, intentionality would have nothing to direct itself towards and there would be no apparent or sensible form for which sense could be constituted as such. It is from this anteriority of giving and givenness over all other instances which are engaged in the operation of the phenomenological reduction that Marion derives the axiom with which his argument concludes: 'so much reduction, so much givenness' (Marion 1989: 303; 1998: 203). The more one reduces or brackets off, the more one isolates that which is given and the giving of the given as irreducible, unconditional and absolute: 'Givenness alone is absolute, free and without condition, precisely because it gives' (Marion 1989: 53–4; 1998: 33).

It is at this point that the Cartesian dimension of Marion's thought perhaps makes itself most clearly felt and that his radicalization of Husserl appears more as a radicalization of that which is most Cartesian in Husserl (Husserl 1999). Givenness, like the Cartesian *cogito*, emerges here as that which resists all possibility of negation or doubt, as that which will necessarily be affirmed as a certainty or evidence when all else can be dismissed as illusion (for even an illusion, falsity, absence, or void must be given in order to be perceived as such).[7] It is because of its absolute irreducibility, unconditionality and indubitability that givenness both precedes and succeeds any other instance or operation of thought. It is also this irreducibility and unconditionality that leads Marion to argue that Husserl, and in his wake Heidegger also, fail to properly pursue the radicality of givenness in their respective phenomenological projects. In each case, Marion argues, both Husserl and Heidegger stop short of fully embracing the full implications of the giving of appearing, the former by inscribing phenomenality within the horizon of objects or 'objectality', the latter by inscribing it within the horizon of being, that is to say, of *Dasein* and its worldly, temporalizing disclosure of beings. Much of the main body of *Reduction and Givenness* is taken up with close readings of Husserl and Heidegger in order to show that givenness is not only anterior to and not conditioned by the instances of intuition, intention and signification, but is prior also to the horizons of objectality and being.

It is here that the radical nature of Marion's phenomenology of givenness really asserts itself. This is radicality understood now, not just as a return to the root or originary moment of phenomenology, but rather as a thoroughgoing and fundamental transformation of its scope and possibilities. The arguments of *Reduction and Givenness* culminate with an identification of what Marion dubs the 'third reduction'. Husserlian phenomenology carries out a first reduction according to which phenomena are reduced in the last instance to their being as objects constituted by the transcendental ego. Heideggerian existential phenomenology carries out the second reduction according to which phenomena are reduced to their disclosure as beings in the ecstatic temporality of *Dasein*. *Carrying the reduction* still further to a third degree, Marion discovers that, in its non-negatability, unconditionality and therefore absolute anteriority, the givenness of phenomena cannot be subsumed into any formal ontology or any horizon of being. As he puts it: 'In the realm of reduction it is no longer a question of Being. . . . Because being never intervenes in order to permit the aboslute givenness in which it plays not the slightest role' (Marion 1989: 69; 1998: 43). In this light, givenness would, for Marion, be prior to and not conditioned by any form of category or relation of any kind whatsoever including, it should be noted, the category of presence. Marion's third reduction, it will become clear, has enormous implications both for the way in which he assimilates key anti-foundationalist critiques of phenomenology, such as Derridean deconstruction, and for the way in which the scope of phenomenality itself is widened to include what he will come to call 'saturated phenomena'. It is this widening of the scope of phenemonality which, in turn, allows his thought to open onto, but (Marion would insist) remain distinct from, theological concerns and the discourse of theology more generally.

Objections and responses: *Being Given* and saturated phenomena

Being Given was published eight years after the appearance of *Reduction and Givenness* and its opening pages, entitled 'Preliminary Responses', indicate the extent to which the work is, at least in part, intended to respond to the debate which was provoked by the earlier work. In this context, *Being Given* can be seen as a re-engagement with, or repetition of, some of the key concerns of *Reduction and Givenness*, as a response to some of the more or less polemical objections raised to it, and as an attempt to develop further the radicality of its insights. Marion begins by claiming for the earlier work a rather modest ambition: 'At that time, I thought only to proceed with a simple historical examination of the development of the phenomenological method' (Marion 1997: 7; 2002c: 2). Readers familiar with the technical detail and scope of Husserlian and Heideggerian thought may find such a protest unconvincing, given the objections which can and, as will become clear, were raised in relation to his reading of Husserl in particular.

Yet, as has been indicated, it would be wrong to suggest that *Being Given* is a purely reactive text. In particular, Marion explores more fully the implications of the third reduction and does so in relation to the question of being. He begins by reiterating a number of key points: that the third reduction has led to a new definition of the phenomenon, 'no longer as object or being, but as given' (Marion

1997: 8; 2002c: 3), that it returns phenomena to their 'pure given status, according to radically non-metaphysical determinations' (Marion 1997: 8–9; 2002c: 3), and that the pure givenness of the phenomenon is freed from 'the limits of every other authority including those of intuition' (Marion 1997: 28; 2002c: 17). These reiterations lead to a more pointed reformulation of the question of being in relation to givenness. Marion underlines, for instance, that the pure givenness of phenomenal appearance abolishes the traditional opposition between existence and essence (since that which appears does so in the absence of any preceding essence) (Marion 1997: 35; 2002c: 22). He also emphasizes that, if all that appears must nevertheless in some sense be said 'to be', this is only because it is given: 'Appearing itself is, in the end, equivalent to being, but being presupposes given being' (Marion 1997: 40; 2002c: 26; translation modified). Nothing *is* unless it is first given as *being* in the giving of its appearance and therefore once again being is necessarily posed as conditioned by an anterior instance of giving, itself absolute, irreducible and unconditioned. In this context, Heideggerian ontological difference – that is, the difference between beings and the horizon of being – emerges secondarily from givenness: 'Being, insofar as it differs from beings, appears immediately in terms of givenness' (Marion 1997: 53; 2002c: 34). Being is, then, always and only an event of *being given* and nothing can appear, affect us, or be accomplished other than by its being given (Marion 1997: 79; 2002c: 53).

These instances of reiteration and further elaboration of givenness in relation to the question of being are worth highlighting because they are developed in various ways throughout *Being Given* and, in particular, prepare the way for one of its most important philosophical engagements, that is, Marion's critical reading of Derrida, and of Derrida's thinking of the gift as elaborated in *Given Time* (Derrida 1991; 1992). Despite the specificity of this reading, it should not be viewed in narrow terms since the relation of Marion's thought to deconstruction more generally is certainly at stake, as is the status of givenness within phenomenology as a whole.

Given Time, published in 1991, had its origin in a seminar given by Derrida between 1977 and 1978. As such, it preceded Marion's *Reduction and Givennness* by over a decade and cannot be read as an explicit response to it, although Derrida does respond to Marion directly in one specific and rather dense footnote added at the time of publication (Derrida 1991: 72; 1992: 50–2, n. 10). Nevertheless, his arguments relating to the impossibility of 'pure giving' or of an absolutely pure gift cannot but directly call into question the fundamental terms of Marion's broader innovation within phenomenology. For both, the exact status of the gift and the possibility or otherwise of its purity and unconditionality are decisive for the possibility of phenomenology itself. Derrida's argument is well known: if an act of giving is to be pure, then there must be no return to the giver, no debt of recognition may occur in relation to the giver, nothing may be accrued as a result, either in the short term or through some process of deferral. Otherwise, the gift is not a gift but functions as a mode of exchange (Derrida 1991: 18–19; 1992: 7). The presence of the pure gift is withdrawn as it is subsumed into an economy of deferral, a wider circle of exchange and recognition in which no gift is ever purely given. Of course, Derrida argues that a gift can only ever present itself in such an economy of exchange and that: 'the gift is annulled . . . as soon as it appears *as* gift or as soon as it signifies itself as gift, there is no longer any "logic of the gift"' (Derrida 1991: 39; 1992: 24). If this argument is followed through in relation to the giving of appearance or phenomenality, then it becomes clear that Marion is profoundly mistaken to claim that 'givenness' can be irreducible or unconditional. The appearing or manifestation of phenomena would always be conditioned by some kind of economy or process of exchange. Derrida's argument in relation to the gift here is, of course, consistent with his deconstruction of phenomenal presence according to the logic of *différance*, whereby presence only manifests itself as such insofar as it is produced in relation to, and marked or divided by, the trace of an immemorial past (Derrida 1976: 65–73). The temporal economy of *différance* always precedes, conditions and produces presence; therefore presence is always deferred, contaminated by its other and by alterity in general: the gift of appearing is never pure.

Not surprisingly, Marion takes considerable pains to reject any Derridean inspired objections to his phenomenology of giving based on the arguments of *Given Time*. Indeed, the greater part of the second book of *Being Given* is devoted to showing that Derrida's analysis of the impossible gift cannot apply to phenomenological givenness. Derrida's key mistake, he argues, is to conflate phenomenal giving or appearing with a model of giving derived from anthropology and sociology.[8] The latter, of course, cannot but function according to an economy of recognition, whereby to give is to receive within a broader system of exchange. Yet, for Marion, phenomenal giving is in no way economic, since the gift is given according to a fundamental asymmetry or paradoxical logic which he describes in the following terms: 'the given, issued from the process of givenness, appears but leaves concealed givenness itself, which becomes enigmatic' (Marion 1997: 100; 2002c: 68). This perhaps rather Heideggerian formulation describes a mode of giving which would be extracted from any economy of exchange or recognition because the giving itself is absolutely anonymous and without identifiable origin. It may be received and may even incur a sense of debt, but without any identifiable giver the circle of exchange which is so decisive for Derrida is broken. In order to demonstrate that phenomenal giving is different from an economy of giving in this crucial regard, Marion takes each term of the gift in economic exchange, the 'giver', the 'receiver' and the 'exchanged object', and shows that each can be bracketed off or suspended when it is a question of appearance or appearing. His response to Derrida hinges essentially on the possibility of carrying out further operations of the reduction, 'a triple *epokhē* of the transcendental conditions of economic exchange' (Marion 1997: 122; 2002c: 84), in order to show that the phenomenal gift can be coherently thought in the absence of each of the three terms (Marion 1997: 124–60; 2002c: 85–113). Once again, the pure givenness of phenomenal appearance emerges as that which cannot be reduced after all else has been suspended or bracketed off. Once again, the gift is shown to be absolute and unconditioned by any other instance, in this case economic. This leads Marion to conclude decisively against Derrida that: 'the gift . . . gets its "given" character from givenness, that is to say, from itself. The gift gives itself intrinsically from a self giving' (Marion 1997: 161; 2002c: 113). If the phenomenological gift is viewed properly and *phenomenologically* according to the operations of the reduction, then it will become clear that it 'owes nothing to any anthropological or sociological model' (Marion 1997: 161; 2002c: 113).

The ambition and daring of Marion's arguments in *Being Given* are very striking, for they underline what has been more or less implicit from the opening chapters of *Reduction and Givenness*: namely, that all of Derrida's patient and careful readings of Husserl, including his earliest readings of 'The Origin of Geometry' and of voice, sign and signification in *Speech and Phenomena* (Derrida 1996) – indeed, the entire deconstruction of presence throughout the Derridean corpus – none of this can deconstruct phenomenal givenness, the irreducible, absolute and unconditional giving of appearance. In response to the Derridean challenge to a phenomenology of givenness, Marion simply develops the scope and the force of the third reduction even further. Yet, despite the ambition and daring of these arguments, what emerges perhaps most strongly from this encounter between Marion and Derrida is the extent to which their difference from each other hinges on the divergence of their respective readings of Husserl. Marion situates the giving of appearance as primary and unconditioned in his radicalized reading of Husserlian *Gegebenheit*. Derrida argues that phenomenality is produced via the temporal and temporalizing economy of *différance*. Marion would accuse Derrida of a metaphysical gesture insofar as he understands appearance to be conditioned by this prior temporal economy (since appearance is referred to an anterior instance). Derrida would accuse Marion of the same insofar as givenness is endowed with an immediacy, a proximity and continuity with the immanence of the consciousness to which it is given (therefore reproducing a logic of presence despite itself).[9] The question perhaps comes down to a question of temporality. In a perhaps rather cursory and underdeveloped moment of *Being Given*, Marion suggests that temporality can only be produced *from* the event of phenomenal appearance, or from the rhythmic succession of such events. Derrida, of course, would suggest the opposite: that it is an economy of spatializing and temporalizing inscription of the trace that gives appearance and, moreover, that such an economy cannot be reduced to a metaphysical grounding principle since it exceeds all ontological disclosure or possibility of reduction, and therefore all logic of foundation or ground. The question then would be: does the giving of appearance give temporality (Marion) or does temporality give appearance (Derrida)?

It is arguable that the limitations of Marion's phenomenology can begin to be discerned here. His affirmation of givenness as an instance prior to any economy (of the trace, of *différance*) perhaps relies too heavily on an overly formalistic radicalization of the Husserlian phenomenological reduction and in so doing fails to satisfactorily pose the question of the genesis or production of presence, intuition, signification, conceptuality, etc. The manner in which this question of genesis or origin is posed by Derrida is arguably one of the most singular and important achievements of deconstruction in relation to the Husserlian legacy and Marion's work is, by contrast, limited by its insistence on an originary anonymity of the giver and of giving and the absolute and unconditioned givenness of the given (and this, as will become clear, is also what opens his thought most directly onto theology and allows for a problematic blurring of the lines which separate phenomenological and theological discourse). Nevertheless, what is important to note at this stage in the argument is the way in which Marion uses his response to Derridean objections as a means of developing and radicalizing his thought further. The third reduction is tested against the deconstruction of the gift and strengthens further Marion's claim that phenomenality must be viewed as pure unconditioned giving prior to any other horizon, economic, ontological or otherwise. What is true for Marion's response to Derrida is true also for his response to Dominique Janicaud whose objection to the phenomenology of givenness Marion addresses directly over a number of pages just before he comes to his more extended discussion of *Given Time* (Marion 1997: 104–8; 2002c: 71–4).

The objection of *The Theological Turn* to Marion's work is, as Marion himself presents it, twofold: firstly Janicaud accuses the phenomenology of givenness of being too empty and abstract in its understanding of the phenomenon itself. The phenomenon is stripped down to a thin or minimal given and is so to the point that Marion's thinking as a whole emerges as a 'negative' phenomenology (Marion 1997: 104; 2002c: 72). Secondly, this minimalism works in favour of, and prepares the way for, a more maximalist or excessive investment in an overall schema of meaning which allows phenomenality to be invested with theological motifs and concerns (Marion 1997: 104; 2002c: 72). In short, Marion's phenomenology is, as Christina Gschwandtner puts it in summary of Janicaud's position 'a mere negative propaedeutic for his theology' (Gschwandtner 2007: xiv). In a later work which responds to the debate provoked by *The Theological Turn*, Janicaud himself summarizes the criticisms of the earlier book, suggesting that his broader target was the 'methodological displacements or even methodological drifting' of certain contemporary phenomenologists, a drifting which allowed theological transcendence to enter into phenomenology, thereby betraying it and decisively deviating from its legitimate concerns (Janicaud 2005: 14). Thus, while these so-called phenomenologists 'believe they have founded the phenomenon and to have enriched phenomenality, they either overload or bar access to it' (Janicaud 2005: 15). The essence of Janicaud's criticism throughout his debate with Marion is that the latter grossly misreads and misrepresents Husserlian thought.[10]

Marion's response to Janicaud in *Being Given* takes the form of a robust and localized rebuttal of the specific points mentioned above, but arguably also manifests itself in his wider re-elaboration of the phenomenology of givenness. On the specific point relating to the supposed 'thinness' or abstraction of the 'given' phenomenon, he notes pointedly that the given can neither be overly abstract nor 'thin' since it 'gives all that is and appears' (Marion 1997: 104; 2002c: 72). There is no attempt here to reduce the richness or density of phenomenality since, if such richness is given, it will necessarily be accounted for in the operation of the third reduction. On the question of theology somehow being smuggled into the phenomenology of givenness, Marion is no less firm: 'the notion of givenness', he asserts, 'has no need, since Husserl, of a theological weight to intervene in phenomenology' (Marion 1997: 105; 2002c: 72). In each case, he maintains, his arguments are grounded in a demonstrable fidelity to Husserl rather than in a deviation or 'methodological drifting' from him.

Throughout both *Reduction and Givenness* and *Being Given*, Marion takes great pains both to underline this fidelity to Husserlian phenomenology and to maintain a clear line of distinction between his phenomenological and theological concerns. Yet, arguably, the broader arguments of *Being Given* relating to 'saturated' phenomenality do quite unequivocally both deviate from key aspects of Husserlian thought and, in part at least, align themselves with theological motifs.

If the discovery of the third reduction represents the climax of *Reduction and Givenness* then the identification and detailed specification of saturated phenomena certainly provide the key focus for the final chapters of *Being Given*. The central importance Marion comes to confer upon saturated phenomena and the manner in which they come to be characterized is entirely consistent with his radicalization of givenness more generally. It will be recalled that in *Reduction and Givenness* Marion identified intuition as 'originally giving' and, of course, the giving of appearing as that which gives intuition its content prior to all other phenomenologically identifiable instances such as intentionality or signification. In *Being Given*, Marion describes the majority of phenomena as being separable into two distinct categories: those 'poor' in intuition and those said to be 'common-law' phenomena. The former are found, for example, in phenomena such as mathematical formulae or abstract ideas and are constituted according to an excess of concept or signifying intention over sensible intuition (which is either minimal or absent). Common-law phenomena are found, for instance, in technical or manufactured objects and are constituted according to a formalized lack of equivalence or inadequation between intuition and intention: the idea or abstract design of a technical object (intention) will always precede, and lack exact correspondence with, its manufacture or presentation (in sensible intuition). The fact that, according to the third reduction, givenness can be shown to be anterior to intention, signification and any kind of category or concept whatsoever means, for Marion, that one can think of a third type of phenomenon which would be constituted in the reverse manner according to an excess of purely intuitive givenness over any horizon of intentionality or concept. Indeed, Marion wants to argue for the necessary 'possibility of a phenomenon where intuition would give *more, indeed immeasurably more,* than intention would ever have aimed at or foreseen' (Marion 1997:

277; 2002c: 197). Being absolutely unconditioned and prior to intention or signification, it is entirely possible that the intuitive givenness of a phenomenon could give itself in excess of these moments and in an unlimited saturation of intuition. If this is possible, then the phenomenologist has every duty to describe such a phenomenon since, as Marion writes elsewhere, 'in phenomenology the least possibility is binding' (Marion 2005: 57; 2008b: 34).

The principal characteristic of saturated phenomena according to Marion is one of surprise, unexpectedness or unpredictability: 'First, the saturated phenomenon *cannot be aimed at* [*ne peut se viser*]. This impossibility stems from its essentially unforeseeable character' (Marion 1997: 280; 2002c: 199). A saturated phenomenon is not something that can appear according to the intentional directedness of consciousness nor within the horizon of any anticipation or purposiveness. It is not something that can be adequately described or prescribed according to categories, concepts or fixed signifying forms, and certainly it is not something that gives itself up for measurement, verifiable experimentation or scientific determination. Indeed, Marion comes to characterize the saturated phenomenon as an absolute givenness to and of intuition in excess of all determinate or delimiting horizon whatsoever. The saturated phenomenon gives itself, as it were, absolutely and free from any conditioning by or analogy with already understood, lived experience. It does not depend on any existing horizon and is thus an entirely unconditioned phenomenon (Marion 1997: 296; 2002c: 212). Much of the detailed phenomenological description of the saturated phenomenon in *Being Given* aims at a demonstration of this excessive character of absolute givenness. Marion shows, for instance, how such phenomena would appear or give themselves outside of Kantian categories of understanding (of quality, quantity, relation and analogy) (Marion 1997: 280–95; 2002c: 199–212).[11] In excess of any horizon or phenomenological condition of possibility, the saturated phenomenon is paradoxical in the sense of being both impossible and possible at the same time. It is also endowed with a certain ipseity or selfhood: it gives itself autonomously as itself and by itself. Giving itself as and by itself, it is not limited or delimited either by a phenomenological horizon nor by the limits of an I. It is, as it were, self-constituting (Marion 1997: 305; 2002c: 219). The characterization of the saturated phenomenon in these terms is, as has been indicated, entirely consistent with Marion's account of the anteriority and unconditionality of givenness and with his discovery of the third reduction.[12] Indeed, such a characterization confers upon the saturated phenomenon an exemplary and privileged status insofar as it is the autonomous self-giving givenness of the phenomenon which is foregrounded above any other instance. This is phenomenality par excellence, or, as Marion puts it: 'The saturated phenomenon in the end establishes the truth of all phenomenality because it marks, more than any other phenomenon, the givenness from which it comes' (Marion 1997: 317; 2002c: 227).

Yet in strict Husserlian terms Marion's formulations here are at best unorthodox and at worst un- or supra-phenomenological. As Janicaud rightly points out, endowing the phenomenon with an ipseity or selfhood is against both the letter and the spirit of the Husserlian text (Janicaud 2005: 36–7). Perhaps more importantly, the notion of horizon and the dependency of phenomenal appearing upon a horizon are indispensable for Husserl's thinking and for phenomenology more generally. For a phenomenon to appear and be constituted as such, it must do so and against the backdrop of a horizon of referential implications that are drawn in its wake. Without horizonality, one could argue, there is no phenomenality.[13]

Marion's attempt to unbind the saturated phenomenon from its dependence upon any delimiting horizon and his conferral upon it of an ipseity or selfhood appear then to give some reasonable grounds for the charge of 'methodological displacement' or drift levelled by Janicaud in relation to phenomenological orthodoxy. Certainly, his assertions of fidelity to Husserl's text need to be viewed critically and not taken at face value. The question arises here as to whether objects or phenomena are still *constituted* by pure or transcendental consciousness, as the post-Kantian inflection of Husserlian phenomenology would insist, or whether, in a surprising reversal of the spirit and letter of Husserl's text, it is now the case that givenness itself is *constitutive*. The implication of Marion's arguments is that it is consciousness that is now constituted in and by the ipseity and unconditioned givenness of the given. This is arguably a reversal or inversion of the post-Kantian emphasis on the constitutive nature of the subject, of consciousness, or of the transcendental ego. Despite the primary emphasis here on the originary or sensible intuition, there is something in this reversal of the constitutive and the constituted which resembles or echoes the anti-Kantianism of Badiou and Laruelle discussed in chapters 6 and 7. The implications of this will be assessed more fully in the conclusion.

In light of this, it is arguable that the persuasiveness of Janicaud's objections is less apparent when the critical question posed to Marion relates less to phenomenological fidelity and more to the innovative force of his overall transformation of Husserlian thought. Rather than objecting to Marion's lack of fidelity to Husserl, his phenomenology of givenness should perhaps best be judged in terms of the originality of what it allows him to think.

Saturation and the self

Saturated phenomena in Marion are divided into four distinct modalities: the event, the idol, flesh, and the icon. Despite this apparently categorizing gesture, Marion argues that what characterizes each of the moments phenomenologically speaking is an excess of appearing or givenness over all intentional directedness and categorial determination. Each of the four modalities is schematically characterized in the following terms:

1   In the case of the event, something occurs which is not limited to or determinable by a specific instant or place, nor limited to the experience of any one individual. The event here is the historic event, one whose impact will be felt by an entire population and whose meaning cannot be grasped with the scope of any one interpretative gesture. Indeed, it is the very ongoing and non-finite process of deciding upon or interpreting an event which constitutes historical community as such. The event imposes itself upon a collectivity of individuals in excess of any singular intentional directedness or horizon of expectation (Marion 1997: 318–19; 2002c: 228–9).

2   Marion gives the work of art, and more specifically painting, as the privileged example of an idol. A painting gives a sensible intuition or sensory perception which is in excess of any determinate meaning, concept, category or classification. We might bring categories or concepts to the painting but, as with the historical event, no such category will be able definitively to account for the surfeit of sensible (visual) intuition the painting makes manifest (Marion 2005: 158; 2008b: 128); any such definitive accounting of meaning is deferred or rendered non-identical with the excess of phenomenal appearance for which it seeks to account (subject to a logic of *différance*).

3   Prior to any intentional directedness of consciousness to an object, the experience of flesh is one of auto-affection or originary sense impression. Pain, suffering, joy, pleasure, indeed sensation of any kind are all auto-affections of the flesh. In this context, flesh needs

to be understood as the fundamental medium of givenness itself: only in the auto-affection of flesh, in excess of all intention and signification, is any intuition given at all, and perhaps most importantly, the flesh gives the self to itself: 'flesh shows itself only in giving itself – and, in this first "self," it gives me to myself' (Marion 1997: 323; 2002c: 232).

4   Marion describes the icon as that which offers nothing to the gaze and which, inaccessible to the gaze of a spectator, nevertheless imposes its own gaze upon the spectator. The icon is the gaze of the other upon the self: 'it resides precisely in the black holes of two pupils, in the sole and minuscule space where, on the surface of the bodies of others, there is nothing to see . . . in the gaze facing me. The gaze that others cast and make weigh on me therefore does not give itself to my gaze' (Marion 1997: 323–4; 2002c: 232). The icon then is the face of the other; it is not constituted by intentional consciousness but rather imposes itself upon it in and of itself.

Readers familiar with the broader field of recent French thought will no doubt recognize echoes of other thinkers in each of these characterizations. The description of the event may recall Paul Ricoeur's collective hermeneutics of history (Ricoeur 1992; 2006) or even Alain Badiou's conception of the event (discussed in chapter 6). The description of painting by which Marion characterizes the idol strongly resonates with a Derridean thinking of *différance* and perhaps more specifically with Nancy's account of the artwork in texts such as *The Muses* and *The Ground of the Image*. Marion's characterization of flesh recalls Merleau-Ponty's thinking in *The Visible and the Invisible* and, much more directly and specifically, Michel Henry's phenomenology of auto-affective immanent life (Merleau-Ponty 1968; Henry 1973). Likewise, the description of the icon clearly repeats the Lévinassian motif of the face of the Other. Despite these resonances, echoes or repetitions, it would be wrong to dismiss Marion's thinking of saturated phenomena as merely derivative. Rather, what he can be said to have achieved is more of an original synthesis of a number of the key advances in recent French phenomenological and post-phenomenological thought: hermeneutics (Ricoeur), *différance* and artistic-presentation (Derrida/Nancy), auto-affection (Henry), and the gaze of the other (Lévinas). The scope of the phenomenon has been extended by the thought of givenness and saturation in order to incorporate the otherwise elusive and excessive phenomenality of these moments or, as Marion puts it, 'Far from underestimating the most recent advances in phenomenology . . . I am only trying to confirm them by assigning each a precise site within givenness' (Marion 1997: 441; 2002c: 321–2).

With the exception of the idol which manifests a surfeit of visible intuition, Marion's thinking of saturation allows for the incorporation (within the phenomenological scope of the third reduction) of phenomena which cannot appear as visible objects, entities or beings, but which nevertheless demonstrably do make themselves manifest and therefore do require to be thought phenomenologically. None of the four modalities of saturation – event, idol, flesh and icon – can be reduced to a horizon of objectality or beingness (*étantité*); therefore, all four require Marion's broadened notion of the phenomenon as first and foremost that which is *given* in order to be thought.

It is here that the phenomenology of givenness edges most proximally towards theological concerns. Having outlined the different modalities of saturation, the text of *Being Given* immediately moves on to what Marion calls the phenomenon of 'revelation'. Since the space of phenomenality has now been extended to encompass experiences of the invisible and the objectively unpresentable, it is perhaps only logical that revelation should be welcomed into the fold of legitimate phenomenological concerns. With all due probity, Marion insists that phenomenology cannot be the arbiter of whether the experience of revelation can, has or will occur; it can only circumscribe or describe the phenomenality of such an occurrence in terms of how it would occur were it so to do. Yet despite such care, it could be asked, as Janicaud repeatedly does, whether Marion's phenomenological thought does not too neatly prepare the way for Christian, and specifically Roman Catholic, modes of religious experience or theological form. It is true that, when Marion does stray into direct religious references of any kind in his phenomenological writing, they are all without exception references to the Christian Bible and the Christian theological tradition.[14] One might therefore question the extent to which his descriptions of saturated phenomena such as revelation are compatible with non-Christian and/or non-monotheistic religious experience. Alternatively, and given the importance of these issues for the entirety of Marion's phenomenological and theological output, one might wonder how far he is able to account for the fact that what is perhaps most strikingly *given* in religious experience is its cultural specificity and its conditioning or shaping by contingent cultural and historical horizons or forms. Once again, the question of the production or genesis of the gift needs to be posed, together with the specifically Derridean question of whether absolute unconditionality is at all possible and whether the gift is not always an economized (and therefore spatio-temporally contingent and conditioned) instance.

Yet if one decides to be generous and to give Marion the benefit of the doubt here, then his attempt in *Being Given* to rigorously demarcate and keep separate phenomenological and theological concerns needs to be taken seriously. What then emerges as perhaps most interesting and original in the phenomenology of givenness is not its opening onto theological concerns or religious experience, but rather the account Marion gives of the 'self' of givenness.

It is here that the phenomenon of flesh, rather than that of revelation, comes into greater prominence. Flesh, it was noted earlier, is the originary medium of auto-affection and 'gives me to myself' (Marion 1997: 323; 2002c: 232). Yet Marion argues that the self of givenness, that to which giving is given, is no form of grounding or foundational 'subject' (such as emerges in the Cartesian *cogito* for example). Nor is it a transcendental unity of apperception (Kant), nor still a Husserlian transcendental ego or Heideggerian *Dasein*. Since giving is given in excess of objectality and being and in the absence of all metaphysical ground, the self to which it is given in the auto-affection of the flesh is itself also ungrounded and irreducible to any logic of causation or foundation. Across the pages of both *Reduction and Givenness* and *Being Given*, this self which is given to itself only in and through the receipt of givenness is named in a number of different ways: as the *interloqué*, as the 'receiver' (*l'attributaire*) (Marion 1997: 343; 2002c: 249), and also finally as the 'gifted' (*l'adonné*) (Marion 1997: 369; 2002c: 268). Marion repeatedly and explicitly returns to the question posed by Jean-Luc Nancy, namely 'Who comes after the subject?'[15] After the subject, he repeatedly answers, comes the self that receives givenness and is *constituted by* its reception of, or 'devotion' to, givenness. The radicalization of Husserlian *Gegebenheit* allows for the broadening of phenomenality and the rigorous description of a range of invisible, excessive or resolutely paradoxical phenomena but, Marion insists: 'At the centre stands no "subject", but a gifted, he whose function consists in receiving what is immeasurably given to him, and whose privilege is confined to the fact that he is himself received from what he receives' (Marion 1997: 442; 2002c: 322).

As was indicated in a preliminary fashion earlier, the ipseity of the given phenomenon, the fact that it gives itself by and of itself, means that a crucial reversal in the constitution of phenomenality has occurred. To repeat, whereas in Husserl consciousness or the transcendental ego is *constitutive*, in the auto-affection of the flesh which gives the self to itself in its receipt of the self-giving phenomenon, the self is now *constituted* (Marion 1997: 369; 2002c: 268). Flesh gives the self to itself but only insofar as something is given in and to the flesh. Once again, one can begin to discern a wider reversal in the direction of constitution which is marked in different ways in all the thinkers discussed in this book. Badiou and Laruelle have already been mentioned, but a similar case can also be made for other thinkers discussed here, such as Stiegler and Malabou.

In the context of Marion's thinking of saturated phenomenality, of flesh and of self, a number of conclusions can be drawn with regard to the originality or importance of his formulations. Firstly, in his attempt to integrate an overcoming of metaphysics with a philosophy of the unconditional given, Marion, like Michel Henry before him, has created a phenomenology of materiality or of material immanence. For all the alignment of his thinking with theological questions, his thought, and all possibilities of thinking for which it allows, remains rooted in the materiality of the flesh, in affect and in ungrounded auto-affection. Secondly, Marion has at the very same time developed a phenomenological account of finite existence which nevertheless thinks of finitude as constituted only in and through a *de*-limitation of the finite. The saturated phenomenon, that which 'establishes the truth of all phenomenality' (Marion 1997: 317; 2002c: 227), appears unconditionally and in excess of any dependence upon a finite horizon or upon any bounded condition of possibility. Finitude, here, can only be thought in terms of the infinitization of finite existence (and in this respect Marion can interestingly be compared to Nancy's thinking of 'infinitude' as discussed in the next chapter). Thirdly, Marion develops a notion of the self to whom givenness is given which transforms traditional metaphysical notions of subjectivity viewed as a foundation or ground of knowledge, as well as post-Kantian and phenomenological notions of consciousness as constitutive.

These motifs of materiality, infinity, and of an ungrounded self will be repeated and transformed in diverse ways in the thinking of the other philosophers treated by this study. Whether one embraces or refuses the alignment with theology that Marion's philosophy offers, his thinking of givenness, of saturation, of flesh and of self undoubtedly articulates an original post-deconstructive and post-metaphysical reformulation of phenomenology and a powerful reinvigoration of the phenomenological method.

2

Jean-Luc Nancy: The Infinity of Sense

Jean-Luc Nancy has published over sixty books and over four hundred articles in a career which has spanned just over four decades. Although he was initially best known in the anglophone academic world for his work on community published in the 1980s, since the late 1990s there has been a burgeoning interest in his philosophy as a whole and he has emerged as the most prominent and influential French philosopher working in the wake of Derridean deconstruction.[1] Yet, while Nancy's philosophy is certainly a deconstructive or post-deconstructive think-ing, it also, and from a very early stage, decisively diverges from Derrida. Nancy's 'singular-plural' ontology, his thinking of finitude, of shared finite existence, sense and world, uses philosophical terms and figures which would be placed under erasure or arouse a high degree of suspicion when seen from a deconstructive perspective: terms such as 'being', 'presence', 'experience', 'existence', 'truth', 'touch' and even, more recently, theological terms such as 'incarnation' and the 'divine'.

Nancy has sometimes been characterized as a thinker of finitude whose philosophy is most indebted to Heideggerian thought.[2] Yet such a characterization does not do justice to the diversity and breadth of his thinking. On the one hand, it is more true to say that, like Derrida's thought, Nancy's philosophy grows out of phenome-nology in general and could more properly be characterized as *post*-phenomenological. On the other hand, reducing Nancy simply to a thinker of 'finitude' in the Heideggerian mould does not take into account the extent to which he is also, and at the same time, a thinker of infinity, or what one might call the 'infinitude' of finitude. Taken in this light, Nancy should be aligned far more with figures such as

Maurice Blanchot or even Emmanuel Levinas rather than solely or straightforwardly with Heidegger. The diversity of his thought is reflected in its successive periods of development. In the 1970s, Nancy (often with his friend and colleague the late Philippe Lacoue-Labarthe) publishes what are principally philosophical commentaries, on, for instance, Lacan, Hegel, Kant and Descartes. In the 1980s, he begins to develop his important thinking around the question of the political and of community (again with Lacoue-Labarthe).[3] This decade also begins to see the emergence of a more ambitious philosophical thinking in major works such as *The Experience of Freedom* (Nancy 1988a; 1993c). In the 1990s, Nancy publishes the principal works upon which his status as an important philosopher of the late twentieth and early twenty-first century rests. These include a major work of ontology, *Being Singular Plural* (Nancy 1996a; 2000c) and also works which engage ambitiously with the question of thought itself, and with questions of embodiment, world disclosure and sense constitution (*A Finite Thinking* (Nancy 1990a; 2003c), *Corpus* (Nancy 1992a; 2008b), and *The Sense of the World* (Nancy 1993a; 1997e)). From the middle of the 1990s through to the first decade of this century, Nancy develops a sustained engagement with the question of art and with aesthetics. Finally, from the late 1990s onwards, he has also pursued what he calls a 'deconstruction of Christianity', a project which has continued right up to the time of writing this study with the publication of the second of two volumes in early 2010 (Nancy 2005a; 2008c; 2010b). Throughout all these successive stages of his career, Nancy has returned to and reworked elements of his previous work such that, taken as a whole, his philosophy emerges as a complex and sustained engagement with a number of fundamental concerns.

These concerns could be characterized, albeit rather broadly and schematically, as follows. Nancy's philosophy aims to develop an ontology, to think being as coexistence and as a singular plural 'being-with'. It engages in a sustained manner with the interrelated questions of community and of the political. It aims to pose the question of the subject and of a post-deconstructive subjectivity and does so in relation to the questions of embodiment, shared worldly existence, sense perception and sense itself, understood broadly speaking as the pre-symbolic meaningfulness of a shared bodily exposure to the world. It engages with what one might call the 'technicity' of worldly existence and sensory experience and on this basis develops a sustained meditation on the status of the arts. Finally, it aims to think the spacing, sharing and coming to presence of the world in terms of an exposure to/of an infinite excess of sense. There is something in this exposure of worldly existence to, or as, infinite excess that Nancy will come to call divine and to think in his deconstruction of Christianity. What follows here will seek to explore these interrelated concerns further and show that, despite the diversity of Nancy's philosophical corpus, it nevertheless does form a corpus, albeit one which insists on its own fragmentary status, on its status as philosophy which is itself exposed to infinite excess.

Infinitude

Finite thought, embodiment, and sense

Finitude could perhaps be most easily understood in terms of limits, that is, as the state of being finite, bounded or limited. The task of a finite thinking, then, would be to think thought itsclf as that which, without renouncing the values of truth or universality, can only think within and at its own limit, touching at its limit and at its own singularity of thought (Nancy 1990a: 13; 2003c: 5). Towards the beginning of *A Finite Thinking*, Nancy argues that this task is inseparable from the question of 'sense' and of the finitude of sense: 'it could be a question of sense's essential finitude – something that would, in turn, demand an essential finitude of thinking' (Nancy 1990a: 13; 2003c: 4). The use of the term 'sense' here is by no means straightforward and, arguably, the entirety of Nancy's philosophy from the beginning of the 1990s onwards can, in one way or another, be viewed as an attempt to elaborate upon its complex status and meaning. Nevertheless, *A Finite Thinking* does begin within an attempt to give an initial definition of this difficult term: 'By "sense" I mean sense in the singular sense taken absolutely: the sense of life, of Man, of the world, the sense of existence; the sense of existence which is or which makes sense, which without sense would not exist' (Nancy 1990a: 10–11; 2003c: 3). What is clear from the outset is that sense, here, has an ontological or existential status. If a world or anything in it can be said to be or to exist, if it can be perceived, taken as an object of thought or simply experienced as such, then that is because it in some way always already *makes sense*, and does so before or prior to conceptual determination, and prior to our giving it a fixed signification, or attributing to it predicates or characteristics. The implications of the ontological status of sense will be explored further as this discussion progresses.

What is worth underlining at this stage is that finitude, for Nancy, is not conceived as a kind of enclosure of thought within its own limits. He is not trying to argue that finite thinking is some kind of prison house which would deprive thought of any access to truth, or condemn it to be rooted in determinable specificities of historical context or situation. Nancy's finite thinking is not a relativism or perspectivism where one point of view has exactly the same value as any other. Nor is finitude here a limitation of thought which would imply an existence, beyond the limit, of a limitlessness or of an infinite (and therefore theological) transcendence. Already in *A Finite Thinking* Nancy understands finitude in terms of a limitation which is always, one might say always already, delimited or exposed to a certain limitlessness of actual and material worldly existence. Finite thinking is 'not a thinking of limitation, which implies the unlimitedness of a beyond, but a thinking of the limit as that on which, infinitely finite, existence arises [*s'enlève*] and to which it is exposed [*s'expose*]' (Nancy 1990a: 48–9; 2003c: 27). Any understanding of Nancy as a thinker of finitude needs to engage with the difficult logic of the limit which is being articulated here and, in particular, needs to engage with the force and implications of the formulation 'infinitely finite' (*infiniment finie*). Such a formulation is no doubt highly indebted to the thought and writing of Blanchot in texts such as *The Infinite Conversation* (Blanchot 1993) and clearly signals that Nancy's thinking of finitude is in no way reducible to the thought of an existence which would simply be enclosed within finite limits (e.g. those of contingency, mortality, language). At the same time, Nancy's use of French reflexive verb forms such as *s'enlever* and *s'exposer* can appear to be rather opaque, particularly to those unfamiliar with his thought.

The best way to tease out what might be at stake in these perhaps elliptical formulations is to turn to Nancy's thinking of sense and embodiment such as it is developed in texts such as *Corpus*, *The Sense of the World* and elsewhere. As has already been indicated, sense, for Nancy, has an ontological status: sense is always the sense of an existence which in some way always already makes sense. Yet, as the sense *of* existence, sense here is always engaged with a certain kind of materiality or concreteness. This materiality is, first and foremost, that of sensing bodies which perceive a world through the senses and through sensory experience more generally. Nancy is interested in the way that the spatiality of worldly existence is disclosed to us through situated and embodied being. In this context, his ontology of sense is also and at the same time an ontology of bodies. Sense and bodies are co-articulated in a fundamental way which discloses the world to us as existing. In *Corpus*, Nancy speaks of an 'Ontology of the body' and argues that 'bodies are existence, the very act of ex-istence, being' (Nancy 1992a: 20; 2008b: 19). At the same time, he also speaks of the body as a 'body of sense' (Nancy 1992a: 24; 2008b: 25) and argues that '*The body is the architectonics of sense*' (Nancy 1992a: 25; 2008b: 25). Being, then, is disclosed in an organization or structure in which sense and bodies are engaged to form the element in which the existence of a spatial, material world can be experienced as such.

These points are developed further in *The Sense of the World* where Nancy argues that this co-articulation of sense and bodies needs to be understood as 'being-toward-the-world'. The original French term *être-au-monde* can translate both as being-in-the-world and as being-toward-the-world, depending on what kind of inflection one gives to the preposition *à* which can have many meanings, including 'at', 'to', 'with' and 'in'. Nancy is trying to think sense as a horizon of shared meaningfulness to which bodies are *exposed* in their apprehension or perception of a world and in the interaction of bodies with the world and each other: their touching, their contact, their mutual spacing and crossing. In this context the co-articulation of sense and bodies is always a 'toward' rather than simply an 'in', insofar as the meaningfulness of the world is experienced always in a projection of bodily sensory experience towards the world and others or, in Nancy's preferred term, its 'exposure' to them. It should be underlined that sense, here, is not yet signification in any fixed or determinable form; it is not articulated in a relation of signifier to signified or in a symbolic order in the structuralist/Lacanian sense: '"being-toward-the-world", if it takes place (and it does take place), is caught up in sense well before all signification. It makes, demands or proposes sense this side of or beyond all signification . . . Thus, *world* is not merely the correlative of *sense*; it is structured as *sense*, and reciprocally, *sense* is structured as *world*' (Nancy 1993a: 17–18; 1997e: 7–8). Understanding the way in which sense, for Nancy, is a horizon of meaningfulness 'well before all signification' is central to understanding his philosophy as a whole.[4] Proposing the sense of the world as an instance which is prior or anterior to any symbolic order or signifying process is also to confer upon it a certain materiality or concreteness, a materiality which is of a different order than any 'materiality of the signifier' or of discourse as material practice. Nancy is trying to think about the way our embodied sense perception and bodily engagements with a world are always caught up in sense such that something always already makes sense in the very moment that it is sensed or perceived. He articulates this engagement of the senses with sense using the figure of 'touch': 'It is not a matter of signification, but of the sense of the world as its very *concreteness*, that on which our existence *touches* and by which it is *touched*, in all possible senses' (Nancy 1993a: 22; 1997e: 10). As is often the case, Nancy is using an apparently straightforward every-day term in a way which is in fact very complex and which resonates with a philosophical register which has a long history within the canon of European philosophy.[5]

It is impossible, within the context of this short discussion, to do full justice to the richness and complexity of Nancy's use of the figure of touch. Nevertheless, some insight can be gleaned from an important passage in *The Muses*, Nancy's first major book on art published in 1994: 'Touch is nothing other than the touch of sense altogether and of all the senses. It is their sensuality as such . . . touch presents the proper moment of sensible exteriority, it presents it *as such and as sensible*' (Nancy 1994: 35; 1996b: 17). 'Touch *forms one body* with sensing, or it makes of sensing a body, it is simply the *corpus* of the senses' (Nancy 1994: 35–6; 1996b: 17). It is the figure of touch here which acts as the hinge or point of articulation between sense understood as a horizon of meaningfulness and the senses understood in terms of the different forms of bodily sense perception (hearing, seeing, touch, taste, etc.). Touch at once becomes the privileged sense of all the five senses insofar as all five could be said to be a kind of contact or proximity in distance with a sensible exteriority. At the same time, touch becomes the figure by which the always already meaningful dimension of sensible experience can be thought: when we perceive or sense something, we 'touch on' or 'at' its sense in a way which is not yet a determined or determinable signification. One can perhaps begin to see here the way in which Nancy uses the term 'touch' to describe, one might say post-phenomenologically, the sense of the world, the sense which the world *is* insofar as it is both mean-ingful and at the same time embodied, material or concrete. In the figure of touch, Nancy is decisively shifting away from the figures of seeing, viewing and other optical metaphors which run through phe-nomenological discourse: '*world* invites us to no longer think on the level of the phenomenon (as surging forth, appearing, becoming visible, brilliance, occurrence, event), but on the level, let us say for the moment, of disposition (spacing, touching, contact, crossing)' (Nancy 1993a: 34, n. 19; 1997e: 176). The figure of touch, then, reor-ganizes the phenomenological discourse of world disclosure and sense constitution around a language of spacing and the mutual contact of bodies in a shared material world. In this manner, the question of phenomenality gives way to the question of shared mate-rial existence.

Being singular plural

If this thinking of sense and bodies represents a decisive shift away from a phenomenological discourse, it does not, as has already been emphasized, attempt to break with ontology, as would, in different ways, Levinas, Blanchot and Derrida. Again, though, care needs to be taken to understand the way in which Nancy uses the language of being, since, as before, his ontology of finitude is inseparable from a thinking of the infinite. If, for Levinas, ontology and finitude represent a gesture of enclosure (of existence) and, indeed, of violent foreclosure (of the ethical moment), this is decisively not the case for Nancy.[6] This is made very clear in a text such as *Being Singular Plural* where, as the title suggests, ontology occupies a central position. Building upon previous works and, in particular, upon *A Finite Thinking* and *The Sense of the World*, Nancy reiterates the ontological status conferred on sense: 'Being itself is given to us as sense' (Nancy 1996a: 20; 2000c: 2; translation modified). The language of being is used here without inverted commas and without being subjected to any irony or erasure. Yet being is thought in *Being Singular Plural* strictly and rigorously in terms of the infinite and irreducible excess of being over itself. The language Nancy uses to describe this excess of being over itself is that of being-with, coexistence, and the singular plurality of origins deployed within the logic of thinking at the limit of thought discussed above. Despite the lines of polemical opposition that separate the two philosophers, there is much that is shared here with Alain Badiou's ontology of inconsistent multiplicity elaborated in chapter 6. Nancy's thinking of embodiment and sense is clearly unequivocally and diametrically opposed to Badiou's subtractive approach to ontology and to his affirmation of a certain Platonism. However, Nancean singular plurality and Badiou's inconsistent multiplicity both affirm the actual infinity of being, its irreducible excess over itself, and its irreducibility to any horizon of unity, or any mode of substance or ground. Granted, Badiou would say that the Nancean discourse of thinking at the limit is not an *adequate* means to think the infinite excess of being over itself (this is reserved for the discourse of mathematics alone) but this should not detract from the similarity of their respective positions in this regard.

Nancy's arguments run broadly as follows: if being is given to us as sense, this is so only insofar as a fundamental privilege is accorded to the 'us' or the 'we' of this donation and only insofar as sense is always and only an element which is *shared*. As Nancy himself puts it, 'sense is itself the sharing of being' (Nancy 1996a: 20; 2000c: 2). It is worth noting here that, as well as drawing attention to its ontological status, this discussion has also repeatedly described sense as being a 'shared horizon of meaningfulness'. It is this motif of sharing which comes to the foreground in *Being Singular Plural*: '"sense", used absolutely in this way, has become the bared name of our being-with-one-another. We do not "have" sense or meaning any more because we are ourselves sense – entirely, without reserve, infinitely, with no sense other than "us"' (Nancy 1996a: 19; 2000c: 1). Meaningfulness here is not something we can ever experience in isolation. As a shared horizon, sense is pre-subjective in that it is prior to conscious thought or cognition. It is also impersonal in that it is prior to any individual identity. Sense, in its sharing and understood as the being-of-all-with-each-other, is that from which any experience of self-reflexivity, individual subjectivity or of personal individuation can arise as such. Being is therefore always being-with and the 'we', for Nancy, is always primordial.

Yet if sense is what we *are*, special attention also needs to be given to his use of the words 'without reserve, *infinitely*' (my emphasis). The key point to note in this regard is that sense, as a horizon of meaningfulness to which bodies are exposed, or upon which they 'touch' in sensory experience, is never, for Nancy, a homogeneous element which can come to be fully determined within a system of signification. Sense is not something that can return to itself in an instance of self-sameness or in a way which would allow it to form a closed circuit of stable meaning. Neither can it be held in reserve nor gathered into the work of a concept. Sense is always exposed in its irreducible singularity and in the irreducible plurality of its exposure. This 'singular plurality' of sense is nothing other than the multiplicity of bodies which, in each and every instant, live, make and share sense. 'A singularity is always a body', Nancy writes, 'and all bodies are singularities' (Nancy 1996a: 37; 2000c: 18). It is here that the register of the infinite is engaged within Nancy's thinking of finite, corporeal being: '"finitude" signifies: the infinite singularity of sense, the infinite singularity of access to truth. Finitude is the origin, that is, it is an infinity [*une infinitude*] of origins' (Nancy 1996a: 33; 2000c: 15). Sense here is not an enclosed or delimited point of origin or stable and fixed grounding of existence. As that to which bodies are exposed in their touch, contact and spacing, sense is only ever a passage or movement (of exposure), which can never be limited, de-limited or contained. It may be what we are; indeed, it is the very truth of what we are and of our being-of-all-with-each-other. Yet it is so only as an infinite excess of sense over any and all finite limits, as the exposure of bodies to that excess and, with that, as the disclosure of a shared meaningful world.

These are difficult formulations and, to a certain extent, the difficulty of Nancy's thinking here is irreducible, since, on its own terms, it is aiming to elaborate a thought of being which is always in excess of thought. Nancy's is a paradoxical ontology insofar as being (envisaged as being-with) always escapes the conceptual or figural grasp of ontological disclosure. It exceeds any and all possible reductions to the identity or limits of a *logos*. This is the kind of paradoxical or aporetic logic with which readers of much twentieth-century French thought will be familiar.[7] Yet ultimately, perhaps, Nancy is trying to think something that is quite straightforward and accessible, namely that we experience a world together whose meaningfulness is both shared and always already available to us in the most basic material sense of perceptions and worldly interactions. Such concrete meaningfulness is what allows us to have a sense of an individual self and to produce thought, symbolic forms, linguistic meaning or abstract concepts and signification. Yet, at the same time, it is never reducible to any of these instances. It is infinitely refractory, infinitely plural and is so only in the multiplicity of singular bodies which are exposed to sense. It is the emphasis on the singularity and plurality of bodies which means that Nancy's thinking, for all its paradoxical force, and for all its post-deconstructive and post-phenomenological rigour, can also persist with the far more accessible ontological language of being-with, as in, for example, the following sentence: 'In being-with and as being-with, we have always already begun to understand sense, and to understand ourselves and the world as sense. And this understanding is always already completed, whole, full, and infinite' (Nancy 1996a: 122; 2000c: 98). Despite the difficulty of his formulations, Nancy is aiming to think the very straightforward thought that, before we are anything which can resemble an individual self or subject, we *are* firstly together in a shared meaningfulness, and that this being together or sharing overspills any possibility of stable conceptualization, signification or determination.

Yet, from this thinking of shared sense and world in which the 'we' is always primordial, an account of individual subjectivity or self does emerge. In fact, Nancy's attempt to elaborate the conditions of what one might call a post-deconstructive subjectivity dates back to the earliest phase of his career in works such as *Ego Sum* (Nancy 1979).[8] The subject here is, as one might now expect, very much to be understood as a 'body-subject' and recalls in various ways the philosophy of Merleau-Ponty as elaborated in key texts such as *Phenomenology of Perception* and *The Visible and the Invisible* (Merleau-Ponty 1968;

2002). Yet the Nancean body-subject diverges in key ways from the 'body-proper' of Merleau-Pontean phenomenology. Nancy's body, for instance, has no gathered unity or propriety since it is always exposed, projected outside itself, as it touches on the sense of the world. Bodily experience here is irreducibly fractured or fragmented. As has been shown already, the exposure to sense never returns to itself, it occurs as an infinite and non-totalizable plurality of singular instances. In this context, the individual, the subject or the self can never be said to form a coherent unit or substantive ground. Rather they *are formed* in a multiplicity or plurality of singularities always exposed to a worldly exteriority or, as Nancy puts it: 'The individual is an intersection of singularities, the discrete exposition of their simultaneity, an exposition that is both discrete and transitory' (Nancy 1996a: 109; 2000c: 85). Perhaps the best terms to use in this context are 'subject' or 'self' rather than the term 'individual'. This is because the (body-)subject in Nancy emerges only in and through a certain *self*-reflexivity which is made possible by the exposure of finite sensory experience to the infinity of sense.

This self-reflexive structure has been best described by Nancy in a more recent text entitled *Listening* (Nancy 2002b; 2007d). In this short work, the dimension of sound and the faculty of listening is used to think once more the relation of bodily sensing to sense. The question of 'self', of individual consciousness and self-reflexive experience has a central place in the argument of *Listening*. Listening is chosen here insofar as it is paradigmatic of the way in which all the senses, in their exposure to sense, allow what Nancy calls an 'access-to-self', a kind of sensible–intelligible reflexivity of sensory experience which gives us self-awareness or self-consciousness in the first instance: 'All perceptible registers make up this access to "self" (which is also to say, to "sense"). But the fact that they are many – and without any possible totalizing – marks this same access, at once, with an internal diffraction, which perhaps in turn lets itself be analyzed in terms of sending [*renvoi*], echoes, resonances and rhythms' (Nancy 2002b: 31, n. 1; 2007d: 73, n. 23; translation modified). It is interesting to note here that, for Nancy, 'access-to-self' and 'access-to-sense' are more or less co-constitutive or covalent. He is arguing in effect that our sense of self emerges only in and through the exposure of finite sensory experience to the infinity of sense.[9] It is interesting also that this exposure of the finite to the infinite is described in terms of a rhythm, a referral (*renvoi*), or an echoing and resonance. This rhythm or resonance would be that of the successive singular and plural exposures of bodily sensing to sense in each and every instance of sensory experience. The Nancean self, then, emerges as nothing other than this syncopated rhythm of successive instances of exposure to sense. This is not a self which is grounded in any way or formed in any kind of substance. It is not a self endowed with any fixed identity or stability; it is a being-always-already-outside-of-itself or an irreducible exteriority. Nancy articulates this in the following terms: 'Access to self: neither to a proper self (I), nor to the self of another, but to the form or structure of the *self* as such, that is to say, to the form, structure, and movement of an infinite referral [*renvoi*], since it refers to something [itself] that is nothing outside of the referral' (Nancy 2002b: 25; 2007d: 9). Nancy is repeating here the thinking of sense, embodiment and exposure developed in the 1990s in *The Sense of the World* and *Being Singular Plural*. Yet he is doing so using the language of an infinite referral of the senses via the infinity of sense and doing so in such a way as to develop much more his thinking of the singular self, rather, than say, of collective being-with. Clearly, the primordiality of coexistence or being-with has not been abandoned in *Listening*, since the sense engaged in the 'infinite referral [*envoi infini*]' of sense experience is, as ever, a shared element in which existence is given as such and as shared. It might be noted here that, as with the renewed conception of 'self' elaborated by Marion and discussed in the previous chapter, Nancy's 'access to self' appears to be very different from a constitutive (transcendental or phenomenological) ego or consciousness. Once again, this is a self that is constituted rather than constitutive. In this case, though, the self is constituted in the infinite referral of, or exposure to, sense, rather than in the giving of a primordial and absolutely unconditioned givenness.

It might be useful to pause here briefly in order to highlight a potential limitation of Nancy's thinking of sense as being-with. It is arguable that the emphasis he places on a fundamental and originary sharing of sense as the element of communal being does not altogether do justice to, or sufficiently account for, the way in which the share of being is unevenly or unequally distributed or divided. Certainly, Nancy sees in the originary sharing of being a starting point for any political affirmation of justice or equality (Nancy 1991b: 51; 2002a: 73, 177; 2007c: 61, 111). In this context, inequality, oppression or evil would all be understood by Nancy as a form of violence done to, or foreclosure of, a more primordial ontological sharing which is always already shared equally. Yet there is a question as to whether Nancy's affirmation of an originary sharing is not a little too optimistic and whether it is able to articulate a more originary violence or unequal division of the share (on this point, see Howard Caygill in Sheppard and Sparks 1997: 30–1). If this is a thinking of embodied being-with understood as *finitude*, i.e. as an existence marked by birth and death, does it account for the fact that some bodies will be *born into* and *as* an unequal share of material existence? That is to say, bodies are always born into different sites of a material existence that are shared unequally, depending upon the distribution of bodies across different geographical and geopolitical situations, and they are born as bodies bearing different markers of identity that will determine or influence their share of existence (e.g. colour, ethnicity, biological sex and, of course, social class). Arguably, Rancière's thinking of the 'distribution of the sensible' which articulates a fundamental sharing *and* a hierarchical, exclusory or unequal distribution of material sensible–intelligible existence does more to philosophically articulate the violence of ontological sharing than does Nancy's thinking of being-with.

This reservation aside, it should by now be clear the extent to which Nancy's thinking of sense and infinity lies at the very centre of all his thinking, of existence, of world, embodiment, sensory experience and of subjectivity or self. As his philosophy develops from the mid-1990s onwards, it becomes increasingly preoccupied with questions of art and aesthetics and with the question of the legacy of Christianity. However, this shift in emphasis does not necessarily articulate a radical break in his thinking. Indeed, as will become clear, the interrelated motifs of sensory experience, sense and embodiment continue to play a central role, albeit within the context of a seemingly different set of concerns.

Art and incarnation

The arts

The emphasis Nancy places on the multiplicity of the arts has been matched by the diversity and range of his writing in this area. He has written extensively on painting (and specifically on, for example, Christian art and on portraiture), on film, on sculpture and installation art, but also on poetry and on prose literature. Much of this writing takes the form of individual full-length works, for example, *The Muses* (Nancy 1994; 1996b), *Le Regard du portrait* (Nancy 2000a), *Visitation (de la peinture chrétienne)* (Nancy 2001e), *L'Évidence du film* (Nancy 2001c), *The Ground of the Image* (Nancy 2003b; 2005b) and *Noli me tangere* (Nancy 2003a; 2008d). However, Nancy has also written many shorter pieces, often published in exhibition catalogues and in collaboration with artists themselves (some of these pieces have been collected in English translation in the second volume of *The Muses*, entitled *Multiple Arts* (Nancy 2006)).

Yet despite the diversity of this writing on the question of art, a number of distinct tendencies can be discerned. First and foremost, it should be underlined that Nancy's thinking here arises from, and is very closely connected to, his wider thinking about sense experience, embodiment and world disclosure. In this context, one might say that his formulations in relation to aesthetics (i.e. the arts) are inseparable from his thinking about the aesthetic (i.e. sense experience). Nancy, perhaps more than any other contemporary French thinker, restores the philosophical questioning of aesthetics to its original meaning, that of *aisthesis* (the ancient Greek noun referring to perception from the senses).[10] At the same time, and unlike traditional enlightenment aesthetics (of, say, Hegel), Nancy does not aim to subsume the specificity of individual art forms into any unified or overarching concept of Art. All his thinking here is directed towards an affirmation of the irreducible multiplicity of the arts in order then to relate this to the irreducible multiplicity (or singular plurality) of sense experience. This means that Nancy almost always talks about art in relation to a specific art form (painting, film, etc.) and more often than not in relation to the work of a particular artist (e.g. Abbas Kiarostami, On Kawara, Michel Deguy, Titian and so on). This also means, of course, that when he does talk about any one particular art form or comments on an individual artist he is also, through his discussion of a particular instance, aiming also to elaborate a more general philosophical understanding about the multiplicity of the arts. When he more directly engages with the philosophical tradition of aesthetics (as in, for instance, his discussion of Hegel in *The Muses*), he does so in order to deconstruct the unified and all-embracing conceptions of Art that the tradition has in different ways elaborated.[11] To read the full range of Nancy's writings on art is, therefore, to be confronted with a strong sense of diversity (of forms and of individual engagements with artists and artworks). Yet to read his writing on art is also, and at the same time, to encounter a sustained concern to elaborate a logic of aesthetic presentation which informs all artworks and underpins the irreducible plurality of the arts as a whole.

First and foremost, Nancy wants to distance or differentiate his account from any phenomenological understanding of art and he makes this very explicit in *The Muses*, his first major work on the subject: 'The objects of art do not depend on a phenomenology ... because they are prior to the phenomenon itself' (Nancy

1994: 61; 1996b: 33). If artworks present to us some kind of sensible–intelligible form, this is not, Nancy argues, because they are *re-presenting* the world of phenomena according to a logic of mimesis. That is to say, they are not straightforward copies of the objects or people that we recognize or perceive in the world around us, nor are they reproductions of their abstract idea or underlying essence. Nancy's refusal to understand works of art according to any representational logic is fundamental to his account of art as a whole and remains a constant throughout all his writing on the subject. If, however, the objects of art are non-representational and are in some way 'prior to the phenomenon', this is because, Nancy continues: 'They are of the patency of the world [*Elles sont de la patence du monde*]' (Nancy 1994: 61; 1996b: 33). To say that artworks are 'of the patency of the world' may appear to be a rather oblique or obscure formulation. What is meant here can best be understood by returning briefly to Nancy's thinking of sense and world disclosure which, it has already been emphasized, is intimately related to the account he gives of the arts and of artworks.

Nancy, it will be recalled, seeks, in works such as *The Sense of the World*, to move away from the optical metaphors (of seeing, looking, lighting, revealing, etc.) which inform phenomenological accounts of meaning constitution and world disclosure. His use of the terms 'patent' and 'patency' need to be understood within the context of this discursive displacement. In this specific instance, though, it is the language of donation and giving (so central to phenomenology and to a thinker like Marion) which he is aiming to displace. The question of the intelligibility of worldly appearance is addressed once again in *The Muses*. He writes: 'In truth it is not a question of donation, nor of intention, nor even of a signifying. The coming [*venue*] of the world is not even a coming. The world is simply patent [*patent*]' (Nancy 1994: 60; 1996b: 33). The original French term used by Nancy, *patent*, means to be evident or manifest (as in something which is 'evidently' or 'manifestly' obvious).[12] Phenomenal appearance, Nancy argues, is not given as such and nor is it presented according to an event of donation. Rather, the world, and more specifically the sense of the world (which, as has been shown, is what the world *is*) is simply always already available to us as the medium of existence. It is never fully present, presented or given as such, but, as was shown earlier, it is always that upon which we touch when we experience the world as (always already) meaningful. Thus the appearance of an intelligible world is simply evident, manifest, patent. In this context, the objects of art are not at all representational but are rather 'of the patency of world' insofar as they 'touch upon' the sense of the world just as we, albeit in a different manner, also 'touch upon' that sense in our embodied sensory perceptions. An important and revealing comment made by Nancy in *The Sense of the World* may clarify what is at stake here. Sense, he writes, is that which 'exceeds the phenomenon in the phenomenon itself' (Nancy 1993a: 35; 1997e: 17). The images or forms presented by works of art are not representational in that they do not retrace, re-present or copy the exterior forms of phenomena. Rather, the images and forms of art, being prior to the phenomenon, give some kind of access to the sense of the world or, as Nancy himself puts it: 'Art isolates or forces . . . the moment of the world as such, the being-world of the world' (Nancy 1994: 37; 1996b: 16).

Art here enjoys a privileged status insofar as it allows some kind of exposure, or indirect access, to the sense or truth of the world. For if, as was shown earlier, sense is that ungraspable horizon of meaningfulness which is always and only ever an excess over language, thought and representation, art nevertheless touches upon, or is exposed to, that excess. 'Art', Nancy writes, 'forces a sense to touch itself, to be this sense that it is' (Nancy 1994: 42; 1996b: 21). This may appear still to be a rather dense and difficult formulation. Yet what Nancy is trying to think here is, perhaps, entirely simple or straightforward. We know very well that works of art have an impact upon us in an intense and direct (and at times very physical) manner. They make sense in some more or less diffuse fashion and in a way which seems intimately bound up with the refractory nature of our shared experience of the world and with the affective states (both individual and collective) which shape that experience. We are used to the notion that engaging with a work of art can give us access to some form of truth, a truth of what we are or of the way the world is. We may also know that works of art do this in a way which can never be entirely reduced to any single determinate signification, nor any one codified meaning or interpretation. In situating the images and forms of art 'prior to the phenomenon' and in arguing that they expose or touch upon the diffuse horizon of sense that the world is (without ever directly presenting or re-presenting sense), Nancy's account gives a powerful philosophical explanation of all the things we may more intuitively know or feel that art does, and of all the things which have historically given art such a privileged status and value.

It might not be surprising in this context that Nancy has written extensively on the tradition of Christian painting and the relation that art can maintain to the dimension of the sacred or divine transcendence. For if it is true that art touches upon, or is exposed to, the excessive and ungraspable horizon of sense that the world *is*, then its intimate relation to the dimension of transcendence, or to the way in which human culture understands transcendence, would appear to be both necessary and inevitable. However, Nancy's corporeal ontology of sense does not directly invoke the category of transcendence, at least not in any straightforward manner. If, in works such as *The Sense of the World*, sense is an excessive and ungraspable horizon, it is only transcendent insofar as it is also and at the very same time immanent. Insofar as sense infinitely exceeds or transcends the limits of finite existence, it does so only as a material immanence. Sense is therefore what Nancy comes to term a 'trans-immanence'. It is this notion of trans-immanence that he invokes when he comes to elaborate the way in which art 'touches upon' sense in *The Muses*. Art, he writes: 'touches on the immanence and transcendence of touch, or put another way: it touches on the trans-immanence of being-in-the-world' (Nancy 1994: 36; 1996b: 18). To say that art touches on touch may once again appear to be a rather opaque formulation. It should be recalled from earlier in the discussion, however, that touch for Nancy is the key term which articulates our shared experience of the world as a contact(-in-distance) of the horizon of sense and embodied sense perception. So art, for Nancy, touches on that very touch on sense which discloses the world to us in the most fundamental manner. It is in this context that he can argue that art touches the trans-immanent being-to-the-world, or, in a more recent text, that it is a 'concentration of world' (Nancy 2003b: 27; 2005b: 10), or, indeed, that 'art touches the real' (Nancy 2003b: 54; 2005b: 25).

Nancy, then, has developed an account of art which places it outside of any logic of representation or mimesis but which nevertheless affirms the possibility of realism. The critique of representation and realism as developed in the twentieth century by the *nouveau romanciers*, by structuralist and post-structuralist criticism and also by Derridean deconstruction has not been rejected by Nancy in favour of some return to an earlier aesthetic model.[13] Rather, he has developed what Derrida himself termed an 'absolute post-deconstructive realism' (Derrida 2000: 60; 2006: 46). If art 'touches the real', it is not because it can signify or codify worldly experience and re-present it to us (which of course it does, but this codification is a construct and far from real). Art touches the real because its presentation of sensible–intelligible forms disengages the senses from signification and thereby also disengages the world from signification, thus exposing us to 'the moment of the world as such, the being-world of the world' (Nancy 1994: 37; 1996b: 16).

Incarnation

If it is surprising to some that a French philosopher working in the wake of Derridean deconstruction may come to elaborate an, albeit heterodox, realist aesthetic, then it is perhaps even more startling that he should have come over the past decade and a half to engage so closely with Christianity and with questions relating to monotheism more generally. From the beginning of his career, Nancy's thought has aligned itself closely with a variety of philosophical legacies that are distinctly and often virulently anti- or a-theological: for instance, the legacy of the Nietzschean 'death of God', of Heidegger's destruction of 'onto-theology', or of Bataille's 'a-cephalic' thought. Yet we also know that as a youth and at the very beginning of his career, Nancy was an active and engaged Christian and, indeed, his very first published articles in the 1960s appeared in the Catholic journal *Esprit*. However much such biographical knowledge may be thought to be useful here, what rapidly becomes clear when one reads Nancy's writing on Christianity is that it is, like his writing on art, intimately connected to the rest of his work and, in many respects, functions as a means of re-elaborating its central concerns, albeit in a different register and in a rather different context.

Nancy's project of a 'deconstruction of Christianity' was first announced in an article bearing that name published in the journal *Études Philosophiques* in 1998.[14] Since then, he has published two volumes on the topic, *Dis-enclosure* (Nancy 2005a; 2008c) and *L'Adoration* (Nancy 2010b). Perhaps the most important thing to note about this endeavour is that the 'deconstruction' at work here is not construed as something that the sceptical philosopher performs *upon* Christianity by way of a more or less critical or destructive reading of the Bible or of religious or theological doctrines. Rather, Nancy argues, the deconstruction at work here is part of the internal logic and historical unfolding of Christianity itself. That is to say, Christianity is inherently auto- or self-deconstructive. This logic of auto-deconstruction is very similar to the deconstruction of the metaphysics of presence such as it is thought by Derrida. Indeed, even in much earlier texts such as *Corpus*, Christianity is explicitly aligned with the metaphysics of presence. Here, Nancy suggests that the words of the Eucharist, *Hoc est enim corpus meum*, are an assertion, tirelessly repeated in Christian ritual, of the immediate presence of God. The Eucharist is an affirmation that 'God's body is *there*' (Nancy 1992a: 7; 2008b: 3). Such an affirmation of immediate presence reassures the believer about the solidity and reliability of the world of appearances; it calms and soothes, 'allays all our doubts about appearances, conferring, on the real, the final touch of its pure Idea: its reality, its existence' (Nancy 1992a: 8; 2008b: 5).[15] This alignment of Christianity with the metaphysics of presence is taken up once again in *Dis-enclosure: The Deconstruction of Christianity 1*. An affirmation of presence, Nancy argues, lies also at the very heart of the Christian doctrine of incarnation (which itself lies at the very heart of Christianity as a whole). In its most orthodox version, Christian incarnation is the doctrine of '*homoousia*, consubstantiality, the identity or community of being and substance between the Father and the Son' (Nancy 2005a: 219; 2008c: 151). Incarnation is thought here as the 'presencing' of divine spirit in fleshy matter, and this real and immediate presence of the divine is then endlessly reaffirmed in the ritual of the Eucharist. If metaphysics is the gesture by which thought grounds or authenticates the being and presence of beings with reference to some transcendent causal principle, then Christianity is metaphysics par excellence. It is a religion which seemingly installs an affirmation of presence as its first and final gesture.

In this context, Nancy points out towards the beginning of *Dis-enclosure* that all the most vigorous critics of the metaphysical tradition (he cites Nietzsche, Heidegger and Wittgenstein, Derrida and Deleuze) have easily shown that it is from *within* the very structure or system of metaphysics that metaphysics itself is undone. Metaphysics, they show in various ways, is necessarily exposed to an unsettling excess which destabilizes or un-grounds all that would seek to secure a stable foundation for the being of beings (Nancy 2005a: 16–17; 2008c: 7). They have shown, Nancy argues, that 'metaphysics deconstructs itself constitutively, and, in deconstructing itself, it dis-encloses [*déclot*] in itself the presence and certainty of the world founded on reason' (Nancy 2005a: 17; 2008c: 7). Metaphysics can be seen to be a form of closure by which beings, grounded in presence, are therefore in a certain sense 'enclosed' within the determinate finite limits which assure their self-identity. Yet, at the very same time, this instance of closure or enclosure is always and unavoidably exceeded, and metaphysics opens onto an excess or absence of ground. In its constitutive gesture of foundation and closure, metaphysics is inevitably exposed to what Nancy comes to call its 'dis-enclosure': 'closure invariably dis-encloses itself' (Nancy 2005a: 17; 2008c: 7).

As metaphysical through and through, Christianity, Nancy argues, is no different. It necessarily comes, despite itself, to untie the logic of foundation, grounding and presence which it appears so tirelessly to affirm. In order to demonstrate that this is so, Nancy turns to a more sustained analysis of the question of incarnation and, more specifically, to the Pauline doctrine of incarnation conceived of as *kenosis*. This doctrine occupies a rather marginal and disputed status within Christology and Christian theology more generally. As was indicated earlier, the doctrine of 'hypostatic union' provides a far more orthodox understanding of incarnation. The hypostatic union of divine spirit and mortal flesh, it will be recalled, describes the way in which the two would be conjoined in the body of Christ in a manner which affirms their shared essence (*homoousia*) and consubstantiality. *Kenosis*, a more heterodox and marginal doctrine, describes what, for Nancy, is nevertheless most fundamentally at stake in the inner logic of Christian incarnation. It describes the movement by which God is thought to empty or void himself of his divinity in the event of incarnation. That is to say, in becoming flesh (in the body of Christ), God renounces divine status and attributes. Nancy pushes this notion even further by insisting that *kenosis* is the movement by which '"god" made himself "body" in emptying himself of himself.' *Kenosis* is therefore and far more radically 'the emptying-out of God, or his "emptying-himself out-of-himself"' (Nancy 2005a: 127; 2008c: 83). God does not simply renounce divinity or specific divine attributes in becoming incarnate. Rather, the very site, space and substance of divinity themselves are voided or evacuated.

This is maybe a radical reading of the doctrine of *kenosis* but, Nancy argues, the movement of 'emptying out' that it articulates in reality forms the most fundamental core and inner theological structure of Christianity itself. *Kenosis*, therefore, is decisive for Nancy's understanding of Christianity's auto- or self-deconstruction. From the perspective of this seeming marginal but in fact central doctrine, the Christian God is not a God of presence who is able to guarantee or ground the being of beings. Rather He is a God who alienates, atheizes or atheologizes himself in the very act of incarnation: in 'emptying' themselves out into matter, both God and the divine, as transcendent or founding principles, are emptied of substance, presence and auto-sufficiency. God becomes nothing, and that 'something' which He becomes (Christ's body and, by extension, all material bodies or beings) is devoid of all foundation or guarantee of presence. As Nancy puts it: 'The "body" of the "incarnation" is therefore the place, or rather the taking place, the event, of that disappearance' (Nancy 2005a: 127; 2008c: 83).

According to Nancy's reading of *kenosis*, then, the real inner structure of Christian incarnation enacts a withdrawal of presence and an 'emptying out' or vanishing of divine substance. This is extended by

Nancy to include the broader Christian (and indeed monotheistic) understanding of divine creation itself. Seen from a 'kenotic' perspective, the act of creation by which the Christian or monotheistic God brings the universe into being would also be a voiding of divine substance. In becoming world, as in becoming flesh, the space or site of divine substance is 'emptied out' in such a way that material existence is underpinned by nothing other than that void or empty space that has been vacated. That is to say, in rather blunt terms, that material 'created' existence has no transcendent guarantee, ground or foundation whatsoever. From this perspective, the more traditional doctrine of a supremely powerful and supremely present God of efficient causes, one who creates the world of substance from nothing (*ex nihilo*), would be an illusion of metaphysics. Such a supremely powerful and supremely 'substantial' God would simply be the product of a metaphysical appropriation of Christianity. The orthodox doctrine of incarnation conceived as hypostatic union would likewise be the result of such a metaphysical appropriation. Within the inner structure of Christianity itself, therefore, the metaphysical doctrine of creation (as the production of something from nothing) would always conceal or be internally inhabited by the void or 'nothing' of kenotic creation, just as the metaphysical understanding of incarnation would always be doubled or haunted by the doctrine of *kenosis* itself. This inner logic of voiding or absence, indeed of self-atheizing, would be the sombre double of Christianity's affirmation of presence and the very motor of its auto- or self-deconstruction.

These meditations on the inner structure of Christian incarnation and monotheistic creation may appear to be at some considerable remove from the philosophy of sense, embodiment and shared worldly existence which underpins Nancy's ontology of being-with. In fact, they need to be understood as a further development and radicalization of that philosophy. This is so in two distinct yet interrelated ways.

Firstly, the elaboration of Christianity's auto-deconstruction allows Nancy to rethink, albeit speculatively, the entire historical–philosophical framework in which modernity and the destruction or deconstruction of metaphysics can be understood. If Christianity is truly self-deconstructing, then the whole trajectory of modern, secularizing and atheistic thought may come to be viewed differently. For instance, the tradition of scientific humanism (as inaugurated in the work of early modern philosophers such as Descartes) will easily appear from this perspective to be a secular double or logical extension of Christianity's metaphysical moment. Insofar as it aims to establish firm foundations for the empirical study of the natural world and thereby (like the Eucharist) to guarantee the reliability of worldly appearances, scientific humanism would be a metaphysics of presence par excellence. By the same token, the anti-foundationalist tradition – that tradition which is perhaps most dramatically and virulently embodied in the Nietzschean 'death of God' – would appear to be not the antithesis of Christianity, but rather the necessary historical–philosophical unfolding of its most fundamental inner logic. Atheism here, in whatever guise, emerges as an extension and development of Christianity and not as its negation. To this extent, Nancy is very clear that, henceforth, atheism and the theist–atheist opposition need to be understood in an entirely new light. The terms of the theist–atheist opposition are deconstructed insofar the two poles are not pure opposites but contaminate and mutually inhabit each other at the most fundamental level. If, in response to the deconstruction of Christianity, one were to ask Nancy whether he was a theist or an atheist, a believer with faith or a faithless unbeliever, he would no doubt insist that the movement of auto-deconstruction he describes would make the very terms in which such a question is posed redundant or inoperative.[16]

Secondly, Nancy's deconstruction of Christianity offers him a means of replaying, developing and further radicalizing the bodily ontology and the thinking of sense, world and being-with which were discussed earlier in this chapter and which form the very centre of his philosophy as a whole. His finite thinking, it may be recalled, was shown to be a thought of 'infinitude' according to which the being of worldly appearances is disclosed only in an exposure of finite sensory experience to the infinite excess of sense. In his writing on Christianity, Nancy appears to be taking kenotic incarnation as paradigmatic of the shared bodily existence that he elaborated at such great length in the early to mid-1990s. He writes in *Dis-enclosure*, for instance, that the incarnate body is 'ultimately, itself, the ontological void, vacuity as a diversifying opening of appearing. The principle of the world is set or *poised* on this void: nothing else organizes it' (Nancy 2005a: 98; 2008c: 68). What this suggests is that incarnation here should be seen as a model or paradigm of worldly embodied existence coming into being in an absence of ground and in a voiding of substance. Likewise, monotheistic creation in general must also be viewed as a model for this coming into being of worldly appearances. Creation here describes the 'patency' of a world which is opened up over an ontological void.

In this context, it is worth noting that some contemporary critics and philosophers, for example Alain Badiou, have responded critically to Nancy's philosophy of finitude. They have judged it very negatively insofar as finitude itself might arguably *only ever* be under-stood as a form of limitation or enclosure of being (and therefore as a continuation of metaphysics).[17] Against this, Nancy's thinking of *kenosis* and kenotic creation give a sustained re-elaboration of the (in)finitude of embodied existence as 'dis-enclosure' and as an opening onto ontological absence or void. The 'deconstruction of Christianity' therefore re-emphasizes and further radicalizes the central and persistent Nancean argument that 'finiteness does not limit infinity; on the contrary, finiteness should give it its expansion and its truth' (Nancy 2005a: 32; 2008c: 18).

It can be concluded from all this that Nancy's thinking of shared embodied existence has developed in his most recent writing into an a-theology. This is an a-theology which overturns the traditional opposition of theism and atheism. Insofar as he leaves open a space for the divine, he does so only to the extent that the divine itself is understood as the ontological void upon which shared existence is itself opened.[18] By the same token, if this is a philosophy of infinite excess, it is so only insofar as that excess is conceived of as the void which opens up between bodies as they 'touch on' sense. Nancy can therefore write sentences such as: 'Divine is the sharing that creates a world' (Nancy 2005a: 103; 2008c: 72; translation modified). The divine persists in his thought as the emptiness and absence which is opened up in the trans-immanence of being-with.

What this means is that Nancy's 'deconstruction of Christianity' does not in any way signal a simple or straightforward return to the reassurance of theological doctrine, faith or religious observance. It may mean however that, within the overall trajectory of Nancy's post-phenomenological and post-deconstructive philosophy of existence, the site which was once occupied by the sacred, by transcendence and by the absolute demand of divine Law still persists and still occupies a central, albeit empty, position. Yet if such a site or space does persist in Nancy's thought, it does so not just as the opening void of our worldly existence. The 'divine sharing' which makes the world is also an absolute demand made upon us by the infinite excess of being-with. This is a demand which carries with it all the force once exerted by the sacred, by transcendence and by divine Law. It is the demand that we become what we are, that shared (in)finite existence be fully and properly shared.

3

Bernard Stiegler: The Time of Technics

Bernard Stiegler is perhaps best known in the anglophone academic community for the first two volumes of *Technics and Time* which appeared in English translation in 1998 and 2009 respectively (Stiegler 1998; 2009c). Yet, since the publication in French of the final volume of this trilogy in 2002, his output has been prolific and includes a second trilogy of books entitled *Mécréance et discrédit* (Stiegler 2004b; 2006a; 2006b), a two-volume work entitled *De la misère symbolique* (Stiegler 2004a; 2005a), as well as numerous other single authored and edited volumes. To label Stiegler simply as a philosopher of technology would be to misconstrue the scope and ambition of the *Technics and Time* trilogy taken in its own right and, more generally, that of his increasingly prolific output. His philosophical elaboration of 'the technological rooting of all relation to time' (Stiegler 1994: 146; 1998: 135) aims at nothing short of a systematic thinking of the technicity of life in general and of human life in particular. To this end, he gives a highly original reworking of Husserlian, Heideggerian and Derridean thought which draws also upon anthropology and various philosophies of technology, for instance work by figures such as Bertrand Gille, André Leroi-Gourhan and Gilbert Simondon.[1]

This fundamental reconfiguration of the relation of technology to time leads Stiegler to develop a critical-philosophical account of contemporary capitalist, technological society. The trajectory of his thinking from the second volume of *Technics and Time* onwards is informed by this critical response to the socio-economic, political and technological forms which have emerged over the last three decades. From the mid-1990s to the present day, Stiegler has developed a resolutely activist philosophy, a philosophy of the left certainly, but one which sets out to rethink the basis of traditional political economy in its entirety. In this context, he draws on thinkers as diverse as, amongst others, Paul Virilio, Jean-François Lyotard, Michel Foucault and Herbert Marcuse. His ambition in all this is very great indeed. He wishes for nothing less than to think or imagine 'a new industrial model' (Stiegler 2006b: 110). This elaboration of an activist philosophy has been accompanied by a very real and engaged political activism carried out under the umbrella of *Ars Industrialis*, an organization founded by Stiegler and others in 2005. Describing itself as an international association for the promotion of 'an industrial politics of technologies of the mind', *Ars Industrialis* has published four collaborative works to date (Stiegler 2006d; 2006e; 2009a; 2009b). These works take up the challenges raised by Stiegler's philosophical writings and do so in order to engage directly with a wider context of political campaigning and activism.[2]

Despite the breadth and scope of the ambition which informs Stiegler's thinking, the conjoined questions of technology and temporality remain both its central concern and its sustained philosophical underpinning. It is with the three volumes of *Technics and Time*, therefore, that this discussion will primarily concern itself.

Technics and Time

Volume 1: The Fault of Epimetheus

Stiegler's aim in *Technics and Time 1: The Fault of Epimetheus* is arguably twofold: first and foremost, he wishes to demonstrate 'the technological rooting of all relation to time' (Stiegler 1994: 146; 1998: 135). Secondly, he wants to rethink the question of historical time or historicity and thereby open the way towards a philosophical and speculative history of technics. According to such a history, the emergence of man as a technical animal would be both a continuation of a wider economy of technical life and *at the same time* would constitute a new regime or rupture within this wider economy. In other words, for Stiegler, the advent of the human and of human history is a matter of technics: 'the invention of the human is technics' (Stiegler 1994: 148; 1998: 137).

As the evocation of the myth of Epimetheus in the subtitle suggests, this ambition unfolds under the motif of forgetting. According to this myth, Epimetheus was responsible for giving a positive trait or skill to each animal but, forgetful and without foresight, when it came to humans he had run out of traits, leaving humankind lacking in any inbuilt characteristics, such as claws for hunting or fur for keeping warm. His brother, Prometheus, then stole the gift of arts/craft (*tekhnē*) and fire from the gods to give to humans.[3] The myth, then, describes the creation of the human in terms of an originary forgetting *and* an originary lack and, in the context of Prometheus' subsequent theft, it posits *tekhnē* as a specific dimension of the human, or rather, as a dimension that defines human specificity per se. In this context, Stiegler uses the Epimetheus myth as a springboard for a twofold philosophical reflection.

Firstly, he argues that the act of forgetting does not end with the fault of Epimetheus and the Promethean theft. Rather, this initial forgetting has been repeated within thought and philosophy as a forgetting *of technics* insofar as philosophy itself has, from its inception, repressed or marginalized the technical dimension of the human; as Stiegler puts it: 'at its very origin and up until now, philosophy has repressed technics as an object of thought. Technics is the unthought' (Stiegler 1994: 11; 1998: ix). Stiegler is interested in the way that philosophy, in its Greek origin, came both to distinguish and to establish a hierarchy between *ēpistēmē* (knowledge) and *tekhnē* (productive technique, all art and artfulness, including that of language) (Stiegler 1994: 15; 1998: 1). At its origin, then, the goal of philosophy was truth and the foundations of knowledge, its technical dimension (language, discourse, etc.) and technicity per se were accorded a secondary, instrumental status. Seen from this perspective, foregrounding the importance of *tekhnē* rather than *ēpistēmē* in philosophy would lead it into sophistry: the privileging of skilful or rhetorical use of language shorn of its primary relation to truth.[4] As will become increasingly clear, Stiegler is using the myth of Epimetheus and the motif of forgetting to elaborate an account of technics which is similar to, but also different from, Derrida's understanding of writing as that which has been repressed within the history of logocentrism and the metaphysics of presence.[5] Where Derrida frames the history of logocentrism as the repression of writing, arche-writing and the inscription of the trace, Stiegler sees western metaphysics as a history of the repression of technics.

Secondly, and again in a move which is similar but different to Derridean thought, Stiegler reads the fault of Epimetheus as a figure for thinking the human in terms of an originary lack. In this context, then, technics is thought according to a logic of supplementarity in relation to that lack. Technical prostheses as used by humans would be seen not just in terms of utility or ends and means but more

fundamentally as a general economy of sense, meaning and purposive, worldly engagement rooted in a withdrawal or absence of origin.
It is this double understanding of technics both as an instance which
has been repressed at the beginning of philosophy *and* as a supplement to a constitutive lack or absent origin which leads Stiegler to
argue that: 'the division originarily made by philosophy between
tekhnē and *epistēmē* has become problematic' (Stiegler 1994: 35; 1998:
21). Philosophy must therefore respond to: 'the need, today, to forge
another relation to technics, one that rethinks the bond originarily
formed by, and between, humanity, technics, and language' (Stiegler
1994: 27; 1998: 13). Stiegler's reworking and synthesis of phenomenology, deconstruction and anthropology in *The Fault of Epimetheus*
aims to articulate just such a response.

A large part of the first volume of *Technics and Time* is taken up
with a sustained engagement with the philosophies of Husserl and
Heidegger. Specifically, and unsurprisingly, Stiegler is interested in
the way each comes to think the conjoined questions of technology
and temporality. In, for instance, *The Crisis of European Sciences and
Transcendental Phenomenology* (Husserl 1970), Husserl gives a speculative history of modern western knowledge. According to this
account, from the time of Galileo and Descartes onwards, knowledge
becomes dominated by a mathematical projection, a calculating
method and what Husserl comes to call a 'technization' of thought
(Husserl 1970: 48).[6] This dominance of technization and formal–
mathematical calculation blinds knowledge to its rootedness in
everyday world consciousness and world-life. Ultimately, then, it
blinds knowledge to its true phenomenological foundation in more
primordial and pre-technical perceptions, activities and worldly
engagements. This everyday world consciousness has its own specific
temporality which is not that of chronological or clock time. It is this
distinct sphere of consciousness with its own distinct and more primordial temporality that Husserl's phenomenological method is
designed to uncover and bring to light in order to overcome the
technicized blindness of modern knowledge to its own foundations.
Likewise, in Heidegger's thought, a more primordial temporality
(that of the being-towards-death of *Dasein* or of the originary giving
of Being) is again opposed to a temporality which is defined by calculation and chronology. Like Husserl, Heidegger defines modernity
by its attachment to a mode of framing being and time which is calculative, mathematized and technicized. Technics in general, and
modern technology in particular, are assimilated by Heidegger to a
logic of nihilism and a catastrophic modernity which has repressed
or forgotten the question of being as a question.[7]

For Stiegler, Husserl's and Heidegger's thinking about technological modernity and temporality mark the culmination of the history of philosophy's repression of technics. This is because both seek to place technicity and a techno-scientific understanding of the world into a secondary or downgraded position. For both, the dominance of technical and calculative thought within modernity blinds us to a more primordial phenomenological (Husserl) or existential (Heidegger) apprehension of the world and of temporality. This primordial pre-technical dimension is accorded a privileged status in the thought of both. Yet, crucially for Stiegler, as a culminating point in this history of the repression of technics, both thinkers nevertheless offer resources for examining a more 'originary relation between the human and the technical, *qua a phenomenon of temporality*' (Stiegler 1994: 57; 1998: 43). Indeed, his elaboration of this more 'originary relation' is decisively rooted in the phenomenological and existential accounts of temporality as elaborated by Husserl and Heidegger respectively.

According to Husserl's phenomenological perspective, consciousness of time and the experience of duration is primordially constituted in and through a structure of retention and protention. In retention, traces of an immediate past are retained by consciousness as it constitutes and experiences the present moment. In protention, futural elements are anticipated and again this anticipative projection of consciousness constitutes the experience of the present. Time consciousness and the perception of the present is formed, therefore, in an ongoing synthesis of retentions and protentions, recollections of an immediate past and purposive projections towards an imminent future. For Husserl this phenomenological temporality is, as has been emphasized, pre-technical, that is, anterior to the numerical ordering of chronological time and the paradigms of techno-scientific rationality.

By way of a rather schematic summary, it can be said that the crucial point for Stiegler is that this structure of protention and retention, constitutive of time, always passes through, engages and is engaged by an exteriority of technical objects and technical prosthetics. Technical prosthetics or tools in this context are not simply defined by their instrumentality or utility. Rather, they function as material and meaningful traces of a historical past and as certain forms of collective and impersonal memory. As Stiegler himself puts it: 'A tool is, before anything else, memory: if this were not the case, it could never function as a reference of significance' (Stiegler 1994: 259; 1998: 254). It is in this context that Stiegler engages extensively with Heidegger's account of the temporality of *Dasein* as explicated in

Being and Time. For Heidegger, as for Husserl, the experience of time is constituted in temporal projections both forward and backward. Yet Heidegger is more decisively interested in the way these projections are articulated within a worldly circumspectful or purposive engagement. This worldly engagement roots *Dasein* in a past, an already-there, and projects it into a future, thus constituting temporal experience. It does so, however, only insofar as these projections into a past and future, *as-worldly*, thrust *Dasein* outside of itself, or constitute it as always standing outside of itself. The temporal consciousness of *Dasein* is constituted only in and through its relation to an already existing exterior world and *Dasein* is therefore without interiority. Its temporal being-in-the-world is always an exteriority, a standing outside of itself, or 'ek-stasis'. Stiegler adopts this understanding of temporal being-in-the world but also diverges in a decisive manner from Heidegger's account insofar as he views this ecstatic temporality as always, one might say always already, constituted in a relation to the impersonal memory traces embodied in worldly technical objects and prosthetics: 'there is no already-there, and therefore no relation to time, without artificial memory supports' (Stiegler 1994: 168; 1998: 159). For Stiegler, the impersonal memory conserved in our surrounding technical environment constitutes us, at a fundamental level, as temporal beings who are aware of a past, experience a present and anticipate a future. Where both Husserl and Heidegger seek to confer upon the world of technical prosthetics a secondary status in relation to a primordial phenomenological or existential temporality, Stiegler aims to think technics as *already* primordially constitutive of any experience of time. He wishes to allow for 'the constitution of temporality to be apprehended from the standpoint of the emergence of memory elaborated and conserved by the organization of the inorganic' (Stiegler 1994: 154; 1998: 143).

The originality of *The Fault of Epimetheus* lies in the way in which Stiegler synthesizes this reworked understanding of existential–phenomenological temporality with Derridean deconstruction and the anthropological thinking of André Leroi-Gourhan.[8] For Stiegler, the always-already technical constitution of temporality described above is also a structure of *referral* and *deferral*. We experience time through our worldly temporal projections which are engaged by the meanings and impersonal memory traces that are conserved in technical prosthetics. This structure of referral to and through the alterity of technics is also a differing, a spacing *and* a deferring, a temporalizing, and as such is aligned by Stiegler with the Derridean logic of the supplement, of the trace and of *différance*. In short, technical prosthetics, for Stiegler, are a material concretization of Derridean *différance*. Whereas the *trace* for Derrida can never be present nor present itself (it belongs to an immemorial past that resists or exceeds the logic of presence), technical prosthetics, for Stiegler are, in his words, the putting 'into actual play [*mise en jeu effective*]' (Stiegler 1994: 240; 1998: 234) of *différance*.[9]

It is in this context that Stiegler turns to Leroi-Gourhan's account of the upright stance, tool use and the cortical development of early hominids. According to Leroi-Gourhan, humans become human through the process in which the gradual adoption of tool use is accompanied by both a massive increase in the size and complexity of the brain cortex and the development of the language function. In this context, Stiegler argues that the inaugural moment of the human in tool use, corticalization, language and so on should be seen as a rupture or break in the general economy of life that is *différance* such as it is described by Derrida in *Of Grammatology*. In this inaugural text of deconstruction, Derrida argues that arche-writing, the trace and the differing-deferring movement of *différance* form an economy of inscription which includes biological-genetic coding, all kinds of instinctive behaviour, the emergence of alphabetic writing all the way through to cybernetics, 'electronic card-indexes and reading machines' (Derrida 1998: 84). As such, Derridean arche-writing, the trace and so on describe the coding of life in general as a form of originary technicity but this technicity precedes the instance of the human, while at the same time also encompassing the human. Stiegler diverges from Derrida by arguing (via Leroi-Gourhan) that what makes humans distinctive *as* human is their ability to conserve the past through the meanings sedimented in the materiality of technical pros-thetics and to project this past into a future (in a way which consti-tutes the present as such). The human, then, is constituted in a *new regime* of technical life within a wider economy of technical life in general (*différance*).

The name Stiegler gives to this new regime is *epiphylogenesis*.[10] Epiphylogenesis in this context is the process by which successive articulations of human life are conserved, accumulated and sedi-mented within the technical systems which form our individual and collective time consciousness (and therefore form us as human beings). To repeat, it is a specifically human trait to conserve the memory and meaning of the past through our relation to technical apparatus and systems and to form our sense of time in this relation. On this basis, Stiegler wants to demonstrate how human tool use constitutes 'a rupture – a new organization of *différance*, a *différance* of *différance*' (Stiegler 1994: 186; 1998: 178). The advent of the human in tool use is a rupture whereby the supplement, the differing and deferring, the spatializing and temporalizing inscription of the trace, is exteriorized into technical objects, thus constituting a doubling of Derridean *différance*.[11]

Stiegler's account therefore both follows Derrida's formulations but also diverges from them in a decisive manner. Derrida, for instance, would no doubt never countenance this notion of the doubling, or the *différance* of *différance*. It is also certainly true to say that the early reception of Stiegler's work by those close to Derrida (most notably Geoffrey Bennington) was sharply critical (on the range of Derridean objections to the arguments of *Technics and Time*, see James 2010b). Yet, however one comes to judge Stiegler's divergence from Derrida, what is perhaps most important to highlight is the way in which the worldly materialization of the trace makes possible a thinking of originary technicity in *historical* terms. Thinking the 'technological rooting of all relation to time' as epiphylogenesis allows Stiegler to give a historical account of successive articulations of technical systems. It allows him to think the relation of technical systems to the historical and epochal constitution of the human. In so doing, Stiegler is able to specify the way in which different epochs of technics would constitute our experience of time *differently*. It is just this possibility of historicizing the originary technicity of the human which opens the way to the political concerns of the second two volumes of *Technics and Time* and, indeed, the political activism of all Stiegler's subsequent philosophical writing.

Volume 2: Disorientation

In *Disorientation*, Stiegler's principal aim is to delineate the epochal limits of a specific historical culture. This is an epoch which, he argues, has been ours until the latter part of the twentieth century. It is a historical culture which has been rooted in the linearity of writing, that is to say, an alphabetical culture of the letter or a culture of the book in which the retention of the past and collective apprehension of the present and of historical time passes primarily through the technical system of the written word. He then wishes to differentiate this culture from what he perceives as a currently emerging epoch in which the retention of the past passes primarily through the technical systems of analogical, numerical and digital communications media and other technically mediated perceptions. If Stiegler is correct that historical epochs, together with the individual and collective forms of time consciousness which define them, are constituted in and through technical systems and prosthetics, then the stakes of this analysis are indeed high, given the rapid pace of technical development in that latter half of the twentieth century and first decade of the twenty-first.

Stiegler identifies the (European) epoch of alphabetical writing with an awareness of a collective historical time as distinctively *linear*, an awareness which above all privileges the value of *presence*. This, of course, is the metaphysics of presence which is the object of destruction in Heidegger and deconstruction in Derrida. At the same time, he identifies our contemporary historical moment as a moment in which this culture of presence is being suspended. This suspension is effected by the specific temporality or time consciousness produced by emergent information and communication technologies and digital media. The contemporary crisis that Stiegler describes in *Disorientation* is rooted, he argues, in our inability to identify this opening of a new epoch *as such* and thereby to engage in a more lucid confrontation with the culture which is in the process of emerging.

If our experience of historical time is fundamentally rooted in technics, then, Stiegler argues, the movement of history itself would be governed by a process in which dominant technical systems develop into something new and are then subsequently accompanied by the emergence of new cultural forms which are programmed by those new systems. Stiegler calls this process whereby culture is reprogrammed by the emergence of new technical systems 'epochal redoubling [*redoublement épochale*]'. The original French word here, *redoublement*, carries the sense of doubling, beginning once again, overhauling or renewing. It also resonates with the verb *doubler*, meaning to double, repeat, accelerate or overtake (as in a car). All these senses are at play in Stiegler's use of the term and, with this concept of 'epochal redoubling', he is able to pose the central question of *Disorientation*: 'Which idea of today, then, would (improbably) program the *epokhal redoubling* of *différant* analogic, numeric, and biologic identities, thus throwing into crisis the presence of which "*today*" consists?' (Stiegler 1996: 75; 2009c: 61). This question is posed by Stiegler with considerable urgency. For, he suggests, new techno-scientific modes are already reprogramming our ways of retaining the past and anticipating the future and have already begun to inaugurate a different experience of time, a new and different mode of temporalization.

It is this sense of a collective blindness with regard to the exact nature and ongoing course of contemporary epochal change that motivates the rhetoric of urgency which is threaded throughout the entire trilogy of *Technics and Time*.[12] This rhetoric of urgency, while clearly designed to have a persuasive impact on the reader, can also be related directly to the nature of the crisis Stiegler is trying to identify. The crisis is one to which he gives the name of the second volume of *Technics and Time* itself, 'disorientation', and the urgency of his rhetoric can be related to the question of *speed* and what might be termed the speed of the epoch of new technologies. Stiegler puts this in the following terms: 'Contemporary disorientation is the experience of an incapacity to achieve epochal redoubling. It is linked to speed, to the industrialization of memory resulting from the struggle for speed, and to the specifics of the technologies employed in that struggle' (Stiegler 1996: 15; 2009c: 7). On one level, Stiegler identifies the crisis of the contemporary as a disorientation brought about by our inability to 'catch up' with the pace of technical change, to engage lucidly with and to stabilize new cultural programmes or forms: this is our 'incapacity to achieve epochal redoubling'. Yet this incapacity is rooted in the nature of the new technical system itself, the rapidity of its development certainly, but also its very nature as a mode of technical time constitution defined in and through *speed*.

Much of the analysis in *Disorientation* is devoted to the way in which digital technologies, information processing and contemporary communications media constitute a new structure or synthesis of retention and protention which deracinates (disorientates) the temporal unfolding of a linear historical time with its privileging of presence. Overturned also is the constitution of a past, or of the historical event *as* properly historical, only in and after a certain period of delay or deferral (e.g. events are proclaimed to be 'historic' or are constituted in their historical significance in the very moment of their coverage in 'real time' by broadcast media). If our dominant access to, or retention of, the past passes through the diverse media of digital communications and information technologies, then our relation to the perception of a 'historical past' may be profoundly altered. Technologies which transmit 'directly' and in 'real time' (that is, in a mode of transmission where instantaneity and speed are the very essence of transmission itself) will necessarily, according to Stiegler, alter the constitution of the time in which events unfold or are perceived and rendered meaningful as such.

This passage of collective memory or retention of the past in the new digital communications technologies is described as a process of 'the industrialization of memory'. This industrialization of memory, Stiegler argues, is in the process of forming, and will in the future fully articulate, an industrialized synthesis of temporal finitude, that is to say, a dominant mode by which time consciousness is constituted in our emergent epoch. This, he suggests, is an epoch of speed and notes: 'To think the current age through speed is thus to think . . . the general modification of event-ization that is taking place before our in-credulous eyes' (Stiegler 1996: 20; 2009c: 11). Readers familiar with the work of Paul Virilio will immediately recognize some of the key motifs associated with Stiegler's account of disorientation in the second volume of *Technics and Time*. The emphasis on speed, on the transformative nature of digital communications technologies in relation to the perception of time and, indeed, to the very 'eventness' of events themselves, are all eminently Virilian concerns.[13] Like Virilio, Stiegler argues that contemporary media, communications and digital or information technologies engender a wasting of a situated (embodied) experience of space as well as of time.

Indeed, it is precisely the absence of situatedness within the temporal and spatial consciousness constituted by digital technologies that, for Stiegler, defines the disorientation of contemporary experience: 'to live contemporary technics today is less about the structuring of territory than it is about deterritorialization' (Stiegler 1996: 110; 2009c: 90). This deterritorialization is articulated as a wider paradigm of collective spatial and temporal experience. Deterritorialization occurs as a shared structure of perception articulated in the disembodied or virtualized 'real-time' of digital communication. It occurs in the quasi-instantaneity of transmission across the globe which annihilates geographical situatedness just as it annihilates temporal delays. Stiegler argues, along with Virilio, that this overturns or transforms our sense of temporal rhythm, of calendar time modulated by the rhythms of night and day, week and month, month and year. The rhythm of night and day gives way to a perpetual 'false-day' (another term borrowed from Virilio), a day bathed in the continuous electronic light of television and monitor screens and the unceasing transmission of information around the entire space of the globe. This false-day, Stiegler writes, 'marks a different relation of space and time, a different synthesis, and an entirely new question of intuition, leaving the 'body proper' behind and investing in industries of the visionic, of telepresence and of virtual reality' (Stiegler 1996: 120: 2009c: 98).

Again, the key terms used here – 'body proper', 'telepresence' – are taken from Virilio and are fundamental to the Virilian account of contemporary technologies. Stiegler diverges in key respects from Virilio, however, and this divergence is marked in his use of quotation marks around the term 'body proper'. For where Virilio maintains a strong, albeit residual, attachment to the authenticity of situated bodily presence and to the phenomenological conception of the 'body proper' (which he takes from Merleau-Ponty), Stiegler, of course, has no faith at all in the purity of 'presence' since he has already shown the way in which any coming to presence always passes through the alterity of technics. As has been indicated, this passage through technics is, for Stiegler, a differing and deferring which would rupture the purity of the present moment. The nostalgia for presence which marks Virilio's work is therefore absent from Stiegler's account. Indeed, he goes so far as to suggest that the disorientation of the contemporary epoch was already emergent in the preceding epoch of writing which ostensibly privileged linear history and presence. In this sense, disorientation is a fundamental characteristic of technical man and of epiphylogenesis per se: 'Orthographic writing enacts a wrenching out of context that is intensified even further by memory's industrialization (disorientation being precisely this decontextualization, this disappearance of place), which has actually been occurring since epiphylogenesis's origin' (Stiegler 1996: 16; 2009c: 8, translation modified). In the light of this, it is important to underline that the argument of *Disorientation* is not orientated simply towards a condemnation of contemporary media and culture in the name of the virtues of the preceding epoch. Stiegler's demand, urgent though it may be, is a demand that we take the time to think what may be at stake in the rapid development of contemporary technical systems. Above all, it is a demand that the new technical media be thought in such a way as to engage critically with the modes of temporalization they engender, with the time consciousness they may come to constitute, and with the 'programmes', or cultural forms they may produce or be in the process of producing.

Volume 3: Cinematic Time and the Question of Malaise

In the third volume of *Technics and Time*, Stiegler extends his philosophical critique of the technological systems which, he argues, produce an industrialized synthesis of memory within contemporary industrial society. In particular, he is interested in the way in which the diverse technologies underpinning both economic and cultural modes of production have converged in what he terms a 'functional integration'. This convergence constitutes a distinctive stage of industrialization which could be called 'hyper-industrial'. According to Stiegler, the functional integration of hyper-industrial society would be one in which all the technical systems of representation which constitute cultural life and support cultural memory (broadcast media, information technology, cinema, the World Wide Web, etc.) converge with the material modes of production, consumption and economic exchange. The risk of this convergence of technical, economic and cultural production is that it subordinates the entirety of the social and cultural sphere to its own (principally economic) exigencies and necessities. Here Stiegler is taking up in a philosophical register the perhaps familiar contemporary concern about the way in which all spheres of cultural life and communal or social experience are being subsumed into a logic of markets, commodification and economic exchange.

Yet, for Stiegler, this is not just a question of the cultural politics of contemporary capitalism. What most concerns him in this context is the question of individuation. By individuation, he understands that process whereby, within any mass or group of people, individuals differentiate themselves and become more distinctively singular or unique.[14] For, insofar as time consciousness and indeed consciousness itself is constituted in its relation to technical prosthetics, the risk is that the functional integration of hyper-industrial society will homogenize not only the cultural sphere but also the experience of those who participate in that sphere. Stiegler puts this in the following terms: 'the functional integration of the symbolic and logistic industries produces total control of markets as collectivities of a temporal stream of consciousness always in need of being *synchronized*' (Stiegler 2001a: 19–20; 2011: 3). Without the synchronization of consciousness and experience (by way of the convergence of technical and productive systems), mass markets and consumer culture cannot, Stiegler argues, function as such. It is a question of the perception of the present, of memory (retention) and of purposiveness (protention) being formed en masse and more or less homogeneously by information and media technology in the service of markets and economic productivity. In the contemporary synthesis of time consciousness, all those processes which would favour individuation are blocked in favour of those which promote homogenization or, as Stiegler puts it: 'the current prosthetization of consciousness, the systematic industrialization of the entirety of retentional devices, is an obstacle to the very individuation process of which consciousness consists' (Stiegler 2001a: 21; 2011: 4).

It is important to note at this point that the manner in which the temporal flux of consciousness is coordinated en masse in hyper-industrial society is not, for Stiegler, a kind of brainwashing according to which our self-awareness is monolithically programmed or determined by technical systems and the representations they produce. Rather, the synchronization of experience here is viewed more as a conditioning which ensures that, despite the processes of singularization and differentiation which will inevitably be at play, enough people will nevertheless desire and consume in the same way such that mass markets will function. Stiegler makes it clear that 'The coincidence of multiple flux does not mean that all these consciousnesses see or live the same thing(s)' (Stiegler 2001: 187; 2011: 124). He is not saying that the convergence of technical systems 'program the time of consciousness in the sense that it determines it', but rather that 'this programming is a conditioning' and that 'this conditioning is enormously effective' (Stiegler 2001a: 187–8; 2011: 124). It is not a question of determinism, then, but more a question of the organizing processes of hyper-industrial society which synchronize consciousness on a huge scale and do so in a conditioning which is inimical to more heterogeneous processes of individuation, singularization and differentiation. For all the talk of individual freedom, autonomy and choice in contemporary consumer societies, Stiegler argues that these societies are, in fact, 'profoundly hostile to the individuation process, to all heterogeneity, to singularity, and to the exception' (Stiegler 2001a: 157; 2011: 101). This crisis of individuation is, then, the 'malaise' referred to in the subtitle of *Technics and Time 3*.

His arguments here follow on directly from the account he gives of the technical constitution of time consciousness in *The Fault of Epimetheus*. For if temporal experience is constituted in and through the exteriorized sphere of technical prostheticity, then it follows directly that this constitution of experience is susceptible to the large-scale manipulation of technical systems. Stiegler is interested in the way in which the digital technologies and mass media of our own age condition the flux of temporal consciousness since, as a system of technical prostheticity, they are constitutive of it. The flux of temporal consciousness can be seen, he argues, as a material to be manipulated on a global scale (Stiegler 2001a: 121–2; 2011: 77). Despite this, Stiegler argues that, if the large scale information technology systems of contemporary society can be used for the purposes of manipulation, they are also themselves vulnerable to contestation. He insists that what is urgently needed in order to tackle the potential 'annihilation of "self-consciousness"' in contemporary mass culture is a more developed critical understanding of the way in which the technologies of hyper-industrial society affect consciousness.

It is here that his interest in cinema comes into play. Cinema is what Husserl would call a 'temporal object'.[15] These are unified objects which appear to, or in, consciousness in extended duration and whose identity is inseparable from their temporal extension (e.g. a piece of music). As one might expect, temporal objects, for Stiegler, are inseparable from their material support and therefore always function as part of the wider economy of technical prosthetics that constitutes time consciousness as such. Cinema, as one such technical –temporal object, plays a decisive role in the argument of *Technics and Time 3* insofar as it exemplifies very clearly both the danger and the positive potential of technology in relation to the constitution of consciousness and the question of individuation.

Cinema is exemplary here insofar as it is shows very directly the way in which consciousness can be synchronized in the collective apprehension of a technical–temporal object. The experience of a cinema audience unfolds simultaneously in the perceptual field of each spectator and the film narrative will seek to elicit a series of more or less synchronized affective responses, e.g. suspense, laughter, horror, surprise and so on. On the other hand, individuals within the audience will, to a greater or lesser extent, experience any one film differently and with a potentially wide range of divergent responses. Yet, at the same time, Stiegler would argue, a cultural object such as a film will necessarily compose its field of representation very selectively. There will inevitably be a set of criteria which define what elements of collective experience are presented and therefore retained within the field of representation and what elements are excluded. Such criteria would relate to rules of genre and to the values of good story-telling, of course, and to shared values of what is or is not permissible to show. They would relate also to more diffuse and selective forms of cultural memory which are less easy to circumscribe but nevertheless work to shape a collective consciousness of both the present and the past. For example, in the last decades of the twentieth century, a UK audience was far more likely to see a film about Mahatma Gandhi and Indian independence than about the incredibly brutal wars of independence fought in British Africa in the 1960s. This very fact might point towards the way in which a very selective historical memory is formed by cultural objects in a way which supports a shared identity in the present (in this case, a certain post-imperial sense of Britishness). Such selectivity, Stiegler would argue, is in fact a decisive factor in the shaping of individual and collective consciousness by the wider cultural industries in which cinema plays such an important part.

What cinema exemplifies, therefore, is the way in which technical–temporal objects can constitute consciousness at the level of the collective or mass and therefore shape it in a more or less homogeneous fashion. Yet at the very same time such objects can affect us singularly and with an intensity which cannot always be pre-programmed, prescribed or subjected to any form of equivalence in purely economic exchange. There is a tension here between the synchronizing-homogenizing power of the technical–temporal object and its affective, singularizing dimension. It is precisely in this tension that Stiegler locates the potential of a critical and political response to the problem of individuation within hyper-industrial society. Cinema shows us that, while the technical–temporal object can indeed synchronize and condition emotional response, collective consciousness and shared memory, it also has the potential to singularize all these things, or, as Stiegler puts it, 'Understanding the singular way in which temporal objects affect consciousness means beginning to understand what gives cinema its specificity, its force, and its means of transforming life' (Stiegler 2001a: 41; 2011: 17).

In short, Stiegler argues that if we can come to properly understand this double potentiality of mass communications technology, technology which has the potential to be both homogenizing *and* singularizing, then we can begin to develop strategies to engage with the totalizing culture of hyper-industrial society differently and transform our experience of that culture. We can begin, perhaps, to develop a politics of re-appropriation whereby the convergence of technical, cultural and economic production is not exclusively in the service of mass markets but, rather, is in the service of individuation, differentiation and the intensities of singular affects and engagements. This would be a politics in which the question of how we should live, what we should do, and how we should desire, would be uncoupled from the exigencies of economic production. It would be a politics in which cultural production and reproduction would open a space for thought, reflection and action rather than a space ever more oriented towards the necessities of passive consumption. The third volume of *Technics and Time* concludes with a resolute affirmation of the necessity of an engaged politics of technology:

> such a politics must be a politics of technics, a practical thought of becoming capable of furnishing it with an idea projecting into the future in which becoming is the agent . . . A politics of technics should be able to elaborate practical ideas capable of asking and regularizing the question as to *what must be done* within the practical domain. (Stiegler 2001a: 292; 2011: 198–9)

Stiegler's arguments relating to the advent of the human, to epiphylogenesis, the industrial synthesis of memory, to disorientation and hyper-industrialization all culminate in what is effectively a political call to arms. The *Technics and Time* trilogy begins as an ambitious philosophical rethinking of human consciousness, thought and historicity and ends as an attempt to rethink political economy in order to affirm a necessity of political understanding and action. There is a steady progression here from post-phenomenological description and diagnosis to political analysis and activism where the aim is nothing less than to transform the fundamental ways in which contemporary society and culture are organized. It is a question, Stiegler concludes, of creating 'the conditions by which new modalities of reproduction are defined within the processes of hyper-industrialization' (Stiegler 2001a: 325; 2011: 223). The question of a technological politics and of '*what must be done* within the practical domain' (Stiegler 2001a: 292; 2011: 199) therefore becomes the guiding motif of Stiegler's thinking after *Technics and Time*.

What is to be done?

As was indicated at the beginning of this discussion, Stiegler's output has been prolific throughout the first decade of this century. It will be possible to give only a schematic account of his philosophical trajectory in this period, given the richness, diversity and sheer volume of his publications. Perhaps most representative of his recent thinking are the two volumes of *De la misère symbolique* published in 2004. In this work, Stiegler refers to, and to varying degrees draws on, the philosophy of Gilles Deleuze and Félix Guattari, writings by Michel Foucault and Jean-François Lyotard and the work of Gilbert Simondon. He also makes extensive reference back to the trilogy of *Technics and Time* as well as to other more recently published works. This very self-conscious interlinking and cross-referencing of his own work indicates clearly that Stiegler wants his readers to understand the ways in which each successive stage of his philosophical thought develops from and builds upon preceding moments. For example, there is little sustained engagement with Husserl and Heidegger in his recent work. The post-phenomenological thinking of technics and time is taken as an established given upon which further thought can be built. However, as Stiegler points out at the beginning of *De la misère symbolique 2*, the many references to his own work do not simply help to establish a foundation or overall coherence: 'above all it is a question of *providing weapons*: of making an arsenal of concepts from a network of questions with a view to pursuing a struggle' (Stiegler 2005a: 13–14). Such a comment shows quite clearly the extent to which Stiegler views his philosophy as a politically activist thinking committed to uniting thought with struggle and action.

In *De la misère symbolique*, then, Stiegler aims to sketch out two principal and intertwined concepts: that of a 'general organology [*organologie générale*]' and of a 'genealogy of aesthetics' (Stiegler 2004a: 14). Taken together, these will be key weapons in his 'arsenal of concepts'. At the same time, he also wishes to develop further his diagnostic of the 'ill-being' of hyper-industrial societies which is begun in *Technics and Time 3*.

The 'symbolic misery' alluded to in the title refers to the way in which the synchronization of consciousness within hyper-industrial society produces a very specific economy of affective life. This is a generalized economy of libidinal affect which is both impoverished and passive, and an economy in which mechanisms of desire are short-circuited or disrupted. Here, Stiegler is extending his critique of consumer societies driven by the exigencies of mass markets and by the convergence of technical, cultural and economic production. In this context, though, he is interested in the way the culture of mass consumption interferes with what he terms 'primary narcissism'. This term refers to the primary desiring identifications through which we achieve a fully individuated and differentiated sense of self. Stiegler's argument runs as follows: if a whole society and its cultural production are geared towards the desire for and consumption of mass-produced objects, then 'individuals are deprived of their capacity for aesthetic attachment to singularities, to singular objects' (Stiegler 2004a: 25). It follows from this standardization of objects of desire, and therefore of desire itself, that there will emerge a generalized '*loss of symbolic participation*, which is also a sort of *symbolic and affective congestion*, that is to say . . . a structural loss of individuation' (Stiegler 2004a: 31). The endless choice and variety which consumer products appear to offer us conceal the reality that such products are necessarily uniform because produced en masse. Marketing might tell us that the consumption of such products is an expression of individual taste and a gesture of self-fulfilment. The reality of mass consumption, however, is that we remain passive consumers of a homogenized material and symbolic culture. The primary identifications from which an individuated sense of self would be fashioned are diverted towards highly standardized objects and therefore put in the service of an impersonal logic of economic productivity. This, at least, is Stiegler's understanding of our contemporary 'symbolic misery', one which he expresses in the following terms: 'So by symbolic misery I understand the *loss of individuation* that results from the *loss of participation* in the *production of symbols* . . . And I suppose the current state of a generalized loss of individuation can only lead to a *symbolic collapse*, that is to say a collapse of desire' (Stiegler 2004a: 33). Like the third volume of *Technics and Time*, *De la misère symbolique* is primarily concerned with the question of individuation and of whether contemporary society is producing a crisis of individuation. Yet this concern is developed much more explicitly within the context of a thinking of what one might call the 'libidinal economy' of consumer society.[16] He is concerned with the way in which hyper-industrial culture channels the libido of consumers into mechanisms of economic exchange and does so at the expense of the singularity, intensity and force of desire itself and therefore at the expense of the life of the individual.

It is easy to see how some might object to Stiegler's formulations relating to individuation in hyper-industrial culture. From the perspective of Rancière's thought outlined in chapter 5, it could, for instance, be argued that Stiegler's understanding of the way consciousness is conditioned by mass culture may imply a degree of elitism. Also the influence of Marcuse, the Frankfurt School and of the concept of 'Culture Industry' can be felt in Stiegler's formulations here. Criticisms that may be made in relation to Frankfurt School cultural theory could well be applied to Stiegler, that is to say, that it underestimates human agency and ignores the fact that mass culture may be so successful simply because people genuinely enjoy its products, and do so without alienation or false consciousness. In this context, Stiegler's emphasis on singularity, intensity and desire would simply be a Nietzschean-inspired elitism which cannot account for the pleasure mass cultural products give and for the fact that they do so within the context of more or less fulfilled social relationships rather than at their expense. From a Rancièrian (and perhaps rather more realistic) perspective, it could be argued that Stiegler's formulations in relation to hyper-industrial society and its symbolic misery maintain the philosopher of technics in a privileged position. They position him as the key figure who can enlighten the masses and lead them from their enthralment to the channelling of collective libido into a standardizing symbolic economy of mass exchange. In this context, Stiegler would resemble the Marxist-scientist philosopher (i.e. Althusser) whose theoretical analysis and demystification can alone provide the way for any kind of emancipation (again, see chapter 5).

Arguably, though, his arguments relating to hyper-industrial society are more nuanced and complex and do not solely or simply testify to a Frankfurt School and Nietzschean inspired elitism. He also draws, for instance, on the thought of both Michel Foucault (2010) and Gilles Deleuze (1990), and does so in order to suggest that the libidinal economy of consumerist, hyper-industrial culture is a form of 'biopower' which ultimately constitutes society as a society of control rather than one of individual liberty, freedom and choice. The analogical and digital technologies that have made modern media and information culture possible have come to form the substructure of a 'hyperindustrial biopower ... which constitutes the general *organological horizon* with, for, and against which it is necessary to struggle' (Stiegler 2004a: 100). To understand better what is meant here by 'biopower' and 'organological horizon', Stiegler's intertwined concepts of 'general organology' and 'aesthetic genealogy' need to be defined.

In the opening pages of *De la misère symbolique 1*, Stiegler engages at some length with the notion of the aesthetic. In a manner which strongly echoes the formulations of Jean-Luc Nancy discussed in the preceding chapter, he notes that our collective experience always unfolds against the backdrop of a shared sensory world.[17] There exists, he suggests: 'a common aesthetic ground. Being-together is the being of a sensible grouping. A political community is therefore the community of a shared feeling' (Stiegler 2004a: 19). Like Nancy, Stiegler is interested in the double meaning of the term 'aesthetic', referring as it does both to the experience of the embodied senses *and* to the realm of art and artistic production. In this context, he argues that we can imagine an 'aesthetic history' of humanity. This would be a history of the different regimes or systems which organize our collective 'aesthetic force and capability' (Stiegler 2004a: 23). Such a history would unfold in the successive historically contingent structures in which bodily sense organs and physiological organization are conjoined or co-articulated with artificial organs (technical objects, tools, instruments, works of art, etc.). This history of 'aesthetic genealogy' is effectively repeating the thinking of epiphylogenesis and epochal redoubling elaborated in the first two volumes of *Technics and Time*. Yet it does so in order to focus specifically on the way in which the technical systems which shape a historical epoch also form a shared sensory experience, that is to say, the 'common aesthetic ground' upon which political community is based. On this basis, Stiegler suggests that we need to imagine a 'general organology' in order to understand the interaction of bodily and artificial organs. 'General organology' here would be a way of knowing exactly how the interaction between the body and technical prosthetics is structured and articulated within any one political community. In turn, it would also be a way of practically engaging with this structure, a way of approaching the space of interaction between the body and technics as a site of intervention, action, contestation and struggle.

In the twin concepts of 'genealogy of aesthetics' and 'general organology', then, Stiegler wishes to articulate a practical way of knowing and understanding our constitutive relation to technical prosthetics and, on this basis, to circumscribe a specific space of political struggle. These general concepts are formed with the aim of practically determining the specificities of interaction between sensing bodies and the technical systems and objects of hyper-industrial society. They should offer a tool, a conceptual apparatus or, indeed, a weapon which will allow us to 'reply to the necessity of *identifying forces, tendencies, processes and energies against which a struggle must be led*' (Stiegler 2005a: 14). Such a struggle would be in the service of a wider political struggle which would have as its goal: 'a *refunctionalization of the aesthetic* typical of the era of societies of control' (Stiegler 2005a: 80).

It is in this context that the particular value Stiegler gives to art and to the experience of the artwork comes to the fore. Art, here, is that particular form of sensory (aesthetic) experience which, he argues, affects us in a way that is different from mass-produced objects (even if, of course, the artwork itself is mass-produced). The experience of the artwork would be one which favours or more actively produces singular identifications or aesthetic (sensory) attachments to singularities and singular objects. For Stiegler, then, art and the realm of aesthetic (i.e. artistic) experience affirms and promotes the processes of primary narcissism, individuation and the differentiation of identity and self. It is unsurprising therefore that over the last decade he has written a great deal about art and individual artists and it is clear that he reserves a privileged space for art in any 'refunctionalizing of the aesthetic' within hyper-industrial societies of control.

The limited scope of this discussion cannot do justice to the breadth and richness of Stiegler's engagement with art. By way of a more general conclusion, it may be worth underlining, however, that, although the question of art and of the aesthetic has come to occupy an important place within Stiegler's thinking in recent years, he does not reduce his thinking of political struggle to a cultural politics of 'high' art versus popular mass culture. This is therefore not simply an elitist privileging of 'high culture'. He is not suggesting that art, or the cultivation of the arts more generally, is some kind of panacea in relation to the malaise of contemporary society. What is perhaps most important in Stiegler's philosophical approach is the demand that we begin to think about the emerging technological world around us differently. Only then will we be able to understand what is actually occurring in the more or less hidden processes of technologically driven society. Only then will we be able to understand what is to be done. Despite its sustained affirmation of activism and political engagement, the force of Stiegler's philosophy arguably remains a primarily theoretical one. It lies in his attempt to open new philosophical perspectives on technology and contemporary technological society. First and foremost, he elaborates new theoretical, philosophical and political paradigms which will challenge contemporary orthodoxies. He wants to 'open the perspective of a *total organological revolution*' and to 'elaborate a new political economy' (Stiegler 2006a: 100) and wants to do this in order, ultimately, to: 'Think a new industrial model' (Stiegler 2006b: 110). It could be concluded that, although Stiegler's philosophy may certainly want to change the world, the task is firstly to *rethink* it.

4

Catherine Malabou: The Destiny of Form

To date, Catherine Malabou is the author of nine single-authored works and numerous co-authored or edited volumes. On the face of it, her philosophical interests are very diverse and include studies of Hegel and Heidegger, engagements with contemporary neuroscience, the question of psychoanalysis and its future, as well as an interrogation of the place of the feminine within philosophy. Yet, despite this apparent diversity, Malabou's philosophy is consistently organized around the elaboration and development of a single guiding concept: that of *plasticity*. For Malabou, plasticity or the plastic becomes the instance which shapes both Hegelian dialectics and the Heideggerian destruction of metaphysics, but also the structure of the brain and neural interconnectivity and, indeed, all of the mutable forms of thought, matter and being in general. Defined initially as that which is able to both receive and give form, the plastic, for Malabou, lies at the heart of what she herself comes to call a 'new materialism' or what one might also call a metamorphic materialist ontology. The interest and innovative force of this ontology lies in the manner in which it connects unique, post-deconstructive readings of Hegel and Heidegger with recent findings within neurobiology and genetics. In so doing, Malabou's materialism decisively moves beyond the paradigm which would align the empirical concerns of science with the analytic philosophical tradition, with philosophy of mind and with linguistic thought. She brings the tradition of post-phenomenological, deconstructive or 'continental' philosophy into a direct engagement with the empirical findings of contemporary neuroscience in particular and does so in order to rethink in an entirely new way fundamental philosophical questions: the nature of 'essence', the debate surrounding 'nature' versus 'nurture', the relation of thought to matter, the mutability of identity, questions of politics, freedom, gender difference and of the linguistic material and style of philosophy itself.

Plastic reading

Reading plasticity – the plasticity of reading

Malabou's major first work, *The Future of Hegel: Plasticity, Temporality, and Dialectic* (Malabou 1996a; 2005b), began its life as a doctoral dissertation written under the supervision of Jacques Derrida. In this first work, she clearly signals that plasticity is not just a philosophical concept to be elaborated, nor simply a thematic to be interpreted within the work of other philosophers. Rather, plasticity informs the manner in which philosophical texts themselves can be interpreted in what can be called 'plastic reading'. As will become clear, the concept of plastic reading first emerges in Malabou's interpretation of Hegel but is also something which subsequently comes to shape her general philosophical method. In a more recent text, *Plasticity at the Dusk of Writing* (Malabou 2005a; 2010b), she describes her work as an attempt to develop 'a new method of reading' and suggests that this new method be called '*plastic reading*: a new, transformed type of structural approach' (Malabou 2005a: 97; 2010b: 51). More specifically, she suggests that plastic reading be thought as 'the metamorphosis of deconstructive reading' (Malabou 2005a: 98; 2010b: 52). In an explicit manner, therefore, Malabou situates her work in the wake of Derridean deconstruction but, like Stiegler, she suggests that her new, transformed and transformative approach moves beyond what might appear to be the decisive limitations of deconstruction. Instead of a concern with the aporetic logic of texts, the withdrawal of presence and self-identity or the affirmation of an irreducible and absolute alterity, Malabou offers readings which attempt to discern the shape or form of that which remains or survives in the wake of deconstruction: '*The plastic reading of a text is the reading that seeks to reveal the form left in the text through the withdrawing of presence, that is, through its own deconstruction. It is a question of showing how a text lives its deconstruction*' (Malabou 2005a: 99; 2010b: 52). It is this central concern with *form* and with the form that presents itself in the withdrawal of presence which define Malabou's difference from her former teacher, Derrida. Like Derrida, she is deeply engaged with

the question of alterity, the non-self-identity of thought and of signification, but she rejects what commentator Jean-Paul Martinon has
dubbed the 'morbid fascination of the radically other' (Martinon
2007: 25) in deconstruction in order to discern how the destruction
or deconstruction of the metaphysics of presence leads to a mutation
of form, and, indeed, arises necessarily from a fundamental mutability
of form per se.

In this sense, plastic reading is, like plasticity itself, defined as a
movement or passage between the formation and dissolution of form.
A text in its metaphysical moment will appear in one form but, in the
work of deconstruction, will emerge in an another unfamiliar and
perhaps even unrecognizable guise. Derrida, of course, might be
suspicious of the very notion or category of form itself insofar as
it can be said to bear the legacy or traces of that most metaphysical
of oppositions: form and matter. Rooted back in the philosophy of
Aristotle, the form–matter distinction, together with the doctrine of
hylomorphism and its attendant notion of substance, would no doubt,
for Derrida, be inseparable from the metaphysics of presence and the
traditions of logo-, phono- and haptocentrism and so on.[1] For her
part, Malabou would maintain that, if one admits the possibility of a
destruction, overcoming or deconstruction of metaphysics, being and
presence, then one likewise necessarily both admits and affirms that
our understanding of being is fundamentally transformable from one
form to another or always articulated in its primordial possibility of
ontological transformation. One therefore also necessarily admits
that, insofar as forms *do* present themselves both in thought and
experience, they do so only on the basis of this fundamental mutability, and do so always on the basis of a prior withdrawal of substance,
presence, ground and foundation. This understanding of being as
fundamentally mutable, transformable, indeed, as *plastic*, is uncovered in Malabou's 'plastic readings' of Hegel and Heidegger.

Hegel: dialectics and futurity

In *Hegel: The Restlessness of the Negative*, Jean-Luc Nancy affirms
that Hegel is the direct opposite of a totalitarian thinker (Nancy
1997a; 2002c). In so doing, he rejects the common post-war, largely
French, evaluation of Hegelian synthesis as a thinking of the Same
or of totalization which can be aligned with the totalitarian.[2] Published
a year before Nancy's book, Malabou's *The Future of Hegel* shares
its ambition to rethink the Hegelian system in terms of a fundamental

openness to alterity rather than as a form of totalizing closure. As the title of her book suggests, this question of the openness or closure of Hegelian thought can be related to the question of temporality and, more specifically, to the role played by futurity within Hegel's system.

At the beginning of *The Future of Hegel*, the dialectical progression of the human spirit towards absolute knowledge is related directly to the question of futurity and, specifically, to the alterity of the futural event. If the history of spirit is constituted in the pure activity of the human mind which overreaches itself, idealizes and thus brings into the identity of concepts all which is other to it, then the question arises as to whether there is any place for the absolute other, or of a future which would be without identity, wholly imprescribable and unexpected.[3] Malabou formulates this in the following terms:

> Spirit, whose task is to comprehend itself, to anticipate itself in everything that is now and is to come, can never encounter anything wholly other, can never come face to face, one might say, with the *event*. How, then, could there be room in Hegelian thought for the future, if everything has already been permeated by spirit and, in this fashion, already completed? (Malabou 1996a: 15; 2005b: 4)

The question of whether Hegel is a totalizing thinker of identity is reposed in relation to the possibility of his philosophy being able to account for the future and, indeed, of it having a future within the history of philosophy. For if Hegelian dialectics cannot truly account for the other and the alterity of the event, then it can have no place in any thinking which might unfold in the wake of the destruction or deconstruction of metaphysics. If it can only anticipate the future in terms of the identity of the present and view temporality in general as a succession of self-present instances of a 'now', then Hegel's thinking of time can never escape the inauthentic, 'flat' temporality which is displaced by Heidegger in, for instance, *Being and Time*, nor the metaphysics of presence which is deconstructed throughout Derrida's philosophical writing.

Against this understanding of a Hegel who cannot think futurity, Malabou's *The Future of Hegel* turns to the elaboration of plasticity as a concept in order to affirm his future: to affirm that Hegel both has a thinking of the future and that he has a future as a post-metaphysical thinker. By uncovering the central place of the 'plastic' within Hegelian dialectics, Malabou's reading of Hegel will itself be plastic in that it aims to show that the image of a totalizing thinker of the Same can be deconstructed and that in its place a form of thought persists which is different and unexpected, or, more precisely, which can account both for difference and for the unexpected. In affirming the future of Hegel, Malabou asserts at the beginning of her work 'plasticity will be envisaged as the instance which *gives form* to the future and to time' (Malabou 1996a: 16–17; 2005b: 5).

This relation between plasticity and time is uncovered in Malabou's reading as the key instance which informs both dialectical progression and the auto-determination of the subject of absolute knowledge within Hegel's phenomenology. In the early pages of *The Future of Hegel*, Malabou describes plasticity, variably, as the excess of the future over the future, as that which is able to give and receive form, as that which gives way to form while at the same time resisting deformation, and also as 'the unforeseen of Hegelian philosophy' (Malabou 1996a: 19; 2005b: xvii). At the heart of her account lies an attempt to think the dialectical process as a form of plasticity, or, put differently, as the process which governs the plasticity of forms, and then to think this process as the mode by which the Hegelian subject experiences temporality and is itself formed as a subject. In this sense plasticity, for Malabou, is the key principle of the entire Hegelian system insofar as it governs both the temporal movement and the by turns dissolving and synthesizing force of dialectics itself. The processes of plasticity are dialectical insofar as the operations that constitute them, the assumption and dissolution of form, emergence and explosion are all contradictory (Malabou 1996a: 26; 2005b: 12). This reading of contradiction and reconciliation in Hegel, or of negation and synthesis, is striking insofar as it understands the dialectical process neither as a totalizing movement towards identity and the Same, nor simply as an endless process of unresolvable negativity. This is neither the triumphant progress of speculative reason nor the ceaselessly disruptive and interruptive movement of negative dialectics. Rather it is, as Malabou constantly underlines, the process by which form emerges as mutable and emerges only in its fundamental mutability.

As will become increasingly clear throughout Malabou's reading of Hegel and, indeed, her work as a whole, this plasticity, mutability or transformability which underpins the dialectical process is the principle which gives life to *all* forms of any kind whatsoever: to all the variable forms of material life, to those of sense and meaning, as well as to all the forms of conceptual or symbolic thought and communication. In the context of *The Future of Hegel*, the principal form in question is that of the human, and first and foremost, that of the human subject of knowledge. One of the central aims of Malabou's reading is to highlight the manner in which the Hegelian subject is articulated as a structure of anticipation, that is, as a process of temporalization (Malabou 1996a: 179; 2005b: 130). In this context, the Hegelian dialectic is read as a process in which temporality (and specifically the dimension of futurity) and plasticity are co-articulated in a manner which forms the subject: 'The dialectical composition of such concepts as "the future", "plasticity", and "temporality" forms the *anticipatory structure* operating within subjectivity itself as Hegel conceived it' (Malabou 1996a: 27; 2005b: 13). The name Malabou gives this structure of anticipation is 'to see (what is) coming [*voir venir*]'. Jean-Paul Martinon has shown very convincingly that an English translation of *voir venir* is a complex and difficult task which bears the weight of the wider force and problem of Malabou's thinking about plasticity, temporality and form in general.[4] For the purposes of this discussion, what is important to underline is the extent to which *voir venir* is above all a temporalizing synthesis by which the Hegelian subject *takes* form. Malabou puts this in the following terms: 'The *voir venir* stands for the operation of synthetic temporalizing in Hegel's thought, which means it is the structure of anticipation through which subjectivity projects itself in advance of itself, and thereby participates in the process of its own determination' (Malabou 1996a: 34; 2005b: 18). The self-determination of the Hegelian subject occurs, according to Malabou's reading, not as a process in which it anticipates itself as already 'present in all that is now and is to come' (Malabou 1996a: 15; 2005b: 4) but rather as a process in which it projects itself towards and is thus *exposed* to the unexpected and the unforeseeable, the contingent and the accidental. This is, precisely, not anticipation in the mode of mastery or appropriation of the event, but rather a mode of exposure to it, to its ungraspable alterity, and therefore a vulnerability to being deformed, reformed or transformed by it. In this context, the temporalizing, anticipative structure of *voir venir* is more a 'seeing something coming' as it appears suddenly to, and imposes itself on, the subject, rather than a mode of grasping or seizing it in a way which allows the subject to remain secure in the sovereignty or self-sameness of its rational and conceptual activity.[5]

Ultimately, then, Malabou's co-articulation of plasticity, temporality and dialectics is a way of thinking about the formation of the future in Hegel's system in a manner which exceeds or undoes the totalizing ambitions of speculative rationality. It is in this sense that plasticity, for Malabou, can be described both as 'the instance which *gives form* to the future and to time' and as 'the excess of time over time' (Malabou 1996a: 16, 17; 2005b: 5, 6). For if the future imposes itself as the exposure of the subject to an ungraspable futural horizon, it does so only in the imposition or formation of a form, that is, the form of the subject itself engaged in the process of self-determination. This process of subjective self-determination as thought within the Hegelian system emerges in Malabou's reading as an 'originary operation of plasticity' (Malabou 1996a: 16; 2005b: 12). On this basis, and perhaps most importantly, the structure of anticipation which articulates the Hegelian dialectic as a *voir venir* is also the starting point for Malabou's elaboration of an ontology. The originary operation of plasticity articulates a structure which informs 'the relation of substance to its accidents' (Malabou 1996a: 27; 2005b: 11). This is an opening towards an ontology in which the traditional distinctions between essence and accident, the necessary and the contingent, are themselves governed by the principle of plasticity.[6] The oppositional poles of these distinctions are no longer secure within the context of Malabou's reading of the Hegelian dialectic since, in the exposure of the subject to the alterity of the future, in its originary possibility of formation and deformation, human essence is necessarily transformed by accidents and the necessary is essentially exchangeable with the contingent.[7] In short, substance itself, its accidents *and* essences, are formed only in their primordial mutability and transformability.

As has been indicated from the beginning of this discussion, for Malabou the operation of plasticity and its articulation of dialectical progression, temporality and subjectivity governs the entirety of Hegel's system. Neither the movement of negating/conserving synthesis (*Aufhebung*) nor the category of absolute knowledge escapes the transformative power and primordial operation of the plastic. According to Malabou, the movement of *Aufhebung* cannot be understood as a progression towards the absolute identity of spirit and matter, nor a triumph of the identity of conceptual determination and speculative reason. Rather, dialectical negation and sublation are themselves constantly mutating forms of thought, non-self-identical, exposed to alterity, and in that exposure both transformable and mutable in their fundamental operation. As Malabou herself puts it: 'in the entire course of spirit's development, there is no perfect identity between preservation and suppression; they are neither unchangeable nor undifferentiated' (Malabou 1996a: 199; 2005b: 145). Thus, absolute knowledge itself cannot be the end or final term of the Hegelian system in the sense that it would herald the cessation of dialectical negation and conservation, nor, indeed, can it constitute anything like the 'end of history'. Malabou's reading of Hegel can allow only for a ceaseless process of metamorphosis in which any instance of a supposed end, final term, or absolute moment of (self-)determination would necessarily still be subject to transformation into another form. Yet, arguably, this is not simply an endlessly negative dialectic since the overall emphasis is not on the instance of negation, on its disruptive or interruptive force, but rather on *formation*, on the emergence of infinitely malleable and formable form. Here the force of formability and the resistance of form to deformation is just as fundamental to the operation of plasticity as the inevitability of the dissolution of form.

What the Hegelian system yields, then, is not the wisdom of absolute knowledge as a static end to the dialectical progression of spirit in history, but rather a knowledge of the 'formation and dissolution of form' and of plasticity as an 'ontological combustion which liberates the twofold possibility of appearance and the annihilation of presence' (Malabou 1996a: 249; 2005b: 187). Hegel emerges definitively as a thinker of the radical openness of any closed system, its transformability and its receptivity to the unexpected and the different (Malabou 1996a: 255; 2005b: 190), but he emerges also as a thinker of a general economy of being and life: 'it is Hegel who will have discovered before its discovery the plastic materiality of being: that free energy, whether organic or synthetic, which circulates throughout each and every life' (Malabou 1996a: 256; 2005b: 193).

Such is Malabou's 'plastic reading' of Hegel. As should by now be clear, her treatment of Hegelian futurity, plasticity, temporality and dialectics has yielded not only a thinking of the subject and its formation but also a thinking of being, of being as a 'plastic materiality [*matière plastique*]'. It is this emphasis on an ontological dimension which opens the way for her reading of Heidegger, a Heidegger who, like Hegel, emerges in a different and unfamiliar form.

Heidegger: transformation and metamorphosis

If Malabou's reading of dialectics, futurity and subjectivity in *The Future of Hegel* has its issue in a thinking of the plasticity of being, then this point of issue is, unsurprisingly, the starting point and sustained concern of *Le Change Heidegger*. Yet, despite this eminently Heideggerian concern with ontology, Malabou's reading of Heidegger arguably goes much further in making his thinking unfamiliar and unrecognizable than does her reading of Hegel. Like the word 'future' in the title of the earlier work, the 'change' of *Le Change Heidegger* has a polyvalent meaning. In this case, though, Malabou ascribes three possibilities of understanding the signification of her title

(Malabou 2004a: 12–13). The first understanding would take the phrase 'le change Heidegger' as having a genitive force, as describing a mode of belonging: this then would be a study of the theme of change and transformation in his philosophy (i.e. 'le change *de* Heidegger'). The second would carry a nominative force and name the process of change articulated by Heidegger himself and which would therefore bear *his* name (e.g. 'le *change Heidegger*', as in 'The Luzhin Defence' of Nabakov's chess player). The third understanding would articulate what Malabou calls a *verbe appareil*. This would describe the change process in Heidegger and the process of changing his thought. This apparatus would therefore be an exegetical tool or framework of interpretation by which a whole ontological structure and process of transformation in Heidegger would be uncovered in its action or movement and this would, in turn, transform or meta-morphose Heideggerian thought in its entirety.

Arguably, it is the third of these ways of understanding Malabou's title which governs the first two and gives the work as a whole its force and originality. In the opening pages of *Le Change Heidegger*, Malabou asserts that one of its key aims will be to 'change, transform, metamorphose the interpretation of Heidegger's thought in its en-tirety' (Malabou 2004a: 13). She wishes to make Heidegger un-recognizable to her readers, to turn their attention away from the insistent thematic of ontological difference or from the sustained preoccupation with an 'other' thinking and saying of Being/Beyng. The apparatus, exegetical tool or framework which she elaborates throughout *Le Change Heidegger* is centred on the recurrence of three German words which thread themselves insistently, but perhaps rather marginally, throughout the entire corpus of Heideggerian thinking: *Wandeln* (changes), *Wandlungen* (transformations) and *Verwandlungen* (metamorphoses). Malabou's focus, therefore, is not on the exegesis of those central terms which Heidegger himself sets out to rethink, e.g. being, beings, man, *Dasein,* metaphysics, nothing, identity, difference and so on. Rather, she focuses on what she comes to call the 'metabolism' of change and transformation in Heideggerian thought. This metabolism of thought allows all these terms to be transformed one into the other: man becomes *Dasein*, the metaphysi-cal thinking of beings becomes that of Being/Beyng, metaphysics itself becomes another path of thinking and so on. What is at stake in Malabou's reading is not the fraying of a path towards these other modes of thought in order to confirm, continue or understand better Heidegger's texts. Rather, it is a question of uncovering the way in which the three terms, *Wandeln, Wandlungen* and *Verwandlungen* (which are abbreviated to *W, W, V* throughout *Le Change*), articulate the modes of transformation at work in Heidegger's texts and *form* their inner workings.

One important word that Malabou does also directly focus on is that of *Wesen* or essence. This is because it is Heidegger's interrogations of essence (e.g. of ground, of truth) which articulate the processes of change or transformation at work in his thought.[8] His analyses often work by first posing an instance as it is viewed from within the traditional metaphysical perspective, for instance: man thought from an anthropological perspective, being seen as a totality of beings, ground understood as the principle which causally underpins the being of those beings, or truth as the correspondence between a statement about beings and their simple presence at hand. He then uncovers a more fundamental, 'authentic' or originary instance which articulates the essence of something from the perspective of the thinking of Being, e.g. man as *Dasein*, beings as revealed in the temporal horizon of Being, ground as ab-ground, truth as aletheia and so on. Yet what this process reveals to Malabou is not that thought should direct itself towards a further elucidation of this more fundamental or originary thinking but rather that 'to view essence is to view exchange [*regarder l'essence, c'est regarder l'échange*]' (Malabou 2004a: 27). What Heidegger's destruction of metaphysics and elaboration of a fundamental ontology (or, later in his career, his poetic saying of being) reveal is the possibility of ontological regimes being exchangeable one with another. Or as Malabou puts it, Heidegger reveals 'the originary possibility that being and beings have to change into each other' (Malabou 2004a: 29). It is this originary possibility of exchange or transformation which, according to Malabou, Heidegger's thinking uncovers.

To this extent, her reading is very similar to the account she gives of Hegel's system. Just as, in Hegel, the end of history and absolute knowledge were shown to be neither final nor static, so, in Heidegger, the end of metaphysics does not give us a final form of being, nor an ultimate and more 'authentic' thinking or saying of Being (i.e. as articulated solely by Heidegger's idiosyncratic philosophical idiom). Just as Malabou's account of Hegel affirmed an understanding of being as an endlessly mutable *matière plastique*, so *Le Change Heidegger* shows that 'With the end of metaphysics it is not, as one might think, the end of exchange which arrives, but rather a change of the primary change [*un change du premier change*], a new exchangeability of being and beings' (Malabou 2004a: 30). To read Heidegger with Malabou and according to the apparatus of *W, W, V* is to sidestep the pathos and the arguably rather imperious or coercive idiom of Heideggerian thinking and to uncover instead 'the conditions of a new ontological exchange' and a more open-ended thought of 'onto-logical transformability, the migratory and metamorphic mutability of all that is' (Malabou 2004a: 30, 37).

The main body of *Le Change Heidegger* is devoted, therefore, to a careful and detailed elaboration of the metabolism of change and transformation at work in Heideggerian thought. The full scope and extent of Malabou's rereading of Heidegger cannot be treated within the context of this discussion. If this reading can be judged to be suc-cessful, however, then her work deserves to be placed alongside that of Nancy and Stiegler to the extent that it can be said to liberate the Heideggerian legacy from Heidegger himself. Like Nancy's thinking of the (embodied) singular plural of being or Stiegler's account of technics and time, Malabou's work arguably moves the reading of Heidegger beyond any determinable form of Heideggerianism, and, as with her reading of Hegel, opens this historically important body of thought to a different future.

A measure of just how different the concerns opened up by Malabou's reading can be found in the subtitle of *Le Change Heidegger*: *Du fantastique en philosophie* (*On the Fantastic in Philo-sophy*). If her reading of Heidegger is directed towards the claim that '"ontology" is only the name given to an originary migratory and metamorphic tendency' (Malabou 2004a: 344), then this is so only insofar as she also wishes to relate this claim to a thinking of the 'fantastic' within philosophy generally. While the motifs of the phan-tasm, the phantasmatic, the marvellous and the fantastic may have a strong presence within the tradition of twentieth-century French psy-choanalytic thought and within the wider legacy of surrealism in French philosophy, this is not a thematic which one would expect to be associated with a detailed exegesis of Heidegger.[9] Yet, for Malabou, the migratory and metamorphic mutability of all that is is inseparable from the fantastic insofar as *that which is* must present itself in order to be and insofar as the mode of this presentation will always, she contends, be governed at its most fundamental level by the fantastic. In this context, the fantastic is the *form* in which the mutable being of being will present or give itself. Malabou puts this in the following terms: 'the fantastic characterizes the apprehension *and* the regime of the existence of that which cannot be presented, that is to say, that which can only change' (Malabou 2004a: 24). What she is suggesting is that, if being is fundamentally mutable, then the *fundamental* forms in which being appears or presents itself to us must themselves also be mutable, transformable, metamorphic. Being presents itself to thought not in the clarity and exactitude of concepts or conceptual determination, but rather in the plasticity of images and phantasms:

'Fantastic. The place of originary change can only be invested with images. It will always lack concepts' (Malabou 2004a: 95). At the point where (the late) Heidegger would affirm a poetic saying of an originary giving of Beyng, Malabou substitutes the infinitely exchangeable and changeable realm of fantastic images.

This emphasis on the fantastic and on the (ex)changeability of the fundamental forms and images of being allow Malabou's thought to be critically and comparatively situated in relation to other thinkers who this study has shown to be preoccupied with the question of exchange, namely Derrida and Marion. A key difference between Derrida and Marion, it will be recalled, hinges on the way in which the latter insists on the primordiality of the phenomenological gift (i.e. the appearing of that which is given), on its absoluteness, unconditionality and anteriority in relation to any economy or system of exchange. Derrida, conversely, insists that the gift is always given, and therefore never (purely) given, within a differing, deferring spatial and temporal economy. Malabou, for her part, follows Derrida in her affirmation of the gift as an originary locus of exchange: 'at the same time a giving of economy and an economised instance' (Malabou 2004a: 198) in a way which can be directly opposed to Marion's account. For Malabou, the givenness of the gift can never have the absolute and unconditional status accorded to it by Marion: '*The gift will never abolish the mutability of being – or of the gift*' (Malabou 2004a: 198). Conversely, her emphasis on the fantastic understood as those images or forms which occupy the site of an originary mutability of Being distances her from her mentor. This emphasis on Being as mutable form at once locates her thinking within an ontological register which Derrida would seek to deconstruct and at the same time affirms a mode of originary presentation of form which Derrida would no doubt suspect of concealing metaphysical contraband. So, in a divergence from Derrida, Malabou is happy to use the term 'presence' in affirming that 'every presence is a change' (Malabou 2004a: 261) and to pose an economy of being that would be prior to all other possibilities of economy: 'ontological mutability supposes the originary economy of an exchange prior to exchange [*d'un échange d'avant l'échange*] and prior to economy' (Malabou 2004a: 361). Ontological mutability and transformation is a site of exchange and transformation which *precedes* the temporalizing-spatializing economy of the Derridean trace or arche-writing.[10]

Taken together, Malabou's emphasis on ontological mutability and the fantastic give a tonality to her thinking which has a far more Nietzschean quality than it does Heideggerian. Her reading of Heidegger from the perspective of *W, W, V* makes a demand on his thought, the demand that it avow its inner ontological metabolism as 'the plastic power of modification' (Malabou 2004a: 295), and that this metabolism avow itself as the exchangeability of plastic and fantastic images. A Nietzschean thinking of flux and becoming resonates far more strongly here than does a Heideggerian saying of being as, for instance, in phrases such as: '*Being only shows itself behind a mask: this is how it all begins. Being "is" (only as) an archimodification*' (Malabou 2004a: 275). At the same time, thinking ontology as an economy or as an exchange of always already mutable essences might recall Nietzsche's early work, *On Truth and Lies in the Extra-Moral Sense*, where Nietzsche compares truth and value to coins and currency. In this context and given the controversies surrounding Heidegger and his legacy, it will be interesting to see whether Malabou's 'plastic reading' here really convinces those who remain resolutely sceptical or antipathetic to this legacy. At the end of her book, she expresses the hope that her readers will no longer recognize the Heidegger as read through the lens of *W, W, V* and that they will be able to begin, not simply to read, follow, or reject his work but to *imagine* it (Malabou 2004a: 369).

Whether this hope is fulfilled or not, it should be clear that Malabou's method of plastic reading does yield innovative, perhaps surprising and certainly forceful accounts of both the Hegelian system and Heideggerian ontology. It succeeds in opening the work of both philosophers up to a range of unexpected futures and suggests that they are still there to be *read* within contemporary thought. What may for some be more clearly and unequivocally unexpected is the future that Malabou herself opens up for this thinking of plasticity as uncovered in Hegel and Heidegger: a thinking of plasticity that connects this 'continental' tradition to contemporary neuroscience and to what Malabou herself comes to call 'cerebrality'.

Cerebrality

Cerebral plasticity

The concept of neuroplasticity or brain plasticity has evolved rapidly in the past decade and a half of research within neuroscience. As Ira Black points out in *The New Cognitive Neurosciences*, the years separating the second edition (2000) from the third edition (2004) of this work saw a huge change in the manner in which brain plasticity was viewed. While previous scientific research had acknowledged that the brain was adaptable and transformable in multiple ways in the process of the development of the cortex, more recently 'a newly recognized source of plasticity has swept through neuroscience – the genesis of new neurons and ganglia throughout life' (Gazzaniga 2004: 107). Within contemporary neuroscience, then, plasticity is not just a capacity of the brain early in life when neural networks are forming; it designates a mutability of brain structure at every stage of human development.

In *What Should We Do with Our Brain?*, Malabou builds on these recent neuroscientific developments by viewing them through the lens of her own thinking of plasticity. The initial definition of the plastic in *The Future of Hegel* as that which is 'at once capable of receiving and of giving form' (Malabou 1996a: 20; 2005b: 8) would appear to be particularly suited to describing the lifelong giving and receiving of neuronal form as described by the concept of neuroplasticity. At the beginning of her short book, she highlights three distinct areas in which the work of brain plasticity can be discerned: firstly in the development of neural connections in the womb and in childhood, secondly in the further formation of these connections throughout life (most obviously in the activities of learning and memory) and thirdly in the formation or deformation of the brain in the wake of damage, trauma or loss of function. The second of these areas forms the principal focus of attention in *What Should We Do with Our Brain?*, just as the third area (trauma/damage) will be the central preoccupation of her later work, *Les Nouveau blessés* (*The New Injured*).

As the title of her work suggests, Malabou is interested in the wider philosophical implications of the science of brain plasticity. She is interested in the questions that such plasticity poses to us and in the demands it might make upon us. These questions and demands are at once ethical and political as well as fundamentally philosophical. If there indeed exists 'an ongoing reworking of neuronal morphology' (Malabou 2004b: 55; 2008: 25) then we cannot *simply or solely* refer back to genetic or evolutionary factors or so-called 'hardwired' brain structures in order to answer questions which are of a fundamentally ethical, socio-political and philosophical order.[11] Malabou puts this in the following terms: 'It is precisely because . . . the brain is not already made that we must ask what we should do with it, what we should do with this plasticity that makes us, precisely in the sense of a work, sculpture, modelling, architecture' (Malabou 2004b: 20; 2008: 7). In short, neuroplasticity challenges, or at least needs to be put into a critical relation with, claims based on neurobiological or genetic determinism but also challenges our understanding of human freedom and possibility, and, in particular, our possibilities of individual and collective self-fashioning. It will be a question, Malabou argues, of grasping: 'the connection between the role of genetic determinism at work in the constitution of the brain and the possibility of a social and political non-determinism, in a word a new freedom: a new meaning of history' (Malabou 2004b: 32; 2008: 13). The social, political and historical constitution of the human, the existence of freedom and the exercise thereof – these are all questions which can be posed anew by philosophy in response to the new cognitive neuroscience and, more specifically, in response to the fact that neural systems and networks can be formed and reformed in the course of human life. This is by no means to downplay the importance of scientifically determinable (neuro)biological and genetic determinations. Rather, it may suggest that philosophy needs to find a new register or conceptual means by which to think the interplay of biological and social/environmental determinations, means that go beyond the highly reductive terms of the nature vs. nurture debate.

Throughout the pages of *What Should We Do with Our Brain?*, Malabou makes wide-ranging references both to writing by leading neuroscientists and by philosophers who have sought to rethink the question of consciousness in the light of contemporary science. These include, amongst others, works by very well-known figures such as Marc Jeannerod, Jean-Pierre Changeux, Antonio Damasio, Joseph LeDoux and Daniel Dennett. She also refers to key ground-breaking figures of the early to mid-twentieth century, such as Donald Hebb and Jerzy Konorski. One of the contemporary figures she singles out for his importance in this area is Joseph LeDoux whose book *Synaptic Self* (LeDoux 2003) gives the title to the third and final section of *What Should We Do with Our Brain?* ('You are your Synapses'). Malabou takes from LeDoux (and Damasio) the notion of a 'neuronal personality', that is, the idea that the self is a synthesis of all the plastic processes of synaptic formation at work in the brain (Malabou 2004b: 119; 2008: 58). Who we are, our self-reflexive sense of who we are and therefore the way in which we make sense of the world around us, is inseparable from and, indeed, is articulated only in, the structure of our neural connections and interconnections.[12] This might, to some at least, appear to be a dangerously reductive way of thinking about personality, identity and consciousness. Yet the central role played by neuroplasticity in this context might warn us against such a hasty response.

In the final chapter of *Synaptic Self*, LeDoux develops the notion of 'parallel plasticity'. He describes the way in which the brain's various neural systems and networks (e.g. those involved in sensory function, motor control, emotion, thinking, reasoning and so on) all work in parallel with each other in a normally functioning brain. The way in which these systems are connected and interact within each of us 'is distinct, and that uniqueness, in short, is what makes us who we are' (LeDoux 2003: 303). Yet LeDoux also emphasizes that 'synapses in all these systems are capable of being modified by experience' (LeDoux 2003: 303). Just as brain systems function in parallel, so they share a plasticity, a susceptibility to being formed and reformed in a connected unity with each other in the course of experiencing the world. LeDoux outlines a number of key principles governing the work of parallel plasticity. Of key interest here is what he calls 'downward causation', the process 'by which a thought can cause the brain to issue a certain order' (LeDoux 2003: 319). We might otherwise call this intentionality: conscious thoughts instruct our brains and bodies to do things by means of one network of neural activity (e.g. thinking or decision) causing other networks to be active (e.g. motor control). Yet such downward causation can also 'cause another network to change, to be plastic. All that is required to induce plasticity in a synapse is the right kind of synaptic activity' (LeDoux 2003: 319). From this, LeDoux concludes that it is entirely reasonable to suppose that the ways in which we think about ourselves can 'have powerful influences on the way we are, and who we become. One's image is self-perpetuating' (LeDoux 2003: 320).

This empowerment of thought in relation to synaptic activity and plasticity opens up the possibility of a complex interaction between consciousness, experience and the mutable structures of neural networks, i.e. the neurological base that defines 'who we are'. If we think of this neurological base in terms of its plasticity, its susceptibility to formation and reformation in experience and, crucially, in our conscious *responses* to experience, then the concept of the neuronal personality may appear to be far more productive of possibility and potential than it is purely reductive to biological or neurological strata. Malabou takes up the notions of neuronal self, parallel plasticity and downward causation in order to identify *and harness* 'the poetical and aesthetic force that is the fundamental, organizing attribute of plasticity: its power to configure the world' (Malabou 2004b: 82; 2008: 39). In *What Should We Do with Our Brain?* she appears to rely heavily on LeDoux's work, her aim being to produce a reflexive and philosophical consciousness of the brain and its plasticity and to put this in the service of an understanding which would at once be both critical, political and emancipatory (Malabou 2004b: 109; 2008: 53).

Before discussing the political dimension of Malabou's philosophical insights on neuroscientific research, it might be worth posing some questions about her relation to, or appropriation of, brain science more generally. It should be noted, for instance, that some scientific opinion at the time of the publication of Malabou's book is rather more conservative in the claims it makes for plasticity than is LeDoux. For instance, Blakemore and Steven talk tentatively about therapeutic possibilities of brain plasticity and of 'adaptive' plasticity but they also pose the question of 'maladaptive plasticity' and stress 'controversy remains as to whether plastic changes in the cortex are causally related to behavioural changes' (Gazzaniga 2004: 1250). This note of caution clearly signals that different scientists have framed the scope and nature of brain plasticity rather differently in recent years and that the, albeit highly innovative, insights of Malabou's *What Should We Do with Our Brain?* need to be understood in the context of a rapidly changing and developing field of experimental research. In this respect, her relation to science differs greatly from Badiou's alignment of ontology with the mathematics viewed as a 'science of the real' and from Laruelle's more general account of the 'posture of immanence' taken by science in relation to the One (see chapters 6 and 7 respectively). This note of caution needs to be offset by the fact that the English translation of *What Should We Do with Our Brain?* was published with a foreword by one of the world's leading neuroscientists, the late Marc Jeannerod (1935–2011). In his foreword, Jeannerod strongly endorses Malabou's arguments relating to the philosophical implications of brain plasticity and, in particular, affirms the value of the way she develops its political implications (Malabou 2008: xi–xiv).

For Malabou's arguments here, although they begin with questions relating to the plasticity of brain structure and its implications for consciousness, freedom, identity and so on quickly shift into the rather different register of discourse analysis and an enquiry into the nature of contemporary social and political structures. She is interested in the way in which, in recent decades, our understanding and representations of brain function may have converged with our understanding, representations and ways of organizing, social and political forms. Her argument here is based on a, perhaps rather speculative, but certainly provocative claim that there exists a '*neuronal form of political and social functioning*, a form that today deeply coincides with the current face of capitalism' (Malabou 2004b: 26; 2008: 10). In order to make this argument, she highlights the diverse ways in which, throughout the twentieth century, the brain was viewed as an information or communication centre or centralized site of storage and retrieval. Its functioning was viewed by analogy with the functioning of diverse technical apparatuses, from telephone exchanges to computers and cybernetic machines. The fixed and centralized 'command and control' model that inform these metaphors of brain function becomes obsolete when viewed in the light of the parallel and plastic nature of neural systems and interconnectivity.[13] In the last three decades, this progressive displacement of a centralized model of command and control has also undoubtedly informed the development of the social and political formations of contemporary capitalism. Malabou argues that this displacement of centralized command is most obviously present in the convergence between the discourses of neuroscience and of management theory. There is, she suggests, a 'transition point between neuroscientific discourse and the discourse of management, between the functioning of the brain and the functioning of a company' (Malabou 2004b: 85; 2008: 40). This might at first seem like a somewhat fanciful claim, but if one looks closely at key concepts of human resources management – concepts such as 'employee participation', 'involvement mechanisms', 'diversity management', 'organizational learning' and 'organizational change and innovation' – one can see ways in which they do resonate with the more decentralized and networked understanding of structure and form that has emerged within neuroscience in recent decades.

On the basis of this convergence or *point de passage*, Malabou argues that the radical role and political potential of plasticity has yet to be fully grasped within our contemporary moment. She suggests that 'today, the true sense of plasticity is hidden, and we tend constantly to substitute for it its mistaken cognate, *flexibility*' (Malabou 2004b: 29; 2008: 12). If plasticity is about the receiving *and* giving of form, flexibility is, conversely, more passive or reactive insofar as it simply receives form: flexible workers and workforces, for instance, will adapt to whatever conditions are imposed upon them by market conditions and the owners of capital. By analogy, a merely flexible brain would adapt to various modes of biological and environmental conditioning but would not be susceptible to the transformations effected by learning and memory or to a more self-conscious, active and proactive sculpting and modelling.

Ultimately, then, the arguments and polemical force of *What Should We Do with Our Brain?* turn on the possibility of tapping into this more active and proactive potential of plasticity. At stake here is *both* the plasticity of neuronal self *and* that of collective social and political organization. Malabou returns here to the dialectical understanding of plasticity she developed in *The Future of Hegel*. If one understands the transformative processes at work in the interaction of consciousness and the neural systems which give it life in terms of a dialectical plasticity, then all the possible fears of reductionism in relation to the neuronal self will appear to be entirely misplaced. Certainly, our consciousness would be formed only in and by the multiplicity and multiple interconnectedness of brain systems. Yet the central role played by neuroplasticity would mean that mental life could not function as an automaton in relation to its neurological base: 'The transition from the neuronal to the mental supposes negation and resistance . . . The neuronal and the mental resist each other' (Malabou 2004b: 147; 2008: 72). Just as that base forms us in multiple ways, so it is itself formable in response to experience and, in turn, formable also by our extended thought patterns and the downwardly causal activity of higher cognitive networks in relation to other brain systems. Insofar as all these systems might resist deformation before being susceptible to reformation, this process is dialectical in exactly the sense worked out by Malabou in her earlier reading of Hegel. Such dialectical plasticity can by implication be extended to the structure of our social forms and modes of organization. Here the convergence of brain structures and social forms is ultimately to be positively affirmed but only on the basis of full apprehension of the plasticity of both. Malabou puts this in the following terms: 'The mental is not the wise appendix of the neuronal. And the brain is not the natural ideal of globalized economic, political, and social organization; it is the locus of an organic tension that is the basis of our history and our critical activity' (Malabou 2004b: 162–3; 2008: 81). *What Should We Do with Our Brain?* concludes therefore with an affirmation of the neuronal self as dialectically structured and capable of a cultural-historical self-fashioning. This self-fashioning occurs within a fundamental economy of contradiction, resistance, deformation and reformation. It is also a cultural-historical self-fashioning which can occur on both an individual and collective level, but which requires a reflexive and critical consciousness of its own possibility in order to be possible. The new cognitive science and a critical-philosophical reflection on plasticity, Malabou argues, provides just such an opening for this consciousness.

If this account is Hegelian, then it is so in the highly mutated form of a Hegelian future made possible by *The Future of Hegel*. When applied to the field of the social and to that of social and political transformation and change, this account might still appear to some to be more conventionally dialectical and Hegelian insofar as the contradiction between, for example, the mental and the neuronal, or critical activity and history, ultimately might be seen to resolve itself into a process of negation and synthesis rather than the arguably more subtle or complex operations of plasticity. Nevertheless, what is perhaps most striking about Malabou's thinking here is the fact that it offers a resolutely materialist and scientifically grounded account of a neuronal self while at the same time avoiding any possibility of reductionism. To this extent *What Should We Do with Our Brain?* marks a key moment in the development of the 'materialist metamorphic ontology' that was alluded to at the beginning of this discussion. Yet if this material, neuronal self is full of emancipatory potential, it is also an instance which, in its very materiality, is extremely vulnerable and fragile, for, in the words of Joseph LeDoux, 'when [neural] connections change, personality too, can change,' and 'the self can be disassembled by experiences that alter connections' (LeDoux 2003: 307). In short, this neuronal self can all too easily disintegrate or be annihilated.

Destructive plasticity

One of the grounding and iconic moments in the history of modern brain science is the case study of Phineas Gage, a worker involved in the building of the Vermont railroad at the end of the nineteenth century. In an appalling industrial accident, an iron rod passed through Gage's head and cut directly through the prefrontal region of his brain. In a very short period of time, he was transformed from an ostensibly hard-working and upstanding citizen into an irritable, indifferent, and unrestrained individual endowed with a new, entirely unrecognizable personality. The case of Gage is one of a number taken up by Antonio Damasio in his seminal work, *Descartes' Error* (Damasio 2006), in order to demonstrate that damage to the prefrontal cortex can lead to a severe diminution in those mechanisms which allow us to exercise social control and can also, in extreme cases, lead to sociopathic behaviour. Citing Damasio's work at the beginning of *Les Nouveaux blessés*, Malabou also highlights the case of Phineas Gage, underlines its paradigmatic significance and notes the view that it has been as important for neurobiology in general as the Schreber case has been for psychoanalysis (Malabou 2007: 46, n. 43).[14]

If one accepts the concept of 'neuronal personality' such as it is developed by neuroscientists like Damasio and LeDoux, then the wider philosophical implications of the Gage case and others like it are enormous. The notion that we are our neurons, nothing more and nothing less, and therefore that what we are can be very easily altered or destroyed, has particular implications for psychoanalysis. This is because the case of Gage suggests that our behaviour and, indeed, our entire personality might be transformable in a manner which is entirely unrelated to the organization of our affects and drives or to the symbolic structuring of our unconscious desire. As Malabou notes, the motivation underlying the writing of *Les Nouveaux blessés* is personal as well as philosophical: her mother died of Alzheimer's disease and so she has been able to witness at first hand the fragility of a self which is nothing without the properly functioning synaptic connections which give it life. *Les Nouveaux blessés*, as the title implies, is a study which examines the implications of the injured, physically traumatized or diseased brain for our understanding of subjectivity, identity and self. In particular, it stages an encounter between the medical findings of neuroscience and the underlying tenets of Freudian and post-Freudian psychoanalysis. The book, in a sense, is structured around the competing legacies of Gage and Schreber.

It may be over-hasty, though, to assume that the insights of psychoanalysis and other theoretical or philosophical conceptions of identity are entirely incompatible with those of neuroscience. As Jean-Pierre Changeux points out in the preface to *Neuronal Man*, the work was initially conceived after a discussion with the psychoanalyst (and son-in-law of Jacques Lacan) Jacques Alain-Miller, a discussion which, surprisingly, 'demonstrated that the protagonists could talk to each other and even come to an agreement' (Changeux 1997: xvii). Similarly, Joseph LeDoux suggests in *Synaptic Self* that the 'postmodern notion that the self is socially constructed' is not necessarily diametrically opposed to the findings of neuroscience 'since brains are responsible for both the behaviours that collectively constitute the social milieu, and for the reception by each individual of the information conveyed by this milieu' (LeDoux 2003: 20). Nevertheless, Malabou identifies a key fault line which separates psychoanalysis from the medical and scientific tradition after Phineas Gage: the question of the aetiology of psychopathology, that is, the root causes of mental illnesses, disturbances and aberrations. Where psychoanalysis will look to the symbolic activity of the subject, to the symbolic structuring of desire or to the unconscious signifying structures by which the subject is articulated *as* subject, neuroscientific medical approaches will look at cerebral activity and structure, the existence of lesions, cortical malformations, mis-adaptation of specific functions and so on. Malabou argues that these two approaches are based in two separate paradigms of understanding the aetiology of psychical malfunction. Psychoanalysis has the paradigm of *sexuality*, neuroscience that of *cerebrality*, and these two paradigms are in competition:

'Sexuality and cerebrality thus appear today as competing economies of the psyche's exposure to injury' (Malabou 2007: 28). Indeed, she goes so far as to suggest that, throughout their respective histories sexuality and cerebrality have waged 'a fratricidal war for etiological domination' (Malabou 2007: 60).

Freud, of course, began his professional life in the 1880s as a medical neurobiologist. Yet as he developed psychoanalysis as a science in its own right, distinct from neurobiology, he came to see the brain itself as a material base, a base which would be distinct and separate from the economy of affects, drives and symbolic represen-tations which constitute the psychical apparatus that analysis will take as its object of study and therapeutic concern. It is this emphasis on a symbolically structured psychic apparatus which is irreducible to pure brain function that underpins the scission between sexuality and cerebrality. The problem psychoanalysis faces, Malabou argues, is that such an understanding of the brain as the material support for a distinct economy of symbolic representation is untenable in the light of the findings of contemporary neuroscience: 'the Freudian conception of a brain which is a stranger to symbolic activity, a pure material base . . . is today being thoroughly reassessed' (Malabou 2007: 76). Malabou describes at some length the way in which the brain has been shown to have an auto-regulative function based in affective, emotional and therefore also *representational* activity. Brain function is coordinated by emotions in what one might call a kind of cerebral homeostasis.[15] This vital functioning of the brain, which allows us to be who we are and do what we do, is grounded in an activity of auto-affection in which the brain is constantly regulating and modifying itself in reflexive processes which are representational in the sense that emotions and affects always carry with them a charge of meaning or sense. These neuroscientific findings lead Malabou to a twofold conclusion:

> In the brain there is therefore no regulation without representation. This double economy precisely defines cerebral identity as a constant synthesis of different states of relation between the body and the psyche. (Malabou 2007: 82)

> Cerebral auto-affection is a logical sensuality which makes possible life's attachment to itself; it is the basis of all subsequent investment. (Malabou 2007: 83)

Psychoanalysis, she suggests, has remained blind to this fundamental structure of cerebral auto-excitation and regulation and therefore blind also to the inherently symbolic and representational workings of the neurological structures of our psychical life. In consequence, Malabou claims, sexuality has remained psychoanalysis's sole frame of reference for understanding the aetiology of psychopathology and it has been unable to relate its understandings of symbolic identity or self to the underlying structure of the brain and its activity.

By implication, psychoanalysis would have difficulty in admitting or theorizing the existence of a 'neuronal self' and in conceding the vulnerability of such a self to purely accidental alterations in the synaptic connections which give it life: vulnerability to, for example, alterations in the prefrontal cortex as suffered by Gage or to the wasting of brain tissue that occurs in Alzheimer's disease. Malabou is interested in the way in which, in a condition such as Alzheimer's, an individual's personality can appear to be entirely and irrevocably lost in the process of cerebral degeneration but that the individual can, at least for a time, survive that loss of personality. They can continue living with their fundamental vital functions intact, but they do so as a seemingly different, unrecognizable person, unmarked by the previous history of their conscious and unconscious lives. This can occur also in patients suffering other types of brain damage, trauma or lesions. Such a possibility, the possibility – of the individual surviving beyond the irrevocable loss of the self or personality that makes them who they are – leads Malabou to formulate the central concept of *Les Nouveaux blessés*, that of *destructive plasticity*. 'If there is such a thing as the creation of a post-lesional identity,' she suggests 'then this is a creation through the destruction of form. The plasticity at play here is therefore a destructive plasticity' (Malabou 2007: 49). This destructive form of plasticity would be the sombre double of the plasticity described in *What Should We Do with Our Brain?* (i.e. the plasticity which constructs, sculpts and models neuronal connections) (Malabou 2007: 15). It would engender the creation of a new identity in the total loss of a previous identity and in the loss of any relation to a past, a primal scene, an Oedipal structuring or symbolic economy of subjectivity or self. Destructive plasticity is, Malabou contends, '*a thinking of the destruction of the psyche which is different to that of psychoanalysis*' (Malabou 2007: 146).

Yet if Malabou's thinking of cerebrality, cerebral auto-affection, and destructive plasticity collectively articulate a confrontation between neuroscience and psychoanalysis, she does not simply wish to affirm that psychoanalysis has had its day, that it is an obsolete paradigm that should be left back in the twentieth century where it began. Rather she suggests that there might be a fruitful cross-fertilisation of the one with the other in an opening towards a future 'neuro-psychoanalysis'. A future neuro-psychoanalysis would provide a model of self which would indeed be a neuronal self such as it is thought by Damasio and LeDoux. As a self formed in and by the parallel activity of neural networks or in the symbolic economy of cerebral auto-affection, it would also have an unconscious. The unconscious of the neuronal self would, however, be a *cerebral* unconscious constituted in the fundamental processes of auto-affection which regulate the life of the brain. Such a neuro-psychoanalysis is definitely only suggested as a futural possibility in *Les Nouveaux blessés*, rather than being theorized in any great detail. Malabou does go so far as to suggest that the Lacanian triad of Real–Symbolic–Imaginary be supplemented by a fourth instance, the 'Material'. The Material, in this context, would be an instance in excess of the Lacan's triad insofar as a rupture or destruction of the material, cerebral base of the subject would interrupt the entire economy and structure of the Real–Symbolic–Imaginary. Malabou's comments here are thought-provoking and full of potential but remain provisional and undeveloped. All one can say perhaps is that a future neuro-psychoanalysis would by implication seek to think ways in which the economies of cerebrality and sexuality could interact, be interrelated or be synthesized each with the other.

What is more immediately significant in this context is that Malabou affirms a material, affective *and* symbolic economy of the self which would be prior to the symbolic economy of subjectivity as traditionally thought by psychoanalysis. In this affirmation, she gathers together and develops further her entire thinking about materiality, plasticity and subjectivity which has informed her philosophy from *L'Avenir de Hegel* onwards. With the publication of *Les Nouveaux blessés*, the outlines of Malabou's materialist metamorphic ontology come into even sharper relief. This is an ontology which unites the insights of a post-deconstructive philosophy with the discoveries of neuroscience and some of the most innovative recent theoretical speculations of neuroscientists themselves. Yet once again, as was the case with Marion, Nancy and Stiegler, we are preoccupied with the question of the subject, with the question of 'who comes after' the subject of metaphysics, and with a subject conceived in resolutely bodily and materialistic terms. Taken together, *What Should We Do with Our Brain?* and *Les Nouveaux blessés* are not just concerned with the implications of creative and destructive plasticity for personal and collective identity. They are concerned with the elaboration of a new and radically materialist understanding of thought and subjectivity in the wake of deconstruction. As Malabou herself puts it towards the end of *Les Nouveaux blessés*, 'Is not cerebrality the accomplishment of the deconstruction of subjectivity?' (Malabou 2007: 339).

Plasticity, writing, and changing difference

It should be underlined here that, for all its materiality, cerebrality, for Malabou, is not a substance or ground. The neuronal self does allow philosophy to retreat back to the reassurance of a subject viewed as site and source of meaning or as a supposedly secure bedrock or foundation for thought. Cerebrality may indeed give life to a subject whose identity is shaped by biological factors, both in the womb and then also throughout life; factors such as the expression of genes, the influence of hormones and other manifold biochemical mechanisms or processes. Yet it is also a subject formed in synaptic interconnections, in processes of cerebral auto-affection, in symbolic cerebral activity. These processes of formation occur in exposure to the environment and in the experience of a shared world. This means that the cerebral subject is without preformed essence or fixity. Its identity and form remains formable and deformable throughout life and is always fragile and vulnerable. It is exposed to the accidents of the world, to the absolute alterity of the event and to a future which is *without* identity. In short, such a subject is as much a product of the aleatory events and sense of the shared historical world in which it is placed as it is a product of genetic and biochemical processes. Indeed, the opposition between the two, between 'nature' and 'nurture', becomes more or less redundant in this context since the formative influences of both worldly sense *and* biochemical determination are functions of the same plasticity, that is to say, the susceptibility of material life to the giving and receiving of form. There is no source or origin here, no fixed essence, only an unending process of transformation and differentiation, of formation and deformation, in which essences and accidents are exchangeable in a metamorphic economy of material existence.

In *Plasticity at the Dusk of Writing* (Malabou 2005a; 2010b), Malabou underlines that what is at stake in her plastic readings within philosophy is the possibility of making visible 'the form that comes after presence' (Malabou 2005a: 106; 2010b: 57). This is true for her metamorphic materialist ontology as a whole. Her philosophy tells us that, in the wake of the destruction of metaphysics and the deconstruction of presence, form has transformed itself: '*Today, form reveals its true colors: form is plastic*' (Malabou 2005a: 11; 2010b: 1).

This plasticity of form is always at stake in the life of the subject exposed to the accidents of the world and to a future without identity, just as it is at stake in the mutable economy of being more generally. What Malabou's plastic readings of Hegel, Heidegger and contemporary neuroscience have sought to show is that all presentation and coming into presence, all emergence and dissolution of form and all articulations of structure, or economies of difference and differentiation are preceded by what she calls: 'the first *metabolè*' (Malabou 2005a: 63; 2010b: 30), and 'an essentially material plasticity' (Malabou 2005a: 86; 2010b: 45). This material plasticity of being is anterior to the temporalizing-spatializing economy of the Derridean trace or arche-writing just as it is anterior to the triadic economy of the Lacanian Real–Symbolic–Imaginary. Dialectical transformation, the transformation of being in the destruction or deconstruction of metaphysics are both articulated in and by this primary metabolism of change.

This anteriority of plasticity leads Malabou to a conclusion which gives the title to *Plasticity at the Dusk of Writing*, namely that 'writing', the figures of 'gramma' and 'graphism', of the trace, of signifier and signified all no longer provide a governing image for the production of thought, meaning, form or presence (Malabou 2005a: 36; 2010b: 15). She suggests that: 'The constitution of writing as a motor scheme was the result of a progressive movement which started with structuralism and was then anchored in linguistics, genetics and cybernetics: a pure linguistic image, that of spacing or difference was progressively imposed as the schema of an ontological organization' (Malabou 2005a: 108; 2010b: 58). Malabou is not, however, suggesting that the Derridean thinking of writing, arche-writing or trace is erroneous or redundant. Rather, she is arguing that thought needs to situate itself within 'a symbolic rupture between the plastic and the graphic elements of thought' (Malabou 2005a: 16; 2010b: 3). In so doing, thought needs to reveal the exchangeability of the plastic and the graphic elements which taken together make thought possible. For Malabou, the Derridean economy of the trace or arche-writing is thinkable only insofar as it articulates or makes possible the presentation of forms, of forms which are presented in excess of any logic of presence or self-identity. This necessarily presupposes the mutual convertibility or exchangeability of trace and form. In excess of presence or presentation, the trace nevertheless ceaselessly produces forms in the spatializing and temporalizing movement of *différance*. This exchangeability can occur, Malabou has repeatedly affirmed, only in an economy of change and transformation which operates prior to the Derridean economy of writing. Plasticity, then, becomes the governing figure of thought. Writing withdraws from its paramount position and retires into its twilight hours.

Ultimately, then, Malabou's philosophy of plasticity has as its ambition the articulation of a different philosophical thinking of difference itself. She wants to change the thinking of difference that has dominated so much French philosophy in the last four decades of the twentieth century. This changed thinking of difference is perhaps best summed up by Malabou herself in the closing pages of *What Shall We Do with Our Brain?*: 'To exist is to be able to change difference while respecting the difference of change: the difference between continuous change, without limits, without adventure, without negativity, and a formative change that tells an effective story and proceeds by rupture, conflicts, dilemmas' (Malabou 2004b: 159–60; 2008: 79). In Malabou's philosophy, the changed thinking of difference turns ceaselessly on a differentiated thinking of change. Plasticity articulates both a joyous quasi-Nietzschean becoming of form *and* a potentially more violent possibility of rupture, deformation and reformation. More than anything, though, her commitment to plasticity is first and foremost a commitment to a radical materialism, an attempt to put an end to 'a certain *dematerialization* . . . of contemporary philosophical thought' (Malabou 2005a: 87; 2010b: 45).

If, then, the philosophy of plasticity has a future in allowing thought to develop, change and transform itself in the wake of Hegel, Heidegger and Derrida, this will only be possible, Malabou would no doubt contend, if we can come to fully understand and affirm the plastic materiality of thought itself.

5

Jacques Rancière: The Space of Equality

Jacques Rancière's philosophy of equality arguably represents one of the most important and original contributions to political thought of the late twentieth and early twenty-first centuries. Since the early 1970s, this philosophy of equality has been elaborated in relation to a wide range of different concerns: firstly, and perhaps decisively, as a critique of Althusserian theory, and then subsequently in relation to questions of education and pedagogy, to problems of history, historiography and historical agency (in particular that of the working classes) and then later, in his mature philosophy, to questions concerning politics, and social or political agency and organization. Over the past ten to fifteen years, Rancière's thought has become increasingly concerned with art and aesthetics and the relation of these to politics and to possibilities of political participation, transformation and emancipation.

Rancière began his career as a participant in Louis Althusser's reading group on Marx's *Capital* which was held between January and April at the École Normale Supérieure at the Rue d'Ulm in Paris in 1965. His contribution to this seminar was published along with those of the other participants later in the same year (Althusser himself, and also Pierre Macherary, Étienne Balibar and Roger Establet; Althusser 1996). His intellectual beginnings, then, can be clearly situated within the milieu of theoretical and structuralist Marxism of which Althusser was the most prominent and leading exponent.[1] The broader milieu in which Rancière began his career was heavily marked by the social and political radicalism which grew up during and after the Algerian war and which culminated in the revolutionary events of May 1968.[2] Yet it is perhaps Rancière's break from Althusser in the aftermath of 1968 which most decisively shapes the development of his philosophy as a whole and the thinking of radical egalitarianism which underpins it. Arguably, the specific way in which he breaks from Althusserian theory determines both the specificity of his subsequent concerns and the broader difficulty of situating his thinking in any clear disciplinary framework.

The repudiation of Althusser brings Rancière into direct engagement with history, with historical archive work and with questions of historiography and yet he is not writing as a historian, nor is he offering a philosophy of history. The rejection of the Althusserian understanding of ideology and of the 'scientific' status of theory shapes the way in which Rancière comes to think about politics, and political agency or activity, but at the very same time it sharply distinguishes his thought from political philosophy as such. Likewise the shift away from the linguistic paradigm that underpins structuralist theory more generally leads Rancière to centre his thinking upon an affirmation of the material, the concrete and the sensory dimensions of experience, and this in turn informs his subsequent formulations relating to the 'distribution of the sensible', to the aesthetic and to art. Yet for all this, Rancière's thought is not a traditional 'aesthetics' understood as that branch of philosophy which deals with notions of the beautiful and with the concept of art in general. As Peter Hallward has remarked, one of the most consistent aspects of this thinking is its affirmation of a fundamental inconsistency, unclassifiability and instability of experience and a refusal of any gesture of authority or theoretical mastery which would seek to police experience and to maintain it within conventional categories and limits (in Robson 2005: 27). This can be related directly to the uncertain status and unclassifiability of Rancière's thought itself. Rather than abandoning philosophy in favour of another discipline, the practice of writing that Rancière develops questions the protocols, conventions and limits which would allow history, philosophy, political philosophy or aesthetics to maintain themselves as stable categories.[3]

Equality, Althusser and the distribution of the sensible

Equality

The consistent affirmation of the inconsistency, unclassifiability and instability of experience in Rancière is arguably a function of his unique and highly original reformulation of the concept of equality.

Rancière's leading contemporary commentators, Todd May and Oliver Davis, have persuasively demonstrated the way in which his conception of equality substantially differs from more conventional understandings of the term. May, for instance, has shown that Rancière's equality needs to be understood as 'active' and opposed to the 'passive' equality which is the concern of the broad spectrum of contemporary political thinking on the subject. May argues that, in the work of libertarian or liberal political thinkers such as Robert Nozick, John Rawls and Amartya Sen, equality, however variably it may be conceived, is passive because it 'concerns what institutions are obliged to give people, rather than what those people do politically' (May 2008: 4). Being concerned with what people receive rather than what they actively do, the mainstream of liberal political theory, whether of the right or of the left, is part of a wider contemporary culture of passivity, May argues, which leaves states or other larger institutions with the responsibility of meeting the demands of social justice and of equality (through the equal distribution of desired properties, e.g. material goods, rights, opportunities and so on). For May, Rancière's understanding of equality is 'active' insofar as it is *presupposed*, that is to say, an assumption of already existing equality among any and all participants of any situation is taken as a given. Insofar as a particular situation may be structured according to a hierarchy or unequal order, the presupposition of equality is then taken as the starting point from which action or intervention can occur. It is the basis upon which the arbitrariness of the existing hierarchy or unequal order can be actively challenged. Oliver Davis also views Rancière's understanding of equality as being active rather than passive insofar as it is not only presupposed but, on the basis of such a presupposition, is also to be both declared and then verified (Davis 2010: 30). That is to say, once equality has been taken as a given, it needs to be actively affirmed and action taken to demonstrate its existence.

Both May and Davis bring out the unique character of Rancière's conception of equality, namely that it is not, in its essence, an end-state or goal which we should expect to be achieved or guaranteed (in a more or less deferred manner) by state or other institutions. In this sense, equality, for Rancière, is also not an abstract value which can be deduced as being desirable according to rational calculation or ethical judgement.[4] Rather, equality here is, in a certain sense, *structural* insofar as it is seen to be the necessary precondition of any contingent unequal order or hierarchy. For Rancière, it is the fundamental condition of equality of everyone with everyone else within an unequally ordered situation that makes any unequal order possible in the first instance. In what is perhaps his most important book of political thought, *Disagreement* (Rancière 1995a; 1998d), the structural dimension of Rancière understanding of equality is made very clear when he speaks of 'ultimate equality on which any social order rests' (Rancière 1995a: 37; 1998d: 16). His reasoning is that any participation within a hierarchical social order requires members of that order to understand their place within the order itself. All members of an unequal order have to have a shared and equal understanding of the order itself and of specific orders given and received and this must be so whatever one's position within the hierarchy. For subordinate members to understand and obey a hierarchical order, 'you must already be equal to the person who is ordering you', and therefore 'inequality is only possible through equality' (Rancière 1995a: 37; 1998d: 16–17). In this context, equality is not presupposed because it is rationally or ethically desirable; rather, it is presupposed because it is structurally necessary; it is: 'the ultimate secret of every social order, the pure and simple equality of anyone with everyone' (Rancière 1995a: 116; 1998d: 79).

However, if equality is the structural precondition of any unequal social order, it is also and at the same time that which reveals inequality itself to be contingent, unfounded and therefore inherently unstable and always exposed to possibilities of contestation or challenge. Equality will always be a presence making inequality possible, but it is a presence which gnaws away at the foundations of any unequal order (Rancière 1995a: 37; 1998d: 16). This leads Rancière to conclude that 'The social order ultimately rests on the equality that is also its ruination' (Rancière 1995a: 116; 1998d: 79). The implications of this structural understanding of equality are worked out in various ways throughout the entirety of Rancière's philosophical writing and, as will become clear, such an understanding is decisive for the way he comes to define democracy, and more generally politics, political agency and possibilities of political intervention and emancipation. It might usefully be noted at this point that Rancière's formulations on equality and inequality in *Disagreement* are based on the fact of shared communication and understanding; that is to say, all members of an unequal hierarchy must understand their place within it and communicate accordingly for the hierarchy to institute and maintain itself. In this sense, it is clear that his understanding of equality and inequality is very much dependent upon the existence of language and the positions that members of a social order occupy in relation to language (as, for instance, the givers or receivers of orders). At a fundamental level, then, Rancière's conception of equality, inequality and of social order or hierarchy is intrinsically tied up with the human capacity for communication and speech and with the question of how and under what conditions voices are heard or can make themselves heard.[5] There is arguably a tension between Rancière's central emphasis on the bodily and the material (which, as will become clear, is articulated in his understanding of the 'distribution of the sensible') and the signal importance he accords to the *capacity* for speech, thought and the question of voice more generally. On the one hand, he offers a sharp criticism of structuralist notions of discourse, signification and ideology (they are too abstract), while on the other hand he privileges the possession or acquisition of a *logos* as a means of verifying equality and enacting emancipation. This tension arguably has its roots in the early days of Rancière's philosophical career. In particular, it can be seen to result from the way in which he makes a decisive break from the thought of Louis Althusser.

Althusser

In *Althusser's Lesson* published in 1974, Rancière gives a wide-ranging critique of Althusserian theoretical, structuralist Marxism (Rancière 1974; 2011c). In particular, he is critical of what he sees as the conservative implications of the distinction Althusser makes between ideology and science. Crudely and very schematically put, ideology for Althusser represents all those forms of ideas, understanding, beliefs and values which allow individuals to collectively function in a given socio-economic world and which work to sustain the relations of power and domination which underpin that socio-economic order. Ideological values and attitudes constitute an imaginary relation to the socio-economic order which conceals the true nature and objective functioning of that order. In this context, personal beliefs or attitudes, for example religious values or shared social discourse, are seen to be a function of ideology and part of a process in which individuals are 'interpellated' as the subjects of ideology.[6] Moreover, so much of what might pass as philosophy or political theory is also a product of ideology, that is, an imaginary construct or relation which conceals actually existing constructs and relations. To ideology Althusser opposes his specific understanding of Marxist science or theory. For Althusser, scientific knowledge is not ideology, attitude or opinion because it is a theoretical practice which identifies the actually existing structures which, behind the veil of ideological appearance, underpin social, economic and historical forms.[7] In so doing, the task of Althusserian science and that of its practitioners will be the transformation of ideological concepts and forms of understanding into scientific concepts and understanding and, on this basis, the way can be opened for the transformation of oppressive social and economic structures and the power relations and subjectivities which they produce.

The complex detail of Althusser's formulations around ideology and science are beyond the scope of this discussion. The schematic account of this distinction which has just been given is sufficient, however, to explain the grounds of Rancière's critique in the essays of *Althusser's Lesson*. Firstly, and perhaps most obviously, Althusser's conception of science as theoretical practice is open to the charge of elitism, a charge that Rancière makes very explicitly: 'The stakes are clear,' he writes. 'It's a question of preserving philosophy, and "Marxist" philosophy in particular, as a concern of university specialists' (Rancière 1974: 35; 2011c: 11). The clear implication of Althusser's account is that the wider collective of those who are oppressed live their lives in a deluded manner, as subjects who have answered the call of ideology and live within the imaginary realm of its representations. Only the theoretical practitioner, the Marxist scientist, can lead them from this life of delusion. It might be recalled here that, in chapter 3, it was suggested that Stiegler's account of the individuation and conditioning of subjects in hyper-industrial society was broadly comparable to Althusser's account of ideology and the subject. In both cases, the philosopher of technics and the Marxist scientist are accorded a privileged role in emancipating collective consciousness from a wider economy of symbolic or ideological exchange which operates in the service of capitalism. However, Rancière's charge of an elitist privileging of the university philosopher is arguably much more justly levelled at Althusser than it could be at Stiegler. This is because Althusserian theory is much more fundamentally a theory of education (rather than of philosophical activism as is the case with Stiegler). As such, it preserves a structural inequality between the practitioners of the theory itself (who continue to enjoy the privileges of their university position) and the unenlightened masses in whose name Marxist theory is ostensibly being practised (Rancière 1974: 104; 2011c: 52). There is, therefore, a constitutive inequality in Althusserian thought which is rooted in the way ideology itself is conceived and in the way individuals are seen to be interpellated as subjects by ideology. Rancière also argues that the structural conception of ideology (which places it in the realm of imaginary subjective interpellation and identification) lacks any articulated understanding of internal conflict or struggle: 'Ideology is not posited, at the outset, as the site of a struggle. Instead of being related to two antagonists, it is related to a totality, of which it forms a natural element' (Rancière 1974: 237; 2011c: 134). This lack of internal conflict or struggle within the constitution of ideology has the effect, Rancière contends, of naturalizing it and of making it a more or less normal state of affairs; it is 'a theory of ideological normality which can only sustain itself in the reality of normalization' (Rancière 1974: 143; 2011c: 75). The direct upshot of this, of course, is the already mentioned elitism which positions the working class as a necessary recipient of university-based Marxist-scientist pedagogy which alone will provide the means by which social and political emancipation can be aspired to (Rancière 1974: 35; 2011c: 11). More problematically still, for Rancière, this naturalization or normalization of ideology has the effect of more or less infinitely deferring emancipation itself. It preserves the institutional privilege of the practitioners of science as they apply the practice of theory to ideological demystification and thereby defers active struggle and effective emancipation in the here and now. In essence, this means that the voices and demands of the working class are not heard or acknowledged as part of any ongoing or active struggle for emancipation. Thus, Rancière concludes, the Althusserian distinction between science and ideology ultimately leads to a conservative position in which real class struggle mutates into 'a clandestine and infinite ideological struggle: a Kantian *task* whose goal will never be reached in this world' (Rancière 1974: 105; 2011c: 52).

When aimed at one of the most prominent and influential Marxist intellectuals of post-war France, such charges of elitism, conservatism and the normalization of bourgeois ideology could not be more damning nor more damaging. They certainly make it clear the extent to which, for Rancière, the break from Althusser in the late 1960s and early 1970s was irreversible.[8] What is perhaps most important to note here is the manner in which this break also marks a more wide-reaching rupture with the linguistics-based structuralist paradigm which underpins Althusserian theory. In rejecting the conception of ideology that this theory advances, Rancière is also rejecting its status as discourse or semiological construct: 'Ideology is not simply a collection of discourses or a system of representation . . . Dominant ideology is a *power* organized in a collection of institutions' (Rancière 1974: 252–3; 2011c: 142). Some care needs to be taken here to ensure that justice is done to the Althusserian understanding of ideology. In the key essay 'Ideology and Ideological State Apparatuses', for instance, Althusser makes it clear that the imaginary relation of ideology is always endowed with a material existence and that the ideas embodied in ideological discourse exist in a 'material ideological apparatus, prescribing material practices governed by a material ritual, which practices exist in the material actions of a subject' (in Sharma and Gupta 2006: 103). In this context it might seem unfair to accuse Althusser of ignoring the material dimension of ideology in favour of a more abstract linguistic model of discourse. Yet it is clear that, for Rancière, however much the 'ideas' of the Althusserian ideological subject may be embedded or expressed in material forms and practices, the conception of ideology itself as a discourse of 'ideas' or concepts to be demystified by theory is ultimately too abstract, too totalizing and too undifferentiated or devoid of internal contradiction. Rancière is targeting the claim made by Althusser in *For Marx* that ideology is that which 'Human societies secrete as the element and atmosphere indispensable to their historical respiration and life' (Althusser 2005: 232). As a necessary medium of meaning for the functioning of social organization per se ideology here is both abstract (an invisible 'atmosphere') and abstracted from the reality of struggle and class conflict. It is also, once again, normalized to the point of being, for all practical purposes, accepted as a natural state of affairs. For Rancière, 'An objective status can only be given to ideologies by thinking them as a function of class struggle. This implies that ideology does not simply exist in discourses, nor simply in systems, of images, of signs, etc.' (Rancière 1974: 271; 2011c: 151).

In short, Rancière insists, against Althusser and against the static structuralist paradigm that informs Althusserian theory, that ideology be seen as a function of conflict or antagonism and that it can never be solely or entirely reducible to concepts, ideas, sign systems or discourse. It is arguably this rejection of the structuralist-linguistic paradigm which will inform all of Rancière's subsequent thinking.

The distribution of the sensible

The projects which Rancière pursues in the decade which follows the publication of *Althusser's Lesson* in 1974 can be related to the polemical arguments which it advances. Most notably, he publishes a number of works which interrogate the history of working-class political activism and explore the question of working-class agency and consciousness.[9] These can be seen as projects which arise directly from his rejection of any understanding of the working classes as subjects interpellated by ideology and lacking in any ability to be political agents without the mediation of Marxist science. In the same way, Rancière's book devoted to the radical egalitarian teaching of Joseph

Jacottet can be seen as responding directly to his rejection of the elitist pedagogical implication of Althusserian theory.[10] More broadly speaking, Rancière's understanding of the 'distribution of the sensible' which informs so much of his mature work can be related back to his rejection of the structuralist account of ideology as a discourse of ideas or concepts.

The original French phrase is *le partage du sensible* and it articulates the way in which, for Rancière, sense perception and sensible experience are divided up and shared out to form a communal world. The verb *partager* has two meanings, both of which are important to note here. On the one hand, it refers to the act of dividing up a collection of elements so that they can be distributed for different uses (and therefore implies classification and differentiation). On the other hand, *partager* refers to the act of jointly participating in an activity or holding something in common. Both these meanings are decisive for the way in which Rancière comes to understand *le partage du sensible*. This can be seen in the following lengthy quotation in which he describes the distribution of the sensible as:

> the system of self-evident facts of sense perception that simultaneously discloses the existence of something in common and the delimitations that define the respective parts and positions within it. A distribution of the sensible therefore establishes at one and the same time something common that is shared and exclusive parts within it. This apportionment of parts and positions is based on a distribution of spaces, times and forms of activity that determines the very manner in which something in common lends itself to participation in a way that various individuals have a part in this distribution (Rancière 2000: 12; 2004d: 12)

The division and sharing described here articulate a structure of generalized inclusion and specific or localized exclusions. It is a structure of shared participation in a world which is nevertheless internally differentiated and divided up into different sites, perspectives and modes of (potentially hierarchical) relation. Rancière is trying to articulate the way in which, at a fundamental level, our experience of a world is necessarily communal insofar as any world can only be experienced as such on the basis of a horizon of perception which is common to all those who inhabit that world. Within that common horizon, however, sensible experience is differentiated according to the division of sites and spaces which determine where one is positioned within any given world and the specific modes of perception and participation one can have in relation to it. This understanding of the sensible and its distribution into unequally divided or apportioned sites of material–intelligible experience, it will be recalled, can be contrasted with Jean-Luc Nancy's understanding of the 'sharing of sense' as discussed in chapter 2. It should be clear now the extent to which Rancière's understanding of 'the system of self-evident facts of sense perception' goes further than does Nancy's in articulating or accounting for a fundamental violence or unequal ordering of sensible–intelligible experience.

This structure of participation and division articulated by the *partage du sensible* can be opposed to Althusser's understanding of ideology in two key ways. Firstly, Rancière, it will be recalled, was critical of ideology because the system of ideas, beliefs and attitudes that constitute ideological discourse was seen to be too totalizing and too lacking internal differentiation. The term *partage* as used by Rancière has the virtue of articulating a structure of universal and equal inclusion (all inhabitants of a world share its common horizon) which at the same time can account for the existence of internal differentiations of position and perspective (inhabitants of a world occupy different sites or spatial/temporal configurations). This tension between equal, shared participation and differentiated, potentially unequal, positioning is, as will become clear, decisive for the way Rancière articulates his thinking about politics. Secondly, the distribution of the sensible can be opposed to Althusserian ideology insofar as it concerns forms of 'sensible evidence'. It concerns shared structures of spatial and temporal perception, and the division of the world into differentiated spaces or sites which then determine perspective, position and possibilities of participation. The distribution of the sensible, then, is a system of shared worldly appearances which is situated prior to any formalized abstract structure of ideas, concepts, sign systems or discourse. Rather than being first a collection of ideas, beliefs or attitudes which are subsequently embodied in, or inserted into material apparatuses, practices, rituals and so on, the distribution of the sensible articulates what Rancière calls a 'primary aesthetics' (Rancière 2000: 14; 2004d: 13), that is, a fundamental order of sensible–intelligible experience which constitutes world-hood as such and which is articulated on the level of the senses or embodied sense perception before it is formalized into the discourse of ideas, beliefs, concepts and so on.

In opposition to the totalizing, naturalizing and potentially abstract conception of ideology advanced by Althusser, Rancière develops a way of understanding collective experience and social organization which accounts both for internal differentiation and for the fundamentally concrete and material status of that differentiation. This not only allows Rancière to give an account of social and political conflict or antagonism and to do so in a way which engages with the multiplicity and different forms of antagonism which constitute material worlds, it also allows him to develop a highly original understanding of politics and of political agency and organization.

Politics, democracy, subjectivation

Politics

As was indicated earlier, Rancière's 1995 book, *Disagreement*, is perhaps his single most significant work of political thought. In its opening pages, he suggests that our contemporary understanding of politics and of political activity has become disenchanted. In the last decade of the twentieth century, politics, in contemporary western democracies at least, is widely thought not to be a matter for thought itself, for commitment, decision and struggle; rather, it is taken as axiomatic that there is little to be debated and that decisions will impose themselves based on the necessities of economic life: 'the work proper to politics simply involving an opportune adaptability to the demands of the world marketplace and the equitable distribution of the profits and costs of this adaptation' (Rancière 1995a: 10; 1998d: viii). Under these circumstances, political debate, such as it is, will concern the best means by which such an adaptation should be achieved. Rancière wants to challenge this view by giving a different and, he would argue, a more fundamental account of what politics is in its real form.[11] Politics is not understood here as a process of (supposedly) rational calculation according to which the forces of global capital can best be managed. Rather, for Rancière, '[politics] has the rationality of disagreement as its very own rationality' (Rancière 1995a: 15; 1998d: xii). What he may mean by disagreement here is, however, far from straightforward and is not reducible to simple differences of opinion or divergences of political outlook.

In fact, Rancière's understanding of politics as a rationality of disagreement goes well beyond the discursive and political plurality normally ascribed to liberal democratic politics, for example, the diversity of opinions guaranteed by freedom of speech or the limited spectrum of positions adopted within a multi-party electoral system. Disagreement here 'clearly is not to do with words alone. It generally bears on the very situation in which speaking parties find themselves' (Rancière 1995a: 14; 1998d: xi). Once again, Rancière is not laying a primary emphasis on discursive positions or the relative differences of competing ideological discourses. Rather, he is concerned with the concrete and material situation or conditions from which people are able to speak and from which their voices can be heard or understood. Put in the terms of Rancière's later text, disagreement is a function of the distribution of the sensible which divides up the spaces, sites and perspectives of a shared world. As such, disagreement cannot simply be a matter of discursive differences but rather concerns the material sensible ground of intelligibility and communicability upon which such differences may be articulated in the first instance. Rancière expresses this in the following terms: disagreement, he writes, 'is less concerned with arguing than with what can be argued, the presence or the absence of a common object between X and Y. It concerns the sensible presentation of this common object, the very capacity of the interlocutors to present it' (Rancière 1995a: 14; 1998d: xii). Disagreement, then, is not just difference of opinion, misrecognition nor misunderstanding. It concerns fundamentally divergent ways of understanding or encountering any object of disagreement and the relative possibilities of expression and communication which are available to those who may be party to a disagreement.[12]

This needs to be understood in relation to the structural definition of equality and inequality outlined at the beginning of this discussion, as well as in relation to Rancière's conception of the distribution of the sensible as a 'system of sensible evidences'. Indeed, more than a radicalization of discursive or perspectival difference, disagreement here is a function of the unequal social order or hierarchy that a distribution of the sensible can produce. Rancière writes: 'Before the debts that place people who are of no account in a relationship of dependence on the oligarchs, there is the symbolic distribution of bodies that divides them into two categories: those that one sees and those that one does not see, those who have a *logos* . . . and those who have no *logos*' (Rancière 1995a: 44; 1998d: 22). Fundamental to any unequal order, it should be remembered, is the equality of understanding and participation that makes that unequal order possible and functional as such. Yet the essence of an unequal order lies in the unequal distribution of material conditions, situations and positions which will determine possibilities of active participation. This means that the things which may be disputed in Rancière's understanding of disagreement are not disputed by parties who have an equal say in the dispute, nor an equal position from which to shape its terms. Disagreement, therefore, relates not just to the contestation of a disputed object but also to the status and position from which the parties to a disagreement can speak and make themselves heard.

For Rancière, the activity of politics (as disagreement) concerns the inequality of material conditions which determine the possession or otherwise of a voice or *logos*. In this context, then, politics cannot simply be party politics because political parties already participate, have a voice and are assigned a recognized place within the social order. Nor can politics be the more or less competent management of economic forces and resources since this too is a matter for those who are already accounted for (and have been given a privileged role) within the order of society. Nor, for the same reason, can politics be the management of competing interests within a shared political, legal and juridical framework. Rancière wants to underline that politics, properly speaking, is not an activity which is pursued on the basis of any consensus (constitutional or institutional) or on the basis of shared norms or protocols.[13] Politics *properly speaking* occurs, he argues, when 'there is a part of those who have no part [*une part des sans-part*], a part or a party of the poor' (Rancière 1995a, 31; 1998d, 11). Such a definition of politics may seem rather limiting since it excludes the greater part of what we would normally understand by the term.[14] Yet it follows directly from Rancière's understanding of inequality and of the distribution of the sensible. As has been indicated, much of what we might normally call politics involves the participation of those who already have a voice or an allocated position within society and whose interests have already been accounted for within the social order. Yet if such an order really is unequal, hierarchical and built upon domination and exclusion, then what we normally call politics is arguably more a process of management by which the order sustains and perpetuates itself. Rancière sees politics as an activity which brings into play actual or real differences and genuine conflict or antagonism. Accordingly, the management of the competing interests and outlooks of those who already have a comfortably assigned place within an order of domination cannot bear the name of politics.

According to Rancière, the process by which any given social order manages and perpetuates itself is not one of politics but one of policing. When he uses the term 'police' or 'police order', he is not referring to state institutions of law enforcement nor is he implying that any social order at all is similar to what we might understand by the term 'police state'. Rather, a police order, according to Rancière, concerns the way different groups of society are assembled and classified, the way in which power and authority is organized and the way in which functions, positions and systems of legitimation are distributed. Rancière defines 'police' as an order 'which arranges that sensible reality in which bodies are distributed in community'

(Rancière 1995a: 51; 1998d: 28). In this sense, it is clearly an operation of the distribution of the sensible but also plays a reinforcing role by ensuring that only certain positions within any given hierarchical distribution are endowed with capacities for active participation and communication. It ensures that only certain positions or groups are endowed with power and control over themselves and others:

> The police is thus first an order of bodies that defines the allocation of ways of doing, ways of being, and ways of saying, and sees that those bodies are assigned by name to a particular place and task; it is an order of the visible and of the sayable that sees that that particular activity is visible and another is not, that this speech is understood as discourse and another as noise. (Rancière 1995a: 52; 1998d: 29)

This means that all those social, political and economic agents or groupings which already have a voice, who are already recognized and endowed with a legitimacy of active participation are part of the police order and do not constitute actors in politics as such. The greater part of what normally passes as politics – that is, the rivalry of political parties or the management of competing interests, economic forces and resources – are policing activities or operations of a police order.

This means that, in opposition to the order of policing, politics can only really be said to happen in the emergence of a conflictual relation between different parties. This conflictual relation is not grounded in differences or competing interests that the police order has already taken into account. Rather, such a relation is grounded in a more radical difference which subsists between those who have a voice and are already counted by the police order and those who have no voice and have been excluded from participation in that order. Put in different terms, politics can be said to occur in the force by which real difference is introduced into the policing or management of any given hierarchical order. For Rancière, politics is the process by which, within any given police order, those voices which hitherto cannot be heard suddenly makes themselves heard. Politics exists as such only in the interruption of an order of domination and in the emergence or institution of a 'part of those who have no part' (Rancière 1995a: 31; 1998d: 11). A key term here is that of 'wrong' (*tort* in French). A wrong will be a specific instance of oppression, exclusion or dispossession which is produced by a given order of domination. Rancière, remember, understands inequality as being made possible only by an underlying equality which constitutes a community as a whole. This means that those who are deprived of voice and who are locally and, as it were, 'situationally' excluded will, given the fundamental equality of all with all, always have the capacity to identify the specific mechanism of their exclusion, a local 'wrong' which has been done to them and which constitutes the very mechanism of their exclusion. By identifying a specific wrong, articulating it and giving it a voice and place within the hierarchical order, the order itself comes to be contested by that which it hitherto excluded.

The identification of a wrong of exclusion and the giving of a voice to those who have been wronged is the condition for genuine politics and real political activity in Rancière's thought. It is in the context of politics conceived in this very particular way that his thinking about the declaration and verification of equality needs to be understood. It is also in this context that Rancière develops his, also very particular, understanding of democracy.

Democracy and political subjectivation

As should be easily inferable from the account of politics and of the police order given above, Rancière does not take the constitutional, political and legal structures we might normally associate with the healthy functioning of democracy to be sufficient conditions for a properly democratic polity. Such structures are a function of the police order and serve to legitimate existing distributions of power and identity and to guarantee the existing hierarchical disposition of specific groups.[15] They do not, in themselves, facilitate the participation of *une part des sans-part* but rather mitigate against such a participation by reinforcing a system of exclusion. Rancière's understanding of democracy extends beyond a specific type of constitutional, electoral and political arrangement or mode of governance. Rather than being a function of representational structures, e.g. parliaments and executives selected through national and local elections, democracy, for Rancière, is a function of his very specific conception of politics and of what he calls 'political subjectivation'. In this context, he comes to think democracy, not simply as the formal operation of a series of constitutional and electoral arrangements, but rather as a mode of interruption of an existing police order:

> Democracy, in general, is politics' mode of subjectivation ... Democracy more precisely is the name of a singular disruption of this order of distribution of bodies as a community that we proposed to

conceptualize in the broader concept of the police. It is the name of what comes and interrupts the smooth working of this order through a singular mechanism of subjectivation. (Rancière 1995a: 139; 1998d: 99; translation modified)

This is a radical conception of democracy insofar as it is concerned with the more fundamental ordering and agency of the *demos* as a whole, with the way in which it is divided into hierarchically positioned groups, and with the possible appropriation and exercise of power through new forms, sites or spaces of participation. Democracy here concerns the possibility of the current ordering of the *demos* being contested through its interruption in the name of a previously unnamed agency or subjective identification. In this context, democracy above all concerns subjects, or rather the production of subjects through modes of subjectivation. Rancière expresses this in the following terms: subjectivation is 'the production through a series of actions of a body and a capacity for enunciation not previously identifiable within a given field of experience, while identification is part of the reconfiguration of the field of experience' (Rancière 1995a: 59; 1998d: 35). Subjectivation, then, is the means by which politics, the creation of *une part des sans-part*, actually comes about. It is the process through which a voice can be found to identify a wrong and through which the equality of all with all can be declared and verified.

From this perspective, properly democratic political participation therefore involves processes of declassification or de-identification of existing positions and the creation of new positions from which those who have had no voice can come to be heard and to be justly accounted for. Democratic participation is an opening of a hitherto unaccounted for space or site of subjective enunciation which can take into account those who have not been counted, classified or positioned by the existing police order. In this sense, the political subjectivation proper to democracy is as much about reconstituting new forms of order on the basis of new possibilities of inclusion as it is about rupture or interruption: 'political subjectivation redefines the field of experience that gave to each their identity with their lot. It decomposes and recomposes relationships' (Rancière 1995a: 65; 1998d: 40). In this way, political subjectivation refashions the distribution of the sensible of any given community; it reorganizes the division and sharing out of different ways of doing, being and speaking and therefore is the embodiment of politics, properly speaking.

It should be clear that Rancière's conception of politics, and of political or democratic participation and emancipation, is thoroughly dependent upon the notion of capacity. Specifically, his understanding of political subjectivation relies upon 'a capacity for enunciation' which a body or bodies that are excluded within a specific distribution of the sensible can be said to possess. Of central importance here, therefore, is the capacity for voice, speech and for the possession of a *logos*. Earlier in this discussion, it was suggested that Rancière's emphasis on the materiality of sensible–intelligible experience and on the bodily could be viewed as being in a tension with the key emphasis he places on the capacity for speech and voice or on the possession of a *logos*. It could be argued that, while his understanding of the 'distribution of the sensible' successfully critiques and provides a more materialist alternative to the structuralist (Althusserian) conception of ideology, his emphasis upon the capacity for communication, voice and the enunciation of a *logos*, returns or recuperates his thinking back into the more abstract economy of signs, signification and discourse. This is the very symbolic economy which, of course, he seeks to think beyond in his decisive break from Althusser.

More problematically still, it could be argued that Rancière's privileging of capacity as the basis of political subjectivation ignores the extent to which capacity itself may be differently or unequally distributed. For all Rancière's commendable and important insistence on the equality of those humans who possess communication and language (whatever their education or social class), the question arises as to what place there is in the processes of politics, emancipations or any thinking of equality and justice for those without the capacity for speech, for instance, the disabled, the very young or those who may have suffered brain injury or degeneration (as discussed by Malabou; see chapter 4). The question of the animal, of course, needs to be posed in all this. To what extent would Rancière's thinking provide the basis for anything like a politics of human-animal solidarity, of animal rights or liberation? Arguably, then, the importance he accords to the capacity for the enunciation of a *logos* limits his thinking of emancipation and justice to specific modes of participation and excludes the animal. It could therefore be said to perpetuate a more or less unthought legacy of humanism and a logocentric attitude of the kind which is identified and deconstructed within Derridean thought.

Whether one accepts or rejects these criticisms, it should be clear that Rancière's formulations on political and democratic subjectivation are entirely consistent with his structural understanding of equality such as it was outlined at the beginning of this discussion. It will be recalled once again that equality, for Rancière, is both the condition of an unequal or hierarchical order and, at the same time, a principle of instability which reveals that order itself to be contingent and therefore always exposed to possibilities of contestation or challenge. This inherent instability of any hierarchical ordering of society and sensible community means that no order whatsoever can fully legitimate or ground itself. All hierarchical social orders of any kind are contingent and therefore contestable, exposed to a hitherto unclassified and heterogeneous element and therefore to the interruptive emergence of *une part des sans-part*. This is as much true within the political community of liberal democracy, such as we know it, as it is within any other type of regime or mode of governance.

It is taken as axiomatic today by much mainstream political discourse that the constitutional arrangements of advanced western democracies are the best, and perhaps only viable, means of fully legitimating the exercise of governmental and executive power. Rancière's point that no system or form can ever fully legitimate itself aligns his thinking with anarchism insofar as it affirms an absence of origin or ground within any and all political communities. Insofar as his understanding of politics, subjectivation and democracy is articulated from the perspective of an absence of ground, Rancière's political thought can be seen as growing from the tradition of anarchism more generally.[16] The strength and force of his thinking here lies in the fact that he does not align democracy solely with a series of constitutional arrangements or a form of government but with an ever present possibility of contestation and of ongoing emancipation. To this extent, for Rancière, democracy as an ever ongoing process or activity will always have a scandalous or threatening potential in relation to existing forms. As he puts in a more recent work, *Hatred of Democracy*: 'The scandal of democracy consists simply in revealing this: there will never be, under the name of politics, a single principle of community, legitimating the acts of governments based on laws inherent to the coming together of human communities' (Rancière 2005a: 58; 2006b: 51; translation modified). In the absence of an origin, arche, or unique and legitimating principle, all forms of social organization and hierarchy will necessarily be exposed to the scandalous contestation of democratic political activity and to unforeseen and unforeseeable processes of subjectivation.

The regimes of art

The extent to which all of Rancière's formulations relating to the political flow from his conception of the distribution of the sensible should be noted here. Despite its reliance on the capacity for enunciation, Rancière's understanding of politics, subjectivation and of democratic participation is concerned with that division and sharing of material experience which forms a communal world. Equality in this context is not so much a unifying principle or natural law as it is a function or effect of a fundamental and fundamentally shared heterogeneity of a material life which is without essence, arche or ontological ground. Although this shared material heterogeneity makes the common space of sensible community possible, it will also never entirely coincide with the regime of division and sharing imposed by any given distribution of the sensible. By the same token, the voice or *logos* which may be found and then heard in the emergence of *une part des sans-part* and in processes of political subjectivation arises from the heterogeneity of material experience and from concrete conditions of exclusion. This voice is not first and foremost an abstract *logos* or signifying discourse in the manner of Althusserian ideology. At the same time, the 'wrong' or the disagreement that such a voice may come to articulate is a relation to material conditions of exclusion which are collectively experienced and immediately understood. They do not require Marxist science in order to be disclosed or revealed.

This primacy of sensible experience, that is, the *esthétique première* which constitutes communal being, also has a central place within Rancière's discourse on art and his formulation of three distinct 'regimes of art'. From the late 1990s onwards, he has increasingly written about the arts, publishing works on Mallarmé and on the politics of literature more generally but writing extensively also on cinema and visual art. Indeed, Rancière's prominence and importance as a contemporary thinker is as much due to the influence and popularity of his thinking about art and aesthetics as it is due to the impact of his political thought. This is borne out, for instance, in the importance accorded to his work within the art world and by influential international art magazines such as *Artforum*. Rancière is interested in the way in which art forms are modes of inscription of the sense of a community (Rancière 2000: 16; 2004d: 14). That is to say, artworks perform an important function in articulating the distribution of the sensible within any given organization of society. It is within this context that he comes to understand the term 'aesthetic' not just as a mode of primary sense experience but also as a mode of organization of the arts. In this context, the aesthetic, for Rancière, concerns '[a] specific regime for identifying and reflecting on the arts: a mode of articulation between ways of doing and making, their corresponding forms of visibility, and possible ways of thinking about their relationships' (which presupposes a certain idea of thought's effectivity (Rancière 2000: 10; 2004d: 10)

Insofar as the production of artworks might constitute such a regime of identification and therefore articulate ways of seeing, doing and the relations that subsist between them, art here always has a relation to the political, even if it is not a direct articulation of politics in either the conventional or the Rancièrian sense. Works of art and the diverse practices and techniques which produce them are implicated in, or more precisely act directly upon, the general distribution of relations between being, seeing and doing. That is to say, they have the power to directly engage with, and potentially to transform, any given distribution of the sensible.

These insights into the nature and status of artworks lead Rancière to identify three regimes of art: the ethical, the mimetic and the aesthetic. These three regimes can be shown to be the dominant forms of specific eras or epochs but at the same time they describe ways of characterizing certain artistic possibilities or forms which can be found in any era. The three regimes of art, therefore, have an explanatory power which is at once historical and typological. The strength of Rancière's thinking here lies in the way it has allowed him to analyse the development of art forms in an entirely original manner. In relation to modern art, for instance, the very notion of modernity itself, or of the 'avant-garde', is not seen to be in any way helpful in explaining the artistic development of the late nineteenth and early twentieth centuries (Rancière 2000: 26; 2004d: 20). At the same time, such influential categories as the modern and the postmodern cease to be a viable or useful way of understanding the mutations of artistic form that were produced during the latter half of the twentieth century.

The three regimes of art can be characterized in the following broadly schematic terms. Firstly, the ethical regime foregrounds the ethical dimension or status of images. It concerns the way in which such images articulate an ethical knowledge or an ethos, a certain way of being of individuals and communal groups (Rancière 2000: 28; 2004d: 21). This regime, as Oliver Davis has highlighted, is not necessarily strictly a regime of art at all but concerns the way in which practices, be they sculptural, poetic or performance-based, are inserted into communal ways of being and behaving (Davis 2010: 134–5). Insofar as this regime is consistent with, and best described by, Plato's discussion of art in *The Republic*, it is most clearly associated with the ancient era and the various artistic and ritual practices of classical antiquity. Secondly, the mimetic regime of art concerns, as the name implies, the imitative or representational qualities of aesthetic artifacts. This regime is grounded in normative forms or codes which define the conditions under which something will be recognized under the category of 'Art' in the first instance, and then be judged a realistic imitation or representation of the society or world which is presented. For Rancière, the mimetic regime has a prescriptive or normative character which does not simply seek to regulate behaviour or ethical conduct. The imitative or representational forms of art are 'removed at one and the same time from the ordinary control of artistic products by their use and from the legislative reign of truth over discourses and images' (Rancière 2000: 29; 2004d: 21; translation modified). It is not just a question of ethics, then, but of the production of truth as verisimilitude. At the same time, the production of truth is in the service of norms which govern society and the various positions assigned hierarchically within society. The mimetic regime, then, is intrinsically hierarchical, insofar as it represents but also therefore validates, legitimates and thus conserves the diverse positions assigned in an unequal social order. This regime can be seen to broadly characterize the production of art up to the end of the eighteenth century.

Thirdly and finally, the aesthetic regime of art can be said to directly oppose the mimetic regime insofar as it is not grounded in the representational verisimilitude prescribed by specific and socially normative ways of doing and seeing. Rather, and once again as the name implies, this regime concerns the aesthetic dimension of the work of art itself. The work is identified *as art* with reference to the specificity by which it articulates sensible presentation, that is to say, it is identified through its specific articulation of the aesthetic understood as sense experience more generally. Just as the mimetic regime of art was inherently hierarchical in its dependence upon social norms and structures, so, for Rancière, the aesthetic regime is inherently disruptive of norms and therefore more open to possibilities of contestation and de-hierarchization. Being concerned with the singularity of its own sensible form or mode of presentation, the aesthetic regime does not obey normative codes but rather frees art 'from any specific rule, from any hierarchy of the arts, subject matter, and genres' (Rancière 2000: 32–3; 2004d: 23). As such, it constitutes 'the breakdown of the system of representation' (Rancière 2000: 48; 2004d: 32). It is this aesthetic regime which, for Rancière, characterizes the general tendency of art over the past two hundred years. This is a regime in which art foregrounds the question of aesthetic form itself and places the exploration of its own sensible singularity and specificity above the imperative of communication and representation. As such, the aesthetic regime of art, in Rancière's hands, offers the key to understanding what is really at stake in the various forms of artistic modernism, avant-gardism and postmodernism in the nineteenth and twentieth centuries.

The historicizing tendency of Rancière's tripartite division is perhaps at its most useful when he uses the category of the aesthetic regime to analyse artworks produced over the past two hundred years and to think artistic, poetic and literary modernity more generally. As has been indicated, though, he does not wish to rigidly, reductively or exclusively tie these categories to a historicizing analysis. In this respect, it might be possible to view any work of art from any period, ancient or modern, from the perspective of each regime such that it might be seen to have an ethical, mimetic and aesthetic dimension with each element being foregrounded to different degrees. What is perhaps most important to note here is that Rancière's regimes of art articulate the diverse ways in which artworks are inserted into the social world and to a large degree help shape that world or reflect the fundamental sensible–intelligible organization of it. His point is that 'The real must be fictionalized in order to be thought' (Rancière 2000: 61; 2004d: 38) and therefore that the way we create art is intimately bound up with fundamental forms of intelligibility, with material signs and images which describe ways of being, seeing and doing. Art, then, plays a key role in articulating the distribution of the sensible which governs any given social order.

This means that, for Rancière, art and politics are intimately connected insofar as '[p]olitical and literary statements produce effects in reality' (Rancière 2000: 62; 2004d: 39). Both politics and art are activities, processes or modes of production which can intervene directly in a prevailing distribution of the sensible in order to interrupt it and fashion new relations of participation and inclusion. Clearly, art does not necessarily do this. In its ethical and mimetic regimes, it may work more to conserve an existing order rather than to transform it. This is true also, as has been shown, for much of what might more conventionally be understood as politics. Yet in the aesthetic regime and in the processes of political subjectivation and democratic intervention, both art and politics emerge in Rancière's thought as means by which equality is ultimately affirmed as the condition of shared sensible experience. His thinking of sensible materiality – the materiality of bodies that feel, perceive and therefore think together in a shared world – therefore underpins and connects his understanding of aesthetics and politics. In both cases, what is at stake is the heterogeneous materiality of space. This is a space of sensible experience which is always divided and shared in specific hierarchical order but which, as heterogeneous, can never be exhaustively determined by that order. It is arguable, then, that Rancière has not only produced highly original philosophical accounts of both politics and art, he has also produced a powerful ontology of space which frees up individual and collective agency for the production of new spaces. Beyond its analytical and explanatory force, Rancière's account of both art and politics show how the production of new spaces is possible in the service of emancipation and on the basis of a universal equality which is presupposed as the very condition of that production. It is a question of creating 'a space where equality can state its own claim: equality exists somewhere; it is spoken of and written about. It must therefore be verifiable' (Rancière 1998a: 87–8; 1995b: 47). Rancière's greatest achievement arguably lies in the force with which he shows that politics and art both can be the mode and means of such verification.

6

Alain Badiou: The Science of the Real

Since the 1970s, Alain Badiou's work has responded to what he perceives to be some of the decisive impasses or false turns within modern and contemporary European philosophy. Whether it be the (post-)structuralist emphasis on language and discourse, the poetic 'saying' of being or the turn towards literary style within philosophy, the thinking of finitude, the ethics of the 'Other' or, indeed, the identity politics and discursive relativism of 'postmodernity', Badiou's thought has consistently set itself against what he sees as contemporary orthodoxies. Such orthodoxies, he argues, have diverted philosophy from its proper path and true vocation. In opposing them, Badiou has engaged in what is perhaps one of the most radical and ambitious attempts to restore philosophy to systematic thinking and to return it to what he argues are its intrinsic conditions. In so doing, he has sought to revitalize the ambition and claims of philosophy more generally and to restore the dignity and validity of such fundamental categories as truth, universality and objectivity, while maintaining the commitment to materiality and to the concrete which is a key feature of all the thinkers treated in this study.

In general terms, Badiou's thought can be situated within a tradition of European thought which privileges mathematics and an abstract, formalist approach. Although he is keen to underline differences, he is himself happy to acknowledge the key importance to his project of thinkers such as Plato, Descartes, Hegel, Lacan and Althusser. More specifically, he places himself within a trajectory of twentieth-century French philosophy characterized by what he calls 'idealizing mathematism'. Culminating in Lacan, Althusser and Badiou himself, this is a trajectory defined by the work of important, but perhaps less well-known, figures such as Léon Brunschwig, Jean Cavaillès, Albert Lautman and Jean-Toussaint Desanti (Badiou 2006a: 16; 2009c: 7).[1] Yet specifying Badiou's position within a particular tradition or line of filiation should not distract from the originality of his contribution to contemporary philosophy more generally. In this context, one only needs to consider just two of his most important works, *Being and Event* (Badiou 1988; 2005b) and *Logics of Worlds* (Badiou 2006a; 2009c). Of the former, it can be said that it aspires to be nothing less than the most important book on ontology since Heidegger's *Being and Time* (and is recognized by some as being just that). Of the latter, it can be said that it aspires to rival Hegel's *Science of Logic* and that it has as its ambition nothing less than to overturn Kantian finitude and to rethink the limits placed on knowledge by critical philosophy and by the post-Kantian tradition in general.

The key to this ambitious enterprise is without doubt Badiou's mathematical turn. In *Being and Event*, he adopts post-Cantorian set theory as the only viable contemporary discourse on being. More recently, in *Logics of Worlds*, he adopts category theory as a means to articulate the intrinsic logic which orders the phenomenal appearance of specific historical worlds.[2] As will become clear, Badiou is insistent that philosophy be distinguished clearly from ontology, that is to say, from what can be said of being *as* being. Concomitantly, he argues that philosophy itself should aim to think what he terms the 'compossibility' of its four 'generic conditions': the matheme, the political, the poem and love (this will be explained further in the course of this discussion). Yet, despite this appeal to philosophy's fourfold conditioning, the predominance of the mathematical paradigm in Badiou's thought as a whole is, as John Mullarkey has persuasively suggested, indisputable (Mullarkey 2006: 88, 133). What follows, therefore, will aim to highlight the status accorded to mathematics in Badiou's philosophy and the key role it plays in underpinning his arguments relating to truth, ethics, universalism and the 'objectivity' of worldly appearances. Most importantly, perhaps, it will highlight the decisive role it plays in Badiou's thinking of historical change or transformation and his original reconfiguration of the category of the subject.[3]

Being and Event

As Oliver Feltham has argued, the sustained concern of Badiou's philosophy is 'the relationship between the thought of multiplicity and the thought of change' (Feltham 2008: 3). In this context, it is arguable that his mathematical-formalist approach to the ontological question of multiplicity and his sustained commitment to a radical, transformative politics are closely interlinked.[4] This is perhaps nowhere more evident than in *Being and Event*, a text in which Badiou seeks both to firmly establish the ontological essence of mathematics and to think the possibility of decisive historical rupture and transformation under the concept of the 'event'.

Ontology as mathematics

In the introduction to *Being and Event*, Badiou signals that his own contribution to the 'closure of metaphysics' will be to combine three very distinct moments: Heidegger's re-qualification of philosophy via the question of ontology, analytic philosophy's orientation of thought around the mathematical revolution of Frege-Cantor, and the modern theory of the subject (implicitly that of Lacan) (Badiou 1988: 8; 2005b: 2). Situating his contribution in this manner, Badiou seeks to position the thought elaborated in *Being and Event* as a radically new turn within contemporary philosophy, or as a revolution that will ultimately be comparable to the Copernican revolution inaugurated by Kant in the *Critique of Pure Reason*. Badiou opens the way towards this combination of ontology, mathematics/logic and the theory of the subject by arguing that 'philosophy is not centred on ontology – which exists as a separate and exact discipline – rather, it *circulates* between this ontology, the modern theories of the subject and its own history' (Badiou 1988: 9; 2005b: 3). The key to this positioning of philosophy as that which can 'circulate' between distinct moments which are exterior to it is the original separation of philosophy from ontology. There are two principal lines of argument that Badiou pursues in order to insist that mathematics – and not philosophy – is the only viable language of ontology.

Firstly, and as Peter Hallward has pointed out, Badiou's conception of ontology is in keeping with a tradition which goes back to Aristotle, namely that it should say what is sayable of being *as* being (Hallward 2003a: 50). In this context, the 'being' of an object can be said to be that which remains once all its contingent qualities or predicates such as weight, shape, colour, material composition and so on have been subtracted. What something *is*, therefore, is not to be located in its physical or sensuous determinants. Its, as it were, *pure* being is rather something other than its qualities or qualitative characteristics.

Badiou pursues this subtractive approach to its limit by insisting that this qualitative dimension would include the predicate of existence itself (thus he sharply differentiates between being and existence) and, along with this, he rejects the notion that ontology would locate being in the substance, essence or the existing 'thingness' of a thing. What remains after this process of subtractive purification – that is to say 'pure being' – is necessarily not something whose nature can be verified by empirical experience or investigation (since one is aiming to think that which *is* prior to or in the absence of empirical contingency). Therefore, it is clear to Badiou that the question of ontology can be settled only through a decision as to the status of that remainder that being 'is'.[5] For his part, it is clear that, if one pursues the subtractive approach to its limit, in the absence of qualities, characteristics and all sensuous determination, all one is left with is pure multiplicity. Stripped of its contingent qualities and predicates, being 'is' only multiplicity. What we are left with is 'the multiple without any other predicate than its multiplicity' (Badiou 1988: 36; 2005b: 28). Badiou will come to call this 'inconsistent multiplicity', that is to say, a non-unifiable, non-denumerable multiplicity.[6] This leads him to write such decisive sentences as: 'if an ontology is possible ... then it is the situation of the pure multiple, of the multiple "in itself". To be more exact; ontology can be solely *the theory of inconsistent multiplicities as such*' (Badiou 1988: 36; 2005b: 28). Being, then, is ultimately indifferent to everything except pure multiplicity, it is nothing other than multiplicity, and in this sense it *is*, in a certain way, no-thing at all.[7] This insistence on being as 'pure being', stripped of sensible qualities or contingent predicates and then conceived as inconsistent multiplicity allows Badiou's ontology to be characterized as a kind of mathematical Platonism.

The second path pursued by Badiou in order to determine ontology as mathematics is the traditional philosophical question of the one and the multiple. This is the central question posed in the first meditation of *Being and Event*. Here, Badiou argues that, since Parmenides and Plato, 'The reciprocity of the one and being is certainly the inaugural axiom of philosophy' (Badiou 1988: 31; 2005b: 23). This alignment of the figure of the one with being has led philosophy, from its Parmenidean inception, into a tortuous and often paradoxical series of negotiations between the principles of the one and the multiple – principles which appear to mutually exclude each other. For, if being and oneness (unity) are reciprocal, then multiplicity *is not*. Yet, since the presentation of being is always and only a presentation of multiplicity and multiplicity therefore undeniably *is*, the reciprocity of being and oneness would be revoked or compromised. If, then, philosophy does orientate itself according to the axiom that being and the one are reciprocal, then the impasse of the one and the multiple is the exact point where 'philosophy is born and buried' (Badiou 1988: 31; 2005b: 23). Badiou's solution to this is as straightforward as it is powerful, namely, to take the ontological decision (and, as has been suggested already, ontology is necessarily a matter for decision) that 'the one *is not*' (Badiou 1988: 31; 2005b: 23). Badiou decides that the one is not anything that is or exists. Rather, the one is only an operation of counting-as-one. If the presentation of being is always a matter of presented multiples or existing multiplicity, then the oneness of something is only a result of counting or numeration. The one is nothing 'in itself'.

The implications of this decision in favour of being as pure multiplicity and the non-existence of the one are wide-reaching and shape the entirety of Badiou's philosophical endeavour, as well as his insistence on the separation of philosophy from ontology. The most immediate consequence which results from this decision is that being cannot be thought in terms of totality. The multiplicity of being cannot, for instance, be understood in terms of a plurality of entities whose existence would be underpinned by a single governing entity acting as their cause or ground (for example, the One of a Supreme Being or Creator God). This totalization of beings in a unified causal principle is, as has been argued elsewhere in this study, the paradigm of metaphysical thought par excellence. If the one *is not* and results only from an operation of counting, then pure multiplicity understood as being is necessarily in excess of the consistency imposed by counting-as-one or, as Badiou puts it, 'the absolute point of being of the multiple is not its consistency – thus its dependence upon a procedure of the count-as-one – but its inconsistency, a multiple deployment that no unity gathers together' (Badiou 1988: 53; 2005b: 42). Thus, the notion of inconsistent multiplicity lies at the very centre of Badiou's thinking about ontology. A thing or an object can be thought of as a denumerable entity or identity only insofar as it is counted-as-one in a given situation. Its *being* prior to any operation of counting is pure inconsistent multiplicity, non-denumerable and in excess of any horizon of unity or totality.

It is Badiou's subtractive approach to ontology and his decision in favour of being as inconsistent multiplicity which leads him to affirm mathematics as the only viable ontology. For if the decision is that only pure multiplicity remains after the process of ontological subtraction and that only multiplicity (and not the one) *is*, then it follows directly that 'ontology can be solely *the theory of inconsistent multiplicities as such*' (Badiou 1988: 36; 2005b: 28). For Badiou, mathematics, and specifically post-Cantorian set theory, is the only discourse available to us which can take on the role of presenting inconsistent multiplicity *as such*. Although this is a complex and, indeed, inherently mathematical issue, two key points are worth signalling in relation to this privileging of mathematics as ontology.

Firstly, as Badiou makes clear, mathematics is not representational. A mathematical sign does not refer to anything other than the multiplicity it presents and in this sense, Badiou argues, mathematics is nothing other than the presentation of presentation itself. To say x > y, or x = y (whatever the values one ascribes to each term), is to present nothing other than the presentation of unspecified multiples and the relation between them. The emptiness of mathematical presentation, the fact that it presents nothing but presentation (of multiplicity) fits exactly, of course, with Badiou's subtractive approach to being. Mathematical presentation, like pure being, is stripped of all qualitative characteristics. It presents the void of pure number or multiplicity.

Secondly, the notion of 'inconsistent' multiplicity is something which only mathematics can think in any rigorous, consequent or viable way. It should be noted that Badiou takes pains to underline that he is definitely *not* saying that being *is* mathematical or 'composed of mathematical objectivities'. His is 'not a thesis about the world but about discourse' (Badiou 1988: 14; 2005b: 8). It is worth underlining here that to think multiplicity outside of totality or outside of countability is, in a very real way, an impossibility of thought. As Badiou points out, all thought implies a situation, a structuring of entities and identities, that is to say (in his terms at least), the operation of a counting-as-one and the conceptual identity and coherence that results from this. It is only (post-)Cantorian set theory with its specific axioms and operations that offers a rigorous and exact way to think both what is consistent or countable of a multiplicity and the impasse or impossibility of inconsistent multiplicity.[8] If, then, inconsistent multiplicity is 'an ungraspable horizon of being' (Badiou 1988: 44; 2005b: 34), it is only in mathematical presentation that such ungraspability can be presented *as such*. A linguistic, discursive or otherwise conceptual presentation of inconsistent multiplicity would, by implication, necessarily return it to a non-mathematical horizon where the multiple is subordinate to the one (or the operation of counting as one). And so Badiou draws the unwavering conclusion from which he will never depart: mathematics has an ontological essence and ontology, as distinct from philosophy, can only be mathematics.

A number of contextual and critical remarks might usefully be made at this point. Firstly, there is no doubt that Frege and Cantor, in their different ways, represent a revolution or decisive break within the histories of logic and mathematics. By the same token, it can easily be conceded that Badiou's specific adoption and use of set theory is highly innovative and original. Despite this, it should be underlined that his mathematization of ontology and general engagements with Frege, Gödel, Russell and others lie in a relation of direct continuity with the thought of the late Lacan and with Lacan's insistence on a mathematization of the real. This is borne out in comments made by Lacan in his seminar of 2 December 1971: 'The real of which I speak is absolutely inapproachable, except by way of mathematics' (Lacan 2011) as well as by the importance he accords in this seminar to the work of Frege, Gödel and Russell. For this reason, and for the reasons outlined in the Introduction, Badiou's claim, accepted uncritically by many of his sympathizers and commentators, that his philosophy represents the emergence of radical novelty within the situation of contemporary thought needs to be treated with some caution or scepticism, or at least interrogated more critically.

Secondly, questions will inevitably be posed as to whether Badiou's subtractive approach, and the mathematical ontology to which it gives rise, is not too abstract and too platonically idealizing to adequately account for the concrete materiality of the real which his thinking seeks to circumscribe. Clearly, all the thinkers discussed so far in this study place their emphasis on precisely that realm which Badiou's ontology seeks to subtract, namely, the realm of the sensible and the bodily, of bodily intuition and of sense perception more generally. This is true for the auto-affection of the flesh (Marion), the exposure of/access to sense (Nancy), for technical prosthetics (Stiegler), the neuronal self (Malabou) and the distribution of the sensible (Rancière). Badiou's subtractive Platonism might also be opposed to Deleuze's philosophy of immanence and his immanentist doctrine of the 'univocity of Being' and therefore, from the Deleuzian perspective, he might also be accused of an excessively formalistic abstraction (Badiou handles these questions directly in his book *Deleuze: "The Clamor of Being"* (Badiou 1997b; 2000)). It should be noted that some of Badiou's commentators have vigorously and powerfully defended his subtractive approach against the charges of abstraction and empty formalism. Oliver Feltham, for example, seeks to argue that mathematical schematization allows for and most adequately achieves an engagement with that which is most 'concrete' in any situation (Feltham 2008: 84–135).

These critical questions relating to the status or otherwise of Badiou's philosophy as an 'event' within thought and to the abstraction and formalism of his subtractive approach can best be explored by interrogating further his use of set theory and his understanding of an 'ontological situation'.

Situation

Badiou assumes an exact identity between what can be said of the being of any given situation and its description according to the axioms and formal notations of set theory. Thus, the idea of an ontological situation and that of a set are subject to a reciprocity or equivalence. Set theory, of course, as a mathematical theory, studies sets as abstract objects within mathematics. It aims to describe the structure of the mathematical universe and thereby to serve as a foundation for mathematics. Using its basic principles of construction and founding axioms, set theory allows for the definition of mathematical objects, for example, different types of number such as integers, real and complex numbers, but also functions, geometric and topological structures and so on. Sets, then, are, for the working mathematician, mathematical objects which contain mathematical objects. It might therefore seem strange to some that Badiou wants to describe the being of concrete existing situations in the abstraction of mathematical language. Yet, as has been shown, that he should do so follows directly and necessarily from his decision that being is pure multiplicity (mathematics presents nothing else) and that the one is not and results only from an operation of counting.

Any given situation must therefore, ontologically speaking, be seen as a presented multiplicity, articulated according to a regime of counting-as-one, and according to a specific structure of counting, of belonging and of inclusion. On this basis, its being can be formally and exactly described in terms of a constructed set, of the elements which belong to or are included in that set and in terms of its subsets and so on. The elements of a situation/set would be all those identities or entities which are counted within it and are therefore subject to the relation of belonging to and/or inclusion. Crucial for Badiou here is the fact that, since the one is not, a situation/set is not a totality or enclosed unity or, as he puts it, 'every situation implies the nothing of its all. But the nothing is neither a place nor a term of the situation' (Badiou 1988: 67; 2005b: 54). If *pure* being is inconsistent multiplicity then, strictly speaking, it *is* nothing; it is only emptiness or void.

Whatever elements may belong to or be included in a situation (according to the operation of a count), the totality of that situation (its pure being) is nothing. It is emptiness or void and this void 'is neither local nor global, but scattered all over, nowhere and everywhere: it is such that no encounter would authorize it to be held as presentable' (Badiou 1988: 68; 2005b: 55). It is in this context that Badiou comes to say that the proper name of being is the void and that the void of a situation is its 'suture to its being' (Badiou 1988: 68–9; 2005b: 55). Set theory provides an exact axiom and mathematical notation for this concept, that of the empty set ø, a subset containing no elements which is always necessarily included in any and every possible set. In this sense, every countable, structured situation has, as its very being, a ubiquity of the void which empties it of all substance and all possibility of totalization or completion. The void is, Badiou says, the unpresentable of any presentation within a situation, the name of this is the empty set (ø), and this void is everywhere and nowhere within the situation itself.[9]

From his founding ontological decisions relating to multiplicity and the non-being of the one, Badiou systematically builds up an account of the way in which set theory and its axioms can present, exactly and rigorously, the being of situations. The account given here is necessarily highly schematic of course and deliberately non- or meta-mathematical. The technical detail of Badiou's arguments can therefore only be touched upon in a very limited way. However, two further aspects of Cantorian set theory are nevertheless worth highlighting.

Firstly, it should be noted that set theory can first and foremost be characterized as the mathematical science of the infinite. Again, if, as Badiou says, the one of being is not and there is only pure inconsistent multiplicity, then this means that being is infinity. Furthermore, it means that *only* pure being can have the infinite as a predicate since individual entities in their distinct identity result from the consistency of a count. Cantorian set theory with its ability to formalize infinity mathematically and to present a proliferation of different types or quantities of mathematical infinity is once again affirmed as the only adequate means by which to think pure inconsistent multiplicity. Set theory, as the mathematical presentation of the infinite, is the only way in which infinity can be presented in its separation from any horizon of the one (Badiou 1988: 164; 2005b: 145). It is only set theory which permits an adequate thinking of the infinitely excessive nature of infinity, its excess over any and all finite horizons or operations of counting.

Secondly, and perhaps most importantly for *Being and Event* as a whole, Cantorian set theory allows for a mathematical formalization of the excess of any set over itself (i.e. its ultimate inconsistency). This Badiou calls 'the theorem of the point of excess' (Badiou 1988: 98; 2005b: 84). This theorem holds that given a set α containing a certain number of elements, the set which would contain all the subsets of α (noted as $p(\alpha)$) will have an unquantifiably greater number of elements than α. In other words, the set of subsets would always be of a different, and immeasurably greater magnitude than the set itself (or: $p(\alpha) > \alpha$). Or put differently again, the count of the subsets of α is radically distinct from, or inconsistent with, the count of the elements of α itself. This once again means that no multiple can make its elements into a countable whole or totality. Yet also, and crucially for Badiou, it also means that 'there are always sub-multiples which, despite being included in a situation as compositions of multiplicities, cannot be counted in that situation as terms, and which therefore do not exist' (Badiou 1988: 113; 2005b: 97). If a set is always non-totalizable and in excess of itself, it always also includes multiplicities which it does not count or present, and to whose indeterminacy it can therefore, in a certain sense, be exposed. This provides the key to Badiou's differentiation between the being of a situation and the non-being of the event, the event which, arising from the 'unpresented' of a situation, can come to radically transform the situation itself.

State, site, event

The ubiquity of the void and the non-totalizable excess of any situation over itself means that the operation of the count and the structure of a situation are by no means stable or secure. There is, as it were, a constitutive ontological indeterminacy or original anarchy to any given situation.[10] The empty set and the theorem of excess describe in rigorous mathematical terms the way in which the elements of a set are never secure, absolutely determinable or totalizable according to any unified operation of a count. Badiou calls the 'state' of a situation the process of assuring the stable count of its elements, parts, sub-multiples and subsets. The state is a metastructure of the situation which seeks to secure the consistency of all the multiples and sub-multiples counted in it. It is in effect a recount of the terms of the situation which would formally acknowledge their inclusion and which would aim to guarantee the reliability and stability of the counting-as-one which constitutes the situation in the first instance. The state, therefore, is the way in which a situation protects itself from anarchy and disorder. The political resonances of this should be clear and, indeed, Badiou is explicit in his alignment of the state of a situation with the function of the state in the political sense. Both guarantee order and stability where there might otherwise be disorder and chaos.[11]

It is here that the overtly political nature of Badiou's ontology begins to resonate strongly and here also that his thinking of the relation of multiplicity to change is most clearly articulated. Building on the theorem of excess, Badiou can formally identify the existence of an abnormal multiplicity in a situation, one which is presented within it but whose elements are not presented. This he calls an evental site and describes in the following terms: 'I will term *evental site* an entirely abnormal multiple; that is, a multiple such that none of its elements are presented in the situation. The site, itself, is presented, but "beneath" it nothing from which it is composed is presented. As such, the site is not part of the situation' (Badiou 1988: 195; 2005b: 175). The theorem of excess, remember, stated that a set always includes multiplicities which it does not count or present. A site, therefore, is a determinable point within a situation in which such unpresented multiplicities are localized. In effect, it is the point at which the existing count or structure of a situation is exposed to the indeterminacy of the void. As such, the existence of an evental site within a situation is exactly what allows its organizing structure to undergo radical change or transformation. It is what allows a situation to be historical. A properly historical situation, one which can truly undergo decisive breaks within or transformations of its structure, is one which is 'in at least one of its points, on the edge of the void' (Badiou 1988: 197; 2005b: 177).

Badiou's specific understanding of the term 'event' needs to be understood as a function of the exposure of a situation and its state to the indeterminacy of the void. It needs to be understood in terms of the transformative potential of this exposure. In this context, an event is not simply 'what happens' on a day-to-day basis within any given situation. It is that which can, but not necessarily will, happen as a result of the existence of a site. For, since a site is a multiplicity present in a situation whose elements are not presented, it would be the locus of occurrence, agency or action which are not prescribable, verifiable or identifiable according to the prevailing logic of the count and the organizing structure of the situation. As Badiou puts it, 'Every radical transformational action originates *in a point*, which, inside a situation, is an evental site' (Badiou 1988: 197; 2005b: 176). The site is where something can happen which exceeds and transforms the prevailing count and structuring logic of a situation. Such a something would go by the name of 'event': that which forces a radical change or decisive break within the state of a situation.

It should be clear, though, that an event, should it occur, is not anything that can be identified or verified from within the existing structure of a situation. Since it exceeds anything the situation can count or present, the event *as such* cannot possibly be known or verified in advance or even in the moment of its surging or emerging. As supernumerary or in excess of the existing count, it *is* not as far as the situation is concerned since it emerges only from that which, precisely, the count of the situation cannot determine or decide (Badiou 1988: 199, 202; 2005b: 178, 181).[12] This follows necessarily from the fact that an event, if it has occurred, will be that which will have completely transformed the state and structure of the situation and will have done so solely on the basis that the elements of the evental site were not presented in the situation prior to the occurrence of the event itself. We can talk of an event, Badiou argues, only in the sense that 'it can only be *thought* by anticipating its abstract form', and that 'it can only be *revealed* in the retroaction of an interventional practice which is itself entirely thought through' (Badiou 1988: 199; 2005b: 178). So radical changes or decisive breaks in historical situations can and do happen but they cannot be prescribed or known in advance nor fully apprehended in an immediate present. They can only be affirmed retroactively as part of a process of reflective, active and self-conscious intervention in relation to the event. Such a process and the agency engaged in it are what Badiou will come to describe in his specific usage of the terms 'truth', 'fidelity' and 'subject'.

Truth, fidelity, subject

When Badiou says that an event can only be averred in the retroaction of a reflective, intervening practice, he is also saying that its truth, the fact that it occurred *and* the globally transformative power of that occurrence, can only be affirmed in an act of subjective fidelity to the naming of the event as such. Yet what he might mean by 'truth' here is very specific to his understanding of pure being as inconsistent multiplicity and to the formal axioms of his mathematical ontology. We might normally understand truth as the correspondence of a knowledge statement or proposition with an existing and verifiable state of affairs in a given situation. This is truth, Badiou would argue, as truthfulness (*véridicité*) and should be distinguished from truth proper (*vérité*). For Badiou, we can only conceive of truth by way of the concept of the 'generic'. Indeed, he states clearly that the generic founds 'the very being of any truth' (Badiou 1988: 361; 2005b: 327).

What is meant by 'generic' here can best be elaborated in the light of the everyday sense of the term understood as the most general, non-specific characterization of something. The generic aspect of a thing is the most general quality of its whole and not a quality of its specifiable parts. In Badiou's terms, the 'generic' will therefore not be anything that can be specifically determined or known according to the count of a situation, but will be rather that which is *indiscernible* according to the specificity of the count and therefore related to its most general being. Thus he says '"generic" positively designates that what does not allow itself to be discerned is in reality the general truth of a situation, the truth of its being' (Badiou 1988: 361; 2005b: 327). Anything we can know specifically of a situation, anything we can say that is factual, determinable or locally truthful about its elements or parts, will necessarily result from the operations of its count, its existing state or structure. It will result from the existing state of knowledge and will be determined contingently and specifically according to the existing norms of knowledge (this is *véridicité*). The generic, conversely, will have a direct relation with the inconsistent multiplicity of the situation, with the void of its most universal being. This means that truth, for Badiou, cannot be a correspondence of knowledge statement and a verifiable fact but must rather be the giving of a name to the generic being of a situation. This act of nomination is necessarily in excess of all the norms and prescriptions of existing knowledge. In this sense, a truth is both 'that which makes a hole in a knowledge' *and* an 'infinite part of the situation' (Badiou 1988: 361, 370; 2005b: 327, 335).

If it is recalled at this point that an event is that which emerges from an evental site, and that an evental site is a localized exposure of the situation to the void, that is, to the infinity or inconsistent multiplicity of being, then it follows that the naming of an event must also be the naming of a truth of the event. This act of nomination requires a *subject* who names or proclaims a truth. If, for Badiou, a truth is an 'infinite determination of an indiscernible of the situation', then it is therefore also a 'global intrasituational result of the event'. But again, this is so only insofar as a subject: 'generates nominations' or 'uses names to make hypotheses about the truth' (Badiou 1988: 437; 2005b: 399). A subject in an act of retrospective fidelity to the event will name: 'the general truth of a situation, the truth of its being' (Badiou 1988: 361; 2005b: 327). In this context, it should be clear that a truth is therefore something that is *subjectively made* or affirmed in the 'evental' exposure of a situation to its indeterminable, generic or infinite being. Crucially, since a truth is not conditioned by existing knowledge but emerges from the infinity of inconsistent multiplicity, it will therefore necessarily affirm itself as equally and universally applicable to all the elements or parts of that situation (or indeed of any situation whatsoever) (Badiou 2001: 73). This act of naming, this process of pronouncing or making a truth, is what Badiou will call a 'truth procedure' or a 'faithful procedure'. It is 'faithful' insofar as it requires a subject both to name the truth of the event *and* to remain in a relation of fidelity to that process of naming. Such a procedure is necessarily subjective and highly uncertain in outcome since, of course, it is not predetermined by existing knowledge. It should be clear, then, that Badiou's 'subject' is not anything like a phenomeno-logical consciousness; it is not a substance or ground nor a founda-tional 'subject of knowledge' in the traditional sense. It is, rather, any local or specific configuration within a situation which supports a truth (of an event) and which remains faithful to the process of naming that truth.

The theory of the subject as that which would be the agent both of a truth and of a fidelity to an event represents the climax of Badiou's axiomatic and systematic thinking of inconsistent multiplic-ity in *Being and Event*. If the concepts of 'evental site' and 'event' are constructed directly from Badiou's ontological axioms (inconsis-tent multiplicity, the void, the theorem of excess), the possibility of a subject, in turn, results necessarily from the undecidability of an event. Badiou puts this in a very succinct manner: 'The impasse of being, which causes the quantitative excess of the state to err without measure, is in truth the pass of the subject' (Badiou 1988: 469; 2005b: 429). That the ontological indeterminacy or inconsistent multiplicity of a situation can always be localized and then erupt as an event in such a way as to radically transform the situation itself confers on Badiou's subject the task and the privilege of decision. This is a decision as to whether the event may have occurred at all, the decision to name the event and to remain faithful to its generic truth. The subject, like the event, will necessarily be a rarity, an exception to the norm and to the prevailing structure of a situation. However rare they may be, the existence of subjects as the agents of historical transformation is something that follows on ineluctably from the structure of being itself: 'the impasse of being is the point at which a subject convokes itself to a decision' (Badiou 1988: 469; 2005b: 429).

The situation of contemporary thought

Peter Hallward remarked in 2003 that it would not be too much of an exaggeration 'to say that Badiou's work is today almost literally unreadable according to the prevailing codes – both political and philosophical – of the Anglo-American academy' (Hallward 2003a: xxiii). Such a statement resonates with Badiou's own characterization of a truth as that which 'makes a hole in knowledge' and as 'an indiscernible of the situation' (Badiou 1988: 361, 437; 2005b: 327, 399). It might be tempting therefore to interpret both Badiou's philosophy and the work of some of his commentators as examples of specific contemporary truth procedures. The philosopher names the mathematical revolution of Cantor as an event within the situation of contemporary European philosophy and develops the axioms of his mathematical ontology in fidelity to that event. His leading and most respected commentator affirms the name of 'Badiou' as a site of unreadability within the political-philosophical situation of the contemporary Anglo-American academy and by implication, therefore, also affirms that this proper name may herald the advent of something radically new, that is, the emergence of something transformative within that situation. What is certain is that, for Badiou, fidelity to an event and its truth requires a taking of sides against the codes of a prevailing situation and in favour of something which would necessarily be 'literally unreadable' according to the logic of those codes. In *Being and Event*, he is absolutely explicit on this point: 'A real fidelity establishes dependencies which for the state are without concept, and it splits . . . the situation in two . . . what it does is organize, *within* the situation, another legitimacy of inclusions' (Badiou 1988: 263; 2005b: 237–8). Fidelity to a truth procedure is always, therefore, a militant gesture which divides a situation in two and pits the faithful subject against the prevailing state of that situation and does so in the name of an entirely different regime of inclusion.

It is probably not too much of an exaggeration to say that a certain militancy pervades the entirety of Badiou's philosophy and his various characterizations of the state of contemporary thought. Certainly, the examples he gives of political events or truth procedures are all drawn from the canon of revolutionary, insurrectionary and militant situations which historically saw groups pitting themselves against existing state apparatuses and doing so in the name of generic (and therefore universal and egalitarian) truths: the slave rebellion against

Rome in the first century BCE, the French and Bolshevik revolutions, for example, or Maoist revolutionary politics. Indeed, all of the four domains in which Badiou argues that an event or truth can emerge (the political, science, art and love) are areas which can be demonstrably transformed through a decisive, definitive (and therefore militant) break with an existing situation, a break which occurs in the name of a truth. As John Mullarkey has noted, these domains, for Badiou, are four, and only four, because it is only politics, science, art and love which 'can give rise to purely disinterested (universal) ideas that inspire pure subjective conviction' (i.e. truths) (Mullarkey 2006: 85).[13] If then, as Badiou says very clearly in *Being and Event*, 'philosophy alone thinks truth, in what it itself possesses in the way of subtraction from the subtraction of being' (Badiou 1988: 391; 2005b: 355), then the task of philosophy will necessarily be to subtract the truths which emerge from within the four (and only four) domains. It is in exactly this sense that these domains are the 'generic conditions' of philosophy since it is only from them that a 'truth' can emerge and act as the material for philosophy's subtractive operations.[14] As philosophy, therefore, a work such as *Being and Event* can be seen as an attempt to subtract the truth of Cantorian set theory (mathematics as ontology, being as inconsistent multiplicity) in order then to re-qualify philosophy itself as separate from ontology and on that basis to develop a systematic and axiomatic paradigm for philosophical thought in general.

Yet if fidelity to truth is always a matter of militancy, of taking sides against the prevailing codes of a situation which has been 'split into two', then the arguably militant character of philosophy as Badiou conceives and practises it is a necessary outcome of philosophy's subtraction of truths from its generic conditions and its subsequent submission to those truths. Such militancy can be seen in the way that Badiou, at each stage of his philosophical career, is always writing against what he frames as the dominant or orthodox state of the contemporary philosophical situation.

For example, in *Being and Event* Badiou writes against post-Heideggerian 'poetic' ontology, the thinking of finitude in general and the broadly post-Nietzschean or hermeneutic claim that thought can only know significations and interpretations. In a work such as *Ethics* (Badiou 1993; 2001), the prevailing orthodoxy is identified as the humanitarian or value ethics of the post-Enlightenment liberal tradition and as a cultural-political ethics of difference or of the other, all of which, Badiou persuasively argues, conceals a powerful and disavowed violence of the same. In *Saint Paul: The Foundation of Universalism* (Badiou 1997a; 2003c), it is a widespread 'cultural and historical relativism' that he writes against, a relativism which is 'today at once a topic of public opinion, a "political motivation", and a framework for study in the human sciences' (Badiou 1997a: 7; 2003c: 6). In his most recent major work, *Logics of Worlds* (Badiou 2006a; 2009c), Badiou identifies and opposes the hegemony of a philosophical, political and cultural matrix defined by what he calls 'democratic materialism'. This is a matrix governed by 'the axiom of contemporary conviction', namely that *'There are only bodies and languages'* (Badiou 2006a: 9; 2009c: 1).

In all cases, what is at stake for Badiou are the interwoven philosophical, ideological and cultural-political forms of contemporary (liberal) capitalist society, economy and democracy. What one might loosely term the 'postmodern' would be one of the most prominent recent names for this cultural-political matrix. According to this account, the state of our contemporary situation supports a configuration which, Badiou argues, underpins all of the following philosophical, cultural and political forms: philosophies of finitude and of difference, philosophies of desire and of desiring bodies, all cultural or historical relativism, the linguistic paradigm within philosophy (both continental and analytic), minoritarian or identity politics, the culture and politics of difference, consumer culture and the ideological structures which support it and, of course, the political and economic structures of contemporary liberal-democratic states themselves. In short, so much of what has passed for philosophical or cultural postmodernity (e.g. post-structuralism(s), libidinal philosophy, constructivism, etc.) can be viewed as an expression of the wider logic of liberal capitalism.[15]

Badiou is perhaps guilty here of forcing too much within the scope of a single conceptual category or cultural-philosophical paradigm. This may well be a function of his specific conceptions of fidelity, taking sides, splitting in two and so on but the question must be posed as to what may be lost by way of nuance or differentiated understanding in such a broad assimilation of diverse phenomena under one rubric. Similarly, the ethical question should be posed as to the degree of violence that is inflicted upon the heterogeneity of phenomena in the process of forcing them into a single paradigm and shared logic of 'democratic materialism'. For Badiou, this may be a necessary violence that is required by the militancy of fidelity to the event in order to both inscribe and further a process of change and transformation. Yet, if one takes, for example, his readings of other modern and contemporary philosophers and his assimilation of their thought to the paradigm of democratic materialism, or earlier in his career, to those of sophistry and anti-philosophy, this loss of nuanced understanding and the violence of forcing become all too apparent. As is highlighted very well by Peter Hallward (2003a: 16), most of what passes for contemporary philosophy is, by Badiou's criteria, 'only a generalized sophistry . . . : language games, deconstruction, weak thought, radical heterogeneity, differend and differences, the collapse of reason, the promotion of the fragment' (Badiou 1992a: 76). Badiou can equally assimilate the thinking he characterizes as philosophical sophistry to the category of anti-philosophy also (on this, see Hallward 2003a: 21). Such judgements may make for good polemic but they arguably also make for overly forced philosophical analyses and interpretation since they depend too much on a simple opposition of different philosophical techniques, that is to say, that of logical-mathematical formalism on the one hand and a more literary-philosophical mode of argumentation on the other. In so doing, Badiou's polemical readings of contemporary philosophy tend to lack a more nuanced account of what different and apparently opposed bodies of thought might share and this can cause his readings to be rather reductive. This is true, for instance, of his interpretation of Nancy's philosophy that is alluded to towards the end of chapter 2. Badiou, it might be recalled, straightforwardly places Nancean thought under the governing logic and signifier of finitude and does so without in any way engaging with the logic of infinity, infinitude or excess which plays such a central role in both his philosophy of sense and his later deconstruction of Christianity.[16]

In defence of Badiou's very broad brush approach to a varied or apparently heterogeneous range of cultural and political phenomena, it could be argued that he is engaged in a typically structuralist gesture. This is a gesture which is comparable to Laruelle's all-embracing characterization of philosophy (see chapter 7) and one which follows in a direct continuity with the preceding generation of formalist-structuralist thinking. That is to say, Badiou assimilates a plurality of apparently distinct elements to an underlying structure or form which they all share as their condition of possibility or motor of their production. To defend him more on his own terms, it could be said that he is engaged in an act of subjective nomination. He is naming the state of the contemporary situation (e.g. 'democratic materialism'). He then argues that diverse but prevalent philosophical, cultural and political forms are structured according to the logic of that state. In bringing all those forms together under the same name and declaring against them, he is splitting the situation in two and so deciding in favour of elements which have been excluded from the situation. Thus, the excluded elements would be gathered together under a different name which would support a different logic of inclusion. In *Logics of Worlds*, the name he gives to this different logic is that most foundational concept of traditional Marxism: 'dialectical materialism'.

Logics of Worlds

As was indicated earlier, at first sight, Badiou's abstract formalism and his decision in favour of a mathematical ontology might seem to be incompatible with any affirmation of a more concrete materialism. Yet it is true to say that, since the earliest phase of his career (characterized by what one might call 'materialist epistemology'), such an affirmation has always occupied a very central place in his philosophy.[17] Although his subtractive approach to ontology and his mathematical formalism might appear to lead to abstraction, if they do provide the only viable means to speak of being *as* being, then ultimately and arguably they represent by far the most viable and effective way to approach being in its most concrete materiality. This is because the materiality of being is ultimately to be located in the immanence of its pure inconsistent multiplicity, rather than in its qualitative or predicative characteristics. Bearing Badiou's long-standing commitment to materialism in mind, it is worth highlighting the way in which he frames the distinction made in *Logics of Worlds* between 'democratic materialism' and 'dialectical materialism'. Whereas the former has as its sole affirmation the specifiable and relatively or contingently *situated* materiality of bodies and languages (and thus provides the axiom of cultural, political and philosophical postmodernity), the latter affirms that, although there are only bodies and languages, this is so only insofar as there are also truths. Democratic and dialectical materialism describe the opposing poles of a situation divided into two. The contingent, relative and locally specifiable materiality of bodies and languages has, *immanent to it*, the absolute and infinite materiality of multiple being. As was the case in *Being and Event*, it is only this generic material immanence which can yield or give rise to a truth. Therefore, in his unswerving opposition to democratic materialism, Badiou will come to affirm both that 'Every world is capable of producing its own truth within itself' and that 'The materialist dialectic is an ideology of immanence' (Badiou 2006a: 16, 18; 2009c: 8, 10).

Logics of Worlds, therefore, continues and develops the preoccupation with truth which earlier dominated *Being and Event*. Yet the reworking and reinvigoration of dialectical materialism in this work also articulates a decisive shift in focus and emphasis. In the first instance, this shift could be described in terms of a transition from the saying of being as 'pure being' to the description of being as the 'being-there' of an existing or appearing world. This, then, would be a shift from ontology to a certain kind of phenomenology, or, as Badiou himself puts it, what *Being and Event* did for pure being, *Logics of Worlds* will do for 'being-there, or of appearing, or of worlds' (Badiou 2006a: 16; 2009c: 8). This in turn entails a shift from the mathematics of set theory to the formal logic of category theory. Category theory is very much an evolving area of contemporary mathematics and might be broadly described as a general mathematical theory of structures and of the integration of structures into systems. In this regard, it is particularly well suited for the study of logical systems. It is also, importantly, a very different framework from set theory and can be considered as an alternative to set theory as a means of exploring the foundations of mathematics. So by introducing category theory to talk about the situated and structured consistency of appearing worlds, Badiou is making a very clear distinction between the discourse of pure being (ontology as set theory) and that of being-there or phenomenal worldly existence (the logic of appearing as category theory).[18]

Where the category of 'ontological situation' was central to *Being and Event*, that of 'world' now occupies a central organizing position in the arguments of *Logics of Worlds*. In this work, Badiou is seeking a formal language which would allow him to describe the logical consistency of appearing worlds and the multiplicities which are presented in them. He aims to identify a number of fundamental operators or organizing structures which would describe the phenomenal appearance of any given world in terms of its structured coherence or consistency. The logic of a world will articulate and determine the relative intensities of different appearing elements within that world, as well as the differential relations which structure the interdependence of those intensities. This, then, would be a way of thinking about the structured *relationality* of presented multiplicities, a relationality which is therefore very different from the perhaps more basic ontological relations of either belonging to, or inclusion in, a particular situation/set.[19]

However, this key distinction between being and appearing (or existence) or between the ontological saying of set theory and the logical description of category theory is ultimately in the service of a more refined and sophisticated account of how truths can and do emerge within a specific, given world. Badiou puts this in the following terms:

It is only by examining the general conditions of the inscription of a multiplicity in a world, . . . that we can hope finally to know: first, what the effectiveness of appearing is; then how to grasp, in their upsurge and unfolding, the singularity of those phenomenal exceptions, the truths upon which the possibility of living depends (Badiou 2006a: 45; 2009c: 36)

Category theory allows Badiou to give a rigorous and exact formal description of the logical structures underpinning the specific appearance of a world (he will refer to these structures as the 'transcendental' of a world) and thereby identify the singularities or exceptions (the 'sites', he may once have said) from which truths emerge. *Logics of Worlds* therefore represents a shift in emphasis away from ontology and towards phenomenology but does this in the name of a more developed ability to identify sites of potential change and transformation. This phenomenology is, as Badiou himself emphasizes, a 'calculated phenomenology' (Badiou 2006a: 48; 2009c: 38) and as such is very different in key respects from phenomenology as it might more traditionally be conceived.

This is important to underline since, as was highlighted earlier, Badiou's original subtractive ontology pitted itself against all those elements which phenomenology and existential phenomenology place at the very centre of their enquiry and methodological approach: for example, the constitutive nature of subjective (and intersubjective) consciousness, the qualitative and affective aspects of phenomenal experience (perception and mood), or the sensory aspects of embodied perception.[20] It should be stressed, however, that Badiou's *phénoménologie calculée* does not in any way represent a return to the idea of a constitutive phenomenological consciousness or ego. Indeed, the formal logic of category theory, Badiou argues, allows him to describe the transcendental organization of a structured and consistent appearing world in the absence of any subjective apprehension or constitution. In *Logics of Worlds*, therefore, the subject (thought as the subject of perception, or of perceptual consciousness) is precisely that which is subtracted in the 'calculated' logic of appearing. On this point, Badiou is very explicit: 'The transcendental that is at stake in this book is altogether anterior to every subjective constitution, for it is an immanent given of any situation whatever'; or again: 'the laws of appearing are intrinsic and do not presuppose any subject' (Badiou 2006a: 111, 334; 2009c: 101, 317).[21]

So one of the key aims of *Logics of Worlds* is to demonstrate the way in which category theory can demonstrate that, *in and of itself,* 'A world articulates a cohesion of multiples around a structured operator (the transcendental)' (Badiou 2006a: 112; 2009c: 102). In so doing, category theory can then offer an exact means of describing this transcendental, structured operator, this guarantor of the coherence of phenomenal appearing. As was the case in *Being and Event*, much of *Logics of Worlds* is taken up with strictly mathematical presentations of key arguments: the development of ontological axioms in the former work is superseded by the presentation of logical categories, functions and relational structures in the latter. This *exposition formelle* is supplemented throughout by non-mathematical exposition, what Badiou calls 'didactic phenomenology' (Badiou 2006a: 209; 2009c: 197). The phenomenological descriptions make Badiou's work eminently accessible to the non-mathematician. Yet, despite this, he insists that the rigour and systematic coherence of his arguments lies in the mathematical demonstrations alone and that the logic of category theory is the only objective means to describe the transcendental structuring of a world.

The consequences of this are far-reaching and, Badiou would argue, amount to nothing less than an attempt to overturn and move beyond the entirety of the Kantian and neo-Kantian legacy within European philosophy. In this context, the decisive philosophical break announced by *Being and Event* would achieve its accomplishment in *Logics of Worlds*. For, in his formal–mathematical presentations, Badiou is aiming to describe the structured objectivity of phenomenal appearances in the absence of their subjective apprehension and independently of the role played by any perceiving subject. What he describes as 'the watered-down Kant of limits' (Badiou 2006a: 16; 2009c: 8) is swept aside insofar as the logic of appearing allows for a notion of the worldly object as being: 'entirely independent from that of subject' (Badiou 2006a: 205; 2009c: 193). The entire Kantian project of grounding and limiting our experience of phenomena by demonstrating that it is phenomena alone that we can know in the transcendental unity of apperception (and never the noumena, the things-in-themselves) is overturned in Badiou's formal–mathematical logic of appearing. This is because the transcendental of a world is, as indicated above, 'anterior to every subjective constitution' (Badiou 2006a: 111; 2009c: 101); it is the transcendental *of* a world and not one of a constituting or constitutive subject. This means that Badiou's logic is not and cannot be a logic of linguistic propositions about a world. Logic here is the exact presentation of that world's transcendental structure in the absence of any linguistic or subjective mediation (just as set theory is the exact presentation of being as pure being).

More ambitiously still, Badiou argues that there is a demonstrable correspondence or correlation between the appearing of presented multiplicities as described by the logic of category theory and the being of pure multiplicities as described by set theory: 'For every pure multiplicity A led to be there in the world, we are certain that to the ontological composition A . . . there corresponds its logical composition' (Badiou 2006a: 231; 2009c: 218). Being and appearance, though absolutely distinct (just as the mathematics of set and that of category theory are distinct), can nevertheless be shown to correspond exactly. The formal–mathematical approach allows us to discern 'the intelligibility of returning from the transcendental synthesis in appearing back to the real synthesis in multiple-being' (Badiou 2006a: 305; 2009c: 289; translation modified). Kant's attempt to place the noumenal within the realm of the strictly unknowable is surpassed here as Badiou comes to affirm the possibility of a non-subjective intelligible and logical transition from appearance to being, phenomenon to noumenon. Philosophy here proclaims its liberation from the chains of Kant's Copernican revolution. The possibility of developing an objective and systematic thinking of things 'in-themselves' opens up once more.[22]

This would mean that, in any given world, any two competent logicians, whatever their divergent perspectives or ideological positions, would necessarily produce the same formal–mathematical descriptions of that world's transcendental logic, just as two scientists performing the same experiment under similar conditions would produce the same experimental results always and universally. Clearly, and, given the very recent emergence of Badiou's calculative phenomenology, its incredibly ambitious claims have not been fully tested in the hands of a range of mathematically competent logicians. It could be objected, though, that if *different* formal–mathematical descriptions and *different* evaluations of the ordering and truth of the same appearing world were to emerge, Badiou's claims with regard to the reversal of Kantianism by way of mathematics would need to be revisited.

Nevertheless, in its ambition alone, Badiou's *Logics of Worlds* is a remarkable and extraordinary achievement. As was indicated above, what he comes to call (asserting a rivalry with Hegel) his Grande Logique has as its aim the apprehension and determination of singular phenomenal exceptions within the presented multiplicities of a world, and, through this, the identification of emergent truths. As with *Being and Event*, the arguments of *Logics of Worlds* all move towards the systematic grounding of the concept of truth and that of a subject who would be able support truth in the procedures of fidelity, naming, militancy and so on. The overriding concern then is, as before, the relation of multiplicity to the thought and possibility of change. Here, though, Badiou is concerned to articulate the agent of change, the subject, in terms of its specific materiality. The subject of *Logics of Worlds* therefore comes to be thought as a 'body-subject'.

'*The most significant stake of* Logics of Worlds', Badiou writes, '*is without doubt that of producing a new definition of bodies, understood as bodies of truth, or subjectivizable bodies*' (Badiou 2006a: 44; 2009c: 35). If democratic materialism has as its axiom that there are only bodies and languages, then Badiou's dialectical materialism not only affirms that there are also truths but that specific kinds of material, bodily configuration are required to support those truths, to oppose the existing organization of a world by dividing it in two, by taking sides against the status quo, and thus to bring about substantive change in the transcendental ordering of that organization. A body-subject, then, may be an actual biological body, but it may also be a materially existing organization or movement (a party, a collectively identified struggle). Either way, it is a configuration which would gather together all those material elements able to support and pro-claim an event, a truth and to affirm a contemporaneity with and fidelity to that event and truth. It is in this context that Badiou's materialism must be viewed as dialectical in its form (and not plural-istic or democratic). For only the body-subject, in proclaiming an event and its truth, in dividing a world into two and in opposing the status quo, will have the means to create a new world from the destruction of the old. Badiou asserts clearly and unflinchingly the essence of dialectical negation and synthesis or transformation: 'The opening of a space of creation requires destruction' (Badiou 2006a: 418; 2009c: 396).[23]

Badiou, therefore, has opened up a space within contemporary philosophy which enables a systematic and rigorous formal descrip-tion of the ontological and phenomenological conditions which allow radical change and transformation to occur within any given histo-rical world. He has also, equally systematically and rigorously, arti-culated the *imperative* of being or becoming a subject. His is an affirmation that to be a subject at all is to be incorporated into a material process of destruction and creation and is to be so only in fidelity to the transformative events of generic and universal truths. This, ultimately, is a forceful reaffirmation that philosophy's task is not just to interpret the world but also to change it.

That this systematicity and rigour is so resolutely grounded in the mathematical paradigm and in an attempt to surpass the limitations of Kantian and Heideggerian finitude means that Badiou's philoso-phy is, without any doubt, one of the most significant and intellectu-ally powerful achievements of contemporary French thought and, indeed, of contemporary thought as a whole. His realignment of post-Hegelian and post-phenomenological philosophy with the axioms and logical categories of mathematics avows itself as a radical transformation of the entire situation of contemporary thought. Yet, as has been argued here, if one takes Badiou strictly on his own terms, his success in effecting or precipitating such a transformation of thought is necessarily unverifiable in advance. Whether it succeeds or not will be a matter for those contemporary and future philosophers who, as subjects faithful to the very idea of such a transformation, decide to incorporate themselves into the real and ongoing composition of that transformation itself.

7

François Laruelle: Beginning with the One

Of all the recent attempts made by French philosophers to effect a break or rupture within contemporary thought, there is perhaps none more radical than that made by François Laruelle. Since the early 1980s, Laruelle has sought nothing less than a decisive break from the entirety of philosophy itself. His thinking of radical immanence and of what he calls 'the One' (*l'Un*) unequivocally demands that thought leave the terrain of philosophy, that its structuring principles and fundamental operations be suspended in a new discursive gesture, a new kind of thinking, theory or knowledge. This new discursive gesture, theory or knowledge takes the name of 'non-philosophy'.

Beginning with the publication of his first full-length work in 1971, *La Phénomène et la différence* [*The Phenomenon and Difference*], Laruelle has published twenty works and has explicitly divided his career into five distinct phases: 'Philosophy I', 'Philosophy II', 'Philosophy III' and so on. Each of these phases represents different moments in his self-positioning in relation to philosophy itself. During the first phase, his work can be situated within the context of 1970s' philosophies of difference, libidinal philosophy and in relation to the complex reception of Nietzsche and Heidegger that occurred in France in the wake of Derridean deconstruction (the work of Jean-Luc Nancy and Philippe Lacoue-Labarthe during this period can also be located in this context).[1] It is also in this first phase alone that Laruelle considers himself to be working within philosophy and as a philosopher. From 'Philosophy II' onwards (beginning with the publication of *Le Principe de minorité* (Laruelle 1981)), he persistently seeks to articulate, or, as will become clear, to 'perform', what he comes to call the 'global change of perspective' (Laruelle 1989: 127) and the 'global change of ground' (Laruelle 1996: 4) of non-philosophical thought. It is arguable, therefore, that from 'Philosophy II' onwards his thinking is marked by shifts within a broader continuous concern rather than by really decisive breaks or successive moments of fundamental reorientation.[2]

Laruelle's influences are very diverse and make his thinking difficult to position in relation to any of his immediate predecessors. He has himself aligned his work with the attempt to develop a 'non-Heideggerian deconstruction' (Laruelle 1989: 179–212, 202). This is borne out in, for example, books such as *Philosophies of Difference* (Laruelle 1986; 2010c), an engaged, and not unsympathetic, critique of Nietzsche, Heidegger, Derrida and Deleuze. This book unequivocally seeks to move beyond philosophies of difference but at the same time demonstrates the extent to which Nietzschean, Heideggerian, Derridean and Deleuzian perspectives are important for the development of Laruelle's thinking as a whole (as is also evident in earlier works of the 1970s, such as *Le Déclin de l'écriture* (Laruelle 1977b) and *Nietzsche contre Heidegger* (Laruelle 1977a)). Yet, drawing on a rather different lineage and context, Laruelle's characterization of philosophy as a whole is also a self-avowedly structuralist gesture of a kind which is different from the 'post-structuralist' dynamic to be found in Derrida and Deleuze. His uses of the terms 'science' and 'theory' are far more reminiscent of Louis Althusser's work and of a trajectory which would pass through Lévi-Strauss and Lacan than they are of anything one might find in Nietzsche, Heidegger and so on. At the same time France's most prominent writer on Laruelle has also brought him into close alignment with Emmanuel Levinas, despite the key differences which separate them (Choplin 1997; 2007). If these multiple lines of influence and engagement were not challenging enough, it is also arguable that the work of rather less well-known figures such as Pierre Klossowski (a significant point of reference for Laruelle in the 1970s) leaves its distinctive mark on the key concerns of his mature work right up to the present day.

Another notable, challenging and difficult aspect of Laruelle's non-philosophical writing is its style. This is a writing characterized by a very high degree of rhetorical and discursive complexity and what has also to be recognized as an extraordinary originality. It is also in consequence marked by a (sometimes extreme) difficulty of accessibility.[3] Yet, as Laruelle himself repeatedly remarks, the non-philosophical gesture will necessarily be incomprehensible from the strictly philosophical perspective and philosophy will, by its very nature, resist or reject as illegitimate the (a-)conceptual language of non-philosophy. One of the key arguments of what follows here will be that Laruelle's thinking of radical immanence, of the 'One', of philosophy and non-philosophy, requires him to develop a very different (but on its own terms highly rigorous) discursive gesture or technique, and that non-philosophy is necessarily and inherently a performative mode of writing. Yet it is a mode whose effectivity and transformative potential entirely depend upon the technique of its enunciation. It may, in fact, be possible to imagine a perspective from which Laruelle's writing is not so inaccessible (although it is always complex). That, of course, would be the perspective of non-philosophy itself, if only we would open ourselves to it. The key to approaching Laruelle's non-philosophical writing, then, lies in understanding the way in which he is seeking a discourse which would be adequate for thinking what is 'radical' in radical immanence, or what he also calls 'the real'.[4] As he has remarked in his most recent major work, *Philosophie non-standard* (Laruelle 2010a), his task is to give to immanence, the One, or the real, 'the thought that it merits' (Laruelle 2010a: 99).

Radical immanence and non-philosophy

Immanence and transcendence constitute a key opposition for both philosophical and theological thought. If one takes the religious doctrine of pantheism, for instance, one can see the way in which this opposition is central to divergent ways in which the place of the divine or the existence of a monotheistic God can be conceived. Where more traditional monotheistic accounts would understand God as transcendent to the world, that is to say, exceeding, surpassing or having a continuous existence outside of or exterior to it, pantheism would view God as immanent to the world, that is to say, indwelling, remaining within or being intrinsic to the material universe. The more traditional monotheistic notion of a creator God requires the transcendence of the divine since only in the exteriority of transcendence can the creator precede creation and therefore act as the supremely powerful effective cause of that which is created. In pantheism, the immanence of the divine, that is, its inherence within all that exists, means that the question of God creating the world from nothing becomes redundant since the two principles of creator and created are equivalent. At the same time, from the perspective of the immanence proper to pantheism, the very principle or reality of transcendence itself can be called into question: there is no need to posit the being of a divine entity beyond or outside of the world; indeed, the entire sphere of transcendence can now easily be dismissed as an illusion.

What is true for immanence and transcendence within the theological context could be said to be true also for more strictly philosophical questions relating to being, existence or objective reality, on the one hand, and the concepts, ideas or categories that are used to represent and understand them on the other. In this context, immanence, the principle of indwelling or being intrinsic to something, could be said to characterize the actuality or the 'real existing' of that which is (that is, 'independent' reality prior to any conscious apprehension we may have of it). Transcendence can be understood as the medium of ideality and abstraction proper to concepts, a medium which is necessarily in excess of, exterior to or separate from the 'real' of existence.[5] The transcendence of concepts would therefore be opposed to immanence. The philosophical question which arises from this separation of (immanent) existence and (transcendent) conceptuality would be that of the possible equivalence between the two spheres or of the adequacy of concepts to describe or determine existence (e.g. the questions of truth and error, epistemological foundations and so on).

In taking ('radical') immanence as the guiding thread for his non-philosophical project, Laruelle is therefore arguably working with one of the most important and constitutive oppositions of philosophical thought. This, at least, is what he himself argues in his own general characterization of philosophy. Most obviously and immediately, however, the theme of immanence can be related back to Deleuzian philosophy.[6] Deleuze's thinking of a 'plane of immanence' seeks to articulate an understanding of immanence in a pure or absolute form. According to this understanding, all existence is an expression of the same mode of substance and there is no cut within being, no separation of transcendence and immanence or of ideality and materiality (hence the Deleuzian doctrine of the 'univocity of being').[7] According to Deleuze, all conceptuality, abstraction or ideality is therefore in no way separate or distinct from what we might take to be a more material dimension of existence since both ideality and materiality are expressions of an immanent existence entirely devoid of transcendence. Philosophy's use of concepts or of transcendent (or transcendental) categories would therefore be, at best, a blindness to the univocity and absolute immanence of being, at worst, a blocking of thought which places it in the service of orthodoxies or dominant ideologies. Within Deleuze's 'plane of immanence', therefore, the very opposition of transcendence and immanence would not be an opposition at all in any real sense. The opposition would necessarily be suspended or collapsed into a more all embracing conception of immanence which has no outside, exteriority or 'beyond'.

Where Deleuze speaks of 'pure' and 'absolute' immanence, Laruelle speaks of 'radical' immanence. This, as will become clear, he does because he believes that Deleuze is unable to go far enough to give immanence 'the thought that it merits'.[8] In order to begin to do so, Laruelle proposes that immanence be understood as that which is 'One', as that which is undivided, absolutely autonomous and, of itself, entirely indifferent and resistant to conceptual transcendence and understanding. In this sense, the One of immanence (or of the real) is entirely in excess of all human categorization or conceptualization, and yet, crucially, this is not a transcendence (of alterity), and nor is it a privation, a negation, lack or an abyss of ground, but rather a positivity of content. The One is One in and of itself prior to, and independently of, any conceptual operations of division, negation and so on. As Laruelle himself puts it: 'The One has an absolutely positive content: and it is the One itself as Indivision' (Laruelle 1986: 170; 2010c: 153). At the very same time, the One – as One – is a unity. Yet it is a unity of a very different kind from that with which theology and philosophy may be familiar. From the traditional theological perspective, God would be conceived as an all-embracing Divine Unity, that is, as the supreme entity who, as the creator of all that exists, underpins creation as a unified and unifying principle. Yet this is clearly a unity of transcendence, of a transcendent gathering together the elements of the immanent/transcendent dyad (of the material and the spiritual) and of a transcendent guarantee that their division or opposition can be synthesized into a greater whole. This is also, Laruelle will argue, the kind of unity offered by philosophy as it constructs an identity between categories or concepts and being or existence: the unity of transcendence is a unity which unites or unifies divisible parts. The One of immanence, however, is a radical 'indifference to the Unity of which all the philosophers speak' (Laruelle 1986: 27; 2010c: 12). Laruelle's One is not a unification of that which has previously been divided (transcendence/immanence) but rather an immanence which is 'always already', absolutely and of itself, indivisible: 'The essence or the reality of the One is radical immanence devoid of all transcendence (nothingness, splitting, desire). It is immanence lived prior to all representation' (Laruelle 1991: 19).

It is this characterization of radical immanence as One which organizes Laruelle's understanding of philosophy and non-philosophy respectively. For if immanence (or the real) is One, if it is absolutely autonomous, self-sufficient and indivisible, how can the transcendence of philosophical conceptualization begin to think or speak about it at all? This, as will become clear, Laruelle acknowledges to be one of the central questions that has already been posed by the philosophies of difference and alterity which immediately precede his non-philosophical thinking and with which he most closely engages. Yet, when set in these terms, the question of immanence and of the One becomes an impasse for philosophy as a whole which, Laruelle argues, is as a form constitutively and inextricably bound up with transcendence, with conceptuality and the division or splitting which accompanies conceptual abstraction.

Laruelle takes a globalizing or totalizing approach to the definition of philosophy which has been criticized in some of the most important and original philosophical engagements that have been made with his thought to date. In *Nihil Unbound*, for example, Ray Brassier argues that Laruelle's characterization of philosophy is too close to Heidegger's thinking insofar as he 'uncritically accepts the Heideggerian premise that the entire history of philosophy can be reduced to a single structure' (Brassier 2010: 121). While this criticism quite reasonably questions whether one can ever sensibly talk about philosophy as a whole or understand it as a 'single structure', it does not quite do justice to Laruelle's position. Firstly, and as this study has suggested from the outset, it is a very widespread gesture on the part of French philosophers working in the wake of both Heidegger and Nietzsche to offer broad characterizations of the European philosophical tradition from its Greek origin onwards and to do so as a means of circumscribing the structure of metaphysics and of metaphysical thinking (Marion, Stiegler and Badiou all do this very explicitly). Laruelle is certainly indebted to Heidegger in his characterization of philosophy insofar as he consistently refers to it as a 'technology' and thereby aligns it with the Heideggerian account of ontotheology, nihilism and of modern technology as 'enframing' (Laruelle 1996: 9–10, 52, 259; 1991: 10).[9] Yet his desire to locate a 'single structure' which would inform the operations of *all* philosophical thinking and define philosophy per se is much more explicitly a structuralist rather than a Heideggerian gesture. Laruelle's description of what he calls 'the philosophical decision' is the result of: 'the systematic search for the *invariants* and the irreducible structures which allow us to speak of philosophy *per se* [*qui permettent de parler de* la *philosophie*]' (Laruelle 1991: 17). This is a search for invariant structures which has always characterized structuralism in its various guises, for example: the attempt to discover the essence of 'literariness' carried out by the Russian formalists; the Prague Circle's attempt to define the 'poetic function'; Lévi-Strauss's identification of invariants underpinning kinship structures; or Lacan's use of linguistic and mathematical formalism to describe the structure of the unconscious and of inter-subjectivity. So while Brassier may well be right to be sceptical of this totalizing tendency, he is wrong to portray Laruelle's desire to define philosophy in unified terms as being solely an uncritical or unreflective Heideggerian gesture. This is important to note since Laruelle's structuralist perspective on philosophy is decisive for the way he comes to understand and use the terms 'science' and 'theory'.

So Laruelle can talk about philosophy in general [*la philosophie*] because, he argues, he has been able to formally identify 'The structural rule of the philosophical decision' (Laruelle 1989: 12). This is a decision which holds for *all* philosophy as philosophy in all times and all places. In each of his major works (and in particular those of 'Philosophy II' and 'III'), Laruelle takes pains to give a meticulous description of the structure of the philosophical decision. This lengthy three-point quotation from *En tant qu'un* is typical:

> (a) [philosophy] does not accede to the real in itself . . . , it is simultaneously a knowledge of the real and of ideality, of their mixing; (b) it does not accede to the real through the sole posture of immanence, but also and simultaneously through that of transcendence and of the decision; its theoretical criteria cannot be radically immanent; (c) in consequence it claims to transform the essence of the real through its representation and modify the order of the real in modifying the order of its own thoughts. (Laruelle 1991: 49–50)

The constant or invariant structure that he identifies is one in which immanence and transcendence are 'mixed' and this mixture is 'synthesized'. The transcendence of concepts operate, as it were, instrumentally as a means by which the transcendence/immanence divide (or 'dyad') can be posed as such and then synthesized into a greater unity. Put differently, philosophy poses 'being' or existence on the one hand and its representation in concepts or categories on the other, and it then constructs, or legislates for, the equivalence, identity or unity of these in the universality of philosophical truths and foundations.[10] Philosophy thus positions itself as the unifying transcendent principle which governs the original division or opposition. In this way, it also founds its own authority (in a very circular manner, Laruelle argues) at the very same moment that it founds the 'truth' of being and existence. In this respect, philosophy, for Laruelle, closely resembles the 'transcendent unity' of monotheism described above.

Ray Brassier puts this very succinctly when he suggests that Laruelle's gesture is 'not so much to totalize philosophy as to identify philosophy *with* totalization' (Brassier 2010: 131).[11] Yet this invariant structure of philosophical thinking comes at the price of an (entirely illusory) splitting or division of the real or the One, whereby immanence is represented or appears as 'mixed' with transcendence, and an (equally illusory but also violent) pretension on the part of the philosophical decision to constitute the real in the very operations of philosophy itself.

Thus, for Laruelle, philosophy is always constituted in a mixing of transcendence with immanence and a process of synthesizing and hierarchizing the two in order to achieve its autonomous self-positioning. It thereby poses itself as the instrument by which being or existence can be known, represented, grounded and so on. The way in which this structure of division, mixing and synthesis articulates a gesture of 'auto-positioning' is crucial for Laruelle since it is only in such a supposedly autonomous and unconditioned operation that philosophy has any claim to universality. As Laruelle puts it: 'Through this structure [philosophy] claims to determine itself without reference to its empirical determinations which it takes into account only to the extent they are subordinated to an *auto-positioning* which is its by right, an auto-understanding or auto-legislation, autonomination, etc.' (Laruelle 1996: 5). In this way, the dyad and synthetic structure of the philosophical decision ultimately grounds the pretension of philosophy to be 'first philosophy', that is to say, *prima philosophia*, the discipline that studies being as being in its universality and which therefore both precedes and has legislative authority over all other forms of knowledge and more regional ways of knowing.

In identifying transcendence and transcendent/immanent mixing and synthesis as fundamental to the structure of all philosophy, Laruelle lays the ground for his attempt to articulate a 'non-philosophical' thinking. Indeed, it is only in the context of the invariant structure of the philosophical decision that the 'non' of non-philosophy can be properly understood. Laruelle repeatedly insists that this 'non' should not be understood in negative or destructive terms. Non-philosophy is not 'the absence or the negation of philosophy, it is, on the contrary, its generality or its opening as a correlate of the One rather than of Being' (Laruelle 1991: 20).[12] The most common analogy he draws in this regard is the distinction between Euclidean and non-Euclidean geometry. Non-Euclidean geometries deviate from Euclid's fifth postulate relating to parallel lines on a 'flat' plane or surface, but they do not negate or invalidate Euclidean geometry. Such geometries function according to a different projection of space and a set of mathematical operations which are not those of the Euclidean form (while still observing Euclid's first four postulates). By analogy, one can say that non-philosophy functions according to a different structure than that of the philosophical decision. Rather than being or existence, non-philosophy takes the One in its absolute autonomy and indivision as its first and last point of reference, and thereby takes a different 'non-philosophical' posture in relation to the real, that is, a posture which will not be structured according to a dyad of transcendence and immanence and their 'mixing'/synthesis. The difference between philosophy and non-philosophy can be viewed as structural or topological rather than as a relation of negation or destruction. What Laruelle wishes to postulate is 'A type of experience or Real which escapes auto-positioning, which is not a circle of the Real and of thought, a One which does not unify but remains in-One, a Real which is *immanent (to) itself rather than to a form of thought*, to a logic etc.' (Laruelle 1996: 6). Non-philosophy, then, will aim to work independently of the auto-positioning and circular logic of the philosophical decision, just as non-Euclidean geometry would function independently of the two-dimensional plane assumed by the parallel postulate. Non-philosophical thought must find a topological or conceptual space for thinking the real, one which divorces itself from the pretensions of transcendence. Such a thinking must seek to be a form of knowledge which will in no way seek to represent, qualify, constitute or transform the immanent real according to any of the conceptual operations proper to philosophy.

If non-philosophy is not philosophy but rather something else, then what kind of knowledge is it? The term Laruelle uses to categorize his new way of thinking is 'science'. Yet great care needs to be taken here to determine exactly how he uses this term and what he may understand by it. Indeed, the exact status of 'science' changes in a number of ways as his thinking develops from 'Philosophy II' through to 'Philosophy V'. Once again, the structural(ist) character of Laruelle's thought comes to the fore here. His use of the term science appears analogous to the way it is used by Louis Althusser. Althusser theorized a (Marxist) 'science' of society, that is, a science which would uncover the deep structures of social organization and historical development and which would therefore distinguish itself from 'ideology' (political belief as relative or contingent 'world-view').[13] In a similar fashion, Laruelle develops a science of philosophy, which uncovers its invariant structures and is different from philosophy which now emerges as a kind of ideology (contingent and relative) rather than as *prima philosophia* (universal). So the term 'science' for Laruelle denotes or determines the existence of non-philosophy as a distinct discipline or body of knowledge whose scientificity resides in its theoretical formalism or its structuralism. This is both a science of philosophy (it uncovers its invariant structure or code, the dyad of transcendence and immanence) and a science of the real which opens up the possibility of a non-philosophical perspective insofar as it approaches the real formally and thinks it according to its indivisible Oneness, its absolute autonomy and immanence in, of and for itself. What Laruelle seeks, then, in this scientific opening onto non-philosophy is a '*a representation that is non-thetic (of) the real, altogether distinct from what philosophy imagines as Representation*' (Laruelle 1986: 177; 2010c: 160). Such a science would be 'non-thetic' insofar as its operations and procedures would never at any point seek to divide and then bind the immanence of the real to the work of conceptuality or transcendence. Rather, the operations of non-philosophy would have as their most important task the maintenance of a separation or duality such that the real is never treated as anything upon which concepts can have any purchase whatsoever. The global operation of this non-thetic science of the real is given the name: 'vision-in-One'.

The key to Laruelle's 'vision-in-One' lies in its attempt to perform a discursive and conceptual operation which is the inverse of the philosophical decision. The latter, in its idealism and abstract conceptuality, seeks to bend the real to the operations of thought and refuses the status of being or existence to that which cannot be thought. Conversely or inversely, the former seeks to bend thought to the indivisible and unthinkable real. In the same way, it can be said that the vision-in-One does not think 'from' being but 'from' the One (Laruelle 1989: 53, 54). It might immediately be objected that this project or aspiration of thought falls directly into self-contradiction, incoherence or, at best, irresolvable paradox and aporia. For, bluntly put, how can the One be thought or theoretically determined when it is taken, a priori, to be unthinkable and undeterminable? Or, alternatively, has the One not always already and necessarily been thought and determined (and therefore divided by transcendence) in the very affirmation of its status as unthinkable and undeterminable? In either case, thought fails in its attempt to achieve any kind of coherent rigour which would be adequate to the absolute autonomy and indivisibility of the One such as it is posed by Laruelle a priori. However, such objections, he would argue, are eminently philosophical in nature since it is philosophy and the philosophical decision which requires that thinking and that which is thought be accomplished as a unity or identity. Being philosophical, these objections necessarily pose the vision-in-One as incoherent or self-contradictory but, in so doing, they also necessarily miss the force of thought or the rigour which is specific to it.

In order to begin to understand the vision-in-One on its own terms, its initial status as an axiomatic way of thinking needs to be highlighted.[14] An axiom can be understood as a principle that is taken to be universally and necessarily true a priori and which is then used as the basis for formal or deductive reasoning. The truth taken as axiomatic by the vision-in-One is (as outlined above) that the One of immanence or of the real is autonomous, indivisible and indifferent to the operations of negation and splitting proper to the transcendence of concepts. Seen from this perspective, to affirm that the One is unthinkable and undeterminable is less an incoherence or self-contradiction of thought and far more a straightforward formal deduction from the axiom of indivisibility itself. Laruelle puts this very clearly in *Principes de non-philosophie*:

> This impossibility of turning towards the One is not an insufficiency or forgetting that can be imputed to thought, it is a constraint that the One imposes upon it, the founding axiom of non-philosophy being that the One or the real is foreclosed from thought and is so in and of itself rather than through any failure of thought. (Laruelle 1996: vi)

The question then is not whether the vision-in-One divides or affects the One in the operation of its founding axiom. Rather, it is a question of the extent to which the One, in its indivisibility and consequent foreclosure from thought, necessarily constrains or conditions thought itself in specific and unavoidable ways. It is in this context that the Laruelle of 'Philosophy II' comes to understand the immanence of the real as a 'transcendental'. It is in this context also that his 'vision-in-One' can be understood, not simply as a vision 'according to' or 'from the perspective of' the One, but also as a mode of vision which is placed back 'into' or always necessarily 'in' the One that it envisions.

In *Philosophie et non-philosophie*, Laruelle says of his new non-thetic, scientific thinking that it has the pretension to know the real transcendentally (Laruelle 1989: 101). He also says of the One in the same work that it is 'transcendental like a lived life can be which is only immanent [*transcendantal comme peut l'être un vécu qui n'est qu'immanent*]' (Laruelle 1989: 46). Likewise in the earlier *Philosophies of Difference*, the One is described as '*a non-reflexive transcendental experience or absolutely immediate and non-thetic givenness (of) itself*' (Laruelle 1986: 33; 2010c: 18). In order to shed light on these formulations, the traditional distinction between transcendence and the 'transcendental' needs to be recalled and clearly marked. Transcendence, as was underlined earlier, is a property of that which exceeds and surpasses, of that which is superior or exterior. Transcendental can also mean this but, more specifically, within Kantian philosophy, of course, it refers to the knowledge of the way in which we know things, that is, the knowledge of those elements or structures which condition knowledge itself or function as its condition of possibility. As the conditions (of possibility) of knowledge, such elements precede experience and are therefore given a priori. Of course, for Laruelle, Kantian transcendental arguments remain eminently philosophical insofar as they are structured according to a unifying logic which mixes transcendence and immanence: they offer a logic of the real according to which the a priori structure and empirical fact are given together in a synthetic unity of immanence and transcendence (Brassier 2010: 123). Laruelle is very clear that the development of his non-philosophy has required 'a concept of the transcendental which would be strictly immanent . . . and real rather than logical or even logico-real' (Laruelle 1991: 22). The transcendental of the One, that is to say, of an indivisible, unreflective and immanently lived experience is therefore very different from the Kantian transcendental.

The One of the real is transcendental in Laruelle's new and slightly modified sense insofar as it is *its own* condition. The real does not need anything other than itself and its own indivisibility in order to be what it is: this is its absolute autonomy and self-sufficiency. Yet since the real is real (a lived, 'unreflective' experience), it is also the condition of all being, existence, thought, consciousness, transcendence and so on since all these instances are (in) the real or, put differently, the real is always immanent to them. While the One may be entirely indifferent to and foreclosed from the sphere of transcendence (being, thought, consciousness), that sphere itself is necessarily caused, conditioned and determined by the One. Or, as Laruelle himself puts it, 'transcendental immanence is the real cause of transcendence and transcendence is as much *through* as it is *in* immanence [*celle-ci est* par *autant que* dans *l'immanence*]' (Laruelle 1989: 72). Transcendental immanence is the 'condition or real base for the sphere of effectivity in general' (Laruelle 1989: 87) while *always and at the same time* remaining undivided, autonomous and absolutely foreclosed from the sphere of transcendence. It conditions and determines transcendence according to a unilateral causality and so is never affected or modified by it in return and never in any way participates in or mixes with it. Unlike Kant's transcendental structures, Laruelle's transcendental immanence is entirely shorn of transcendence while at the same time always being that which conditions transcendence in the last instance. This is a one-way street of causality whereby everything which 'is' is necessarily 'in' immanence and caused by it, but never able to exert any reverse causal determining force on the indivisible and autonomous One of immanence itself. All this follows rigorously as a deduction from the axiom of indivisibility which organizes the vision-in-One.

Much of what Laruelle says axiomatically of the One may recall the key terms of the philosophies of difference or theories of the Other with which readers of, for example, Deleuze, Derrida, Lyotard, Levinas or Lacan will be familiar. In different ways, all of these thinkers hold difference, alterity, or the Other to be in excess of the work of the concept, the logic of the Same, and therefore in excess also of all phenomenological, ontological (and therefore philosophical) disclosure. Yet, in his close and sustained reading of philosophies of difference, Laruelle argues that categories such as difference or the Other (and also those of *différance*, alterity, exteriority, etc.) are shot through with transcendence (for example, excess or the Other are posited directly *as* transcendence). The desire of such philosophies to think difference and alterity as primary or originary and to do so *against* the monolithic and unitary pretensions of the Same (presence, substance, identity, etc.) in no way ultimately makes them any less philosophical or any less able to escape the orbit of the philosophical decision. Indeed, Laruelle views the philosophy of difference as the last avatar of philosophy in general. However much the category of difference may itself come to be differently conceived, he argues, it nevertheless remains a 'combination each time, of an immanence and a transcendence, of an ideality and a supposed real' and therefore the thought of difference itself, like all philosophy, is structurally constituted in its 'unitary essence of mixture' (Laruelle 1986: 29; 2010c: 15).

So however much the axiomatic formulations relating to the One might resemble the philosophical thinking of difference, alterity and of the Other, Laruelle would argue that non-philosophy's rejection of the philosophical decision per se and its attempt to structure thought differently in fact makes all the difference. Indeed, the extent to which the internal logic of the vision-in-One is indeed different from that of the philosophies of difference is very clear. The immanent real, it was noted above, is a unilateral cause or condition of transcendence. Transcendence is 'in' immanence and always conditioned by it but can never affect or alter immanence in return. This logic of unilateral causation has huge implications. It means first and foremost that Laruelle's 'science' and the non-philosophical practice which flows from it does not require any foundation of the kind that philosophy always seeks or, rather, seeks to confer upon itself (and does so, it is argued, even in the torsions of anti-foundationalist difference philosophy). The One posed by the vision-in-One is, for Laruelle, 'the essence or the ground [*le fonds*] of the real' (Laruelle 1991: 25) and is so in such a way that Laruellian 'science' 'has no need of a philosophical foundation, it is without foundation because it has a cause: the One, the real-as-Identity: not only an immanent cause, but a *cause-by-immanence*, the causality of radical immanence itself' (Laruelle 1991: 27). Taking the indivisibility and autonomy of the real as its first axiom, and deducing from this its unilaterally causal and conditioning force in relation to all transcendence (being, world, consciousness, etc.), Laruelle is able to affirm that all thought is (always already) 'in' and 'of' the real (that is, caused by it in the last instance) but also, and crucially, that everything we can know or think is ultimately *not* grounded in a subject. Or at least, being caused by the One, it is not in any way dependent upon a subject of knowledge such as philosophy may have conceived it from Descartes onwards. If the One is the essence of, or the *fond du réel*, then it is 'this real rather than Being that the sciences, all sciences, postulate' (Laruelle 1991: 25).[15]

The unilateral causality of the transcendental and immanent real opens the way once again for an overturning of the Kantian philosophical legacy and specifically of the Copernican revolution within philosophy.[16] This is so because consciousness is no longer constitutive of experience and knowledge (in, for example, the transcendental unity of apperception). Rather, the One of the immanent real is the cause, condition and ultimate determining instance for all consciousness, experience and knowledge. Thus, rather than affirming that the real must conform to knowledge (this would be philosophy), non-philosophy affirms unequivocally that our knowledge and experience, *in a certain way and in the last instance*, will always be conditioned by the real since it is always ultimately caused by it. Laruelle calls this operation of unilateral causation 'determination-in-the-last-instance [*détermination-en-dernière-instance*]'. In *Principes de non-philosophie*, he describes this in the following terms: 'knowledge does not determine the real, rather the order of the real determines-in-the-last-instance the order of knowledge' (Laruelle 1996: 149). This logic of unilateral causality and of determination-in-the-last-instance is without doubt one of the most important and powerful aspects of Laruelle's thought. Its stark reversal of the Kantian-Copernican revolution is comparable to Badiou's adoption of mathematics for similar anti-Kantian ends (as discussed in chapter 6) and is of signal importance for the work of contemporary young philosophers, such as Ray Brassier, working to develop the school of thought known as 'speculative realism' (see Brassier 2003; 2010).

Such a reversal follows directly from the logic of unilateral causation that is deduced from the axiom of indivisibility which organizes the vision-in-One. It also signifies that the vision-in-One itself is a form of ultra-realism. This is an ultra-realism which remains realist despite the fact that it understands the real as radically unknowable, indivisible and absolutely autonomous. Or, perhaps more surprisingly and counter-intuitively, it is 'ultra-realist' precisely because it understands the real as a unilaterally causal yet indivisible/unknowable immanence. The ultra-realism of Laruellian science and non-philosophy is worth highlighting since it is decisive for any proper understanding of the consequences which follow on from the vision-in-One. It is decisive also for any critical appreciation of the performative practice of non-philosophy itself.

Equivalence and the material of philosophy

Perhaps the most surprising thought which the ultra-realism of non-philosophy posits is that of the equivalence of different kinds of philosophical decision when considered in relation to the real. For it follows from the indivisibility and absolute autonomy of the One that no single philosophy and no specific form of the philosophical decision can have any greater or lesser purchase on the real than any other (since ultimately they all have none at all). From the perspective of the vision-in-One, *all* philosophical systems and perspectives are equally contingent and their contingency is in each case equally 'in' and 'of' the real. This means, therefore, that all such systems are exactly equivalent in relation to the real or, as Laruelle puts it, different terms belonging to different philosophies are *'equivalent by way of their essence in the One, but contingent. Equivalent therefore once again but this time from the perspective of the One [mais cette fois-ci au regard de l'Un]* (Laruelle 1989: 118). Such a radical equivalence of different philosophies in relation to the real would explain the fact that philosophy itself has historically been produced in so many different, mutually exclusive, but on their own terms perfectly coherent, forms. Philosophical systems, Laruelle would argue, have to be internally self-legitimating and coherent while at the same time being dismissive of other philosophical systems and other ways of structuring the philosophical decision. On its own terms, philosophy is inherently hierarchical, legislative of its own (circular) truths and conflictual in relation to other philosophies since each philosophy must presume that its own particular version of the philosophical decision is superior to any other. From the perspective of the vision-in-One, however: 'There would be for each possible real point [*pour tout point réel possible*] an infinite multiplicity of syntaxes or heterogeneous oppositions' (Laruelle 1989: 112). Each philosophical decision, syntax or structuring of the transcendence/immanence dyad would exist in a state of equality *alongside* all others and equally *alongside* the immanent real. Each would affirm its universality or totality but would do so on an (itself universal) plane of equivalence in relation to the real and would thus participate in a 'radical multiplicity of philosophical decisions' (Laruelle 1989: 112).

Such a radical multiplicity, equality or equivalence might appear to be nothing other than an extreme relativism of the kind that has often been attributed to 'postmodern' thinking by its opponents or detractors. Yet, as has been shown, Laruelle considers his science to be 'ultra-realist'. His affirmation of the real as a transcendental immanence which unilaterally causes or conditions transcendence means that his thought is neither an anti-realism, nor an anti-foundationalism, nor still a radical subjectivism of the kind which is so often associated with relativist positions. In *En tant qu'un*, he argues very clearly that it is not a question of non-philosophy substituting one philosophical ground for another, nor indeed of it positing as relative all ground per se. Rather, it is a question of abandoning the *illusory* ground of philosophy in favour of 'a real base – the only real base', that of the real itself (Laruelle 1991: 193). In order to understand how Laruelle's thinking distinguishes itself from a relativist free-for-all, it should be stressed that he understands all philosophies to be equivalent in relation to the real *only*, and in relation to their determination-in-the-last-instance by the real.[17] He in no way wishes to suggest that different philosophical systems are homogeneous or the same, in for instance, their relation to instances of the world, of consciousness, of subjectivity/objectivity, of the transcendence/immanence dyad and so on. Clearly different philosophies define their specificity precisely in relation to their different conceptions of all these instances. Laruelle wishes to preserve the relative heterogeneity of philosophical decisions and differences. His is not a realism nor a relativism in relation to the world nor in relation to any subjectively or objectively constituted reality which might be available to consciousness or knowledge. Rather, it is a 'realism of the last instance and not an objective viewing or a viewing in the first instance [*et non pas une visée objective ou de première instance*]' (Laruelle 1991: 58).

While different philosophical decisions may be equivalent, Laruelle, in 'Philosophy II' at least, nevertheless reserves a special place for science or theory. This will have been clear from the presentation of Laruellian science as a formalism or structuralism given above. Throughout the period which defines 'Philosophy II', a privileged status is accorded to science in relation to the One of the real which confirms the priority and superiority of science over philosophy. Science, approaching the real formally as an unknowable transcendental, is 'a representation which relates to the real . . . without the mediation of logic or any other *organon*, therefore directly' (Laruelle 1991: 102).[18] Non-philosophy in the period of 'Philosophy II' is therefore 'a systematic project founded in the precession of science over philosophy' (Laruelle 1989: 123). This means that, for all its apparent relativism and for all its affirmation of infinite multiplicity (of philosophical decisions), science and the non-philosophical practice it engenders is nevertheless uniquely privileged in its relation to radical immanence and the transcendental unilateral causality of the One.

In fact, the real significance of the contingency and equivalence of philosophical systems for Laruelle lies in the way in which philosophy itself necessarily comes to provide the materials for non-philosophy. Certainly, and as will become clear, he sets great store by the way non-philosophy can introduce equality and 'democracy' into the sphere of philosophy, now rendered non-hierarchical and contingent rather than legislative and totalizing. Yet, as Hugues Choplin has noted, since it follows from the axiom of indivisibility that the One is absolutely autonomous and indifferent to the operations of thought, non-philosophy cannot call upon the One itself in order to produce its own non-philosophical discourse. Rather, non-philosophy *requires* philosophy, taken now in its contingency and as an inessential form, in order to provide it with the material from which the non-philosophical universe will be made. The One, however much it may be a transcendental cause or determinant-in-the-last-instance of *all* thought, is simply too indivisible and autonomous to generate *specific* terms or content for any particular form of thought, in this case non-philosophy.[19] Thus, it will be the task of non-philosophy to extract the materials offered by philosophy (its different dyads, its diverse a priori elements, its divergent syntactical and linguistic forms) and to 'perform' them differently in such a way that they are shorn of transcendence and 'placed back' into the immanence of the real which conditions them in the last instance. This process of extraction and the performative use of philosophical material it engenders follow directly from the axioms and deductions of the vision-in-One.

Indeed, the performative nature of non-philosophy emerges here as decisive because it is ultimately the sole guarantor of the 'non' of non-philosophy (that is, its distinctness from philosophy itself) but also because the changing performativity of non-philosophical practice defines the different divisions between 'Philosophy II', 'Philosophy III', etc. and therefore determines the development of Laruelle's thought as a whole.

Performance

The non-philosophical performance of the material extracted from philosophy is predicated on the possibility, opened up by the vision-in-One, that thought can proceed on a different basis than that of the philosophical dyad and its mixing of transcendence and immanence. From the perspective of the vision-in-One, the dyads of philosophy are treated not as concepts which have 'split' the real and transformed it according to the logical operations proper to them. Rather, they are treated according to the axiom of indivisibility and in the presupposition that a radical separation or duality subsists between the real and all possible permutations of the philosophical dyad/decision. Laruelle's vision-in-One installs 'a *radical duality*, a duality which is static or without splitting [*sans scission*], that ruptures the continuity of the philosophical dyad' (1989: 70). Throughout the different phases of his thought, this radical duality is maintained as the first and last affirmation and necessity of non-philosophical practice. Indeed, if the axiom of indivisibility and vision-in-One are to have any coherence or discursive rigour at all, the performative effectivity of this duality between thought and the real must be maintained. Thus, when Laruelle extracts or in any way treats philosophical material, he will speak of 'dualyzing' its oppositions, of treating them according to a 'unilateral duality', or of subjecting them to a 'dualysis' (Laruelle 1996: 54, 226). That this is such a constant of his thought is borne out by his insistence in his most recent major work, *Philosophie non-standard*, that non-philosophy maintain itself as a space which is: 'resolutely dualist' and which 'refuses unitary mixes' (Laruelle 2010a: 133).

It is therefore only in the context of a performative dualyzing of philosophical dyads that they can be effectively shorn of transcendence and its pretensions to unity or totalization (the splitting, mixing, synthesis of transcendence and immanence). Yet such a performative maintaining of non-philosophical duality proves to be the most difficult, complex and challenging aspect of non-philosophy itself. It is both a challenge to which Laruelle responds in different ways in each phase of his thought but it is also a challenge faced by his reader who may be confronted by an array of potentially familiar philosophical terms or forms which are nevertheless functioning rather differently from the way they would function in their usual contexts.

The difference between 'Philosophy II' and 'Philosophy III' is illustrative of the way in which Laruelle's non-philosophical discourse transforms itself in order to respond to the demand that a duality be maintained between thought and the real. It was noted above that the immanent real is viewed as a 'transcendental' in a rather different sense from that ascribed to the term by Kant. The real, it will be remembered, is transcendental insofar as it is the condition or unilateral cause of all thought, consciousness, world and so on. Yet it was also noted that the real is affirmed as a transcendental in 'Philosophy II' only. In 'Philosophy III', Laruelle severs the link between the real and the transcendental. This is because 'transcendental' itself is simply too philosophical a term and is too much associated with the operations of thought. Describing the real as a 'transcendental' would imply perhaps that thought can have some purchase upon it after all. There is a risk that such a usage, despite its deployment within the vision-in-One, nevertheless splits the real and affirms its participation, albeit minimally, in thought and thus fails to maintain the necessary duality between thought and the real that non-philosophy must maintain. This alteration may appear slight but in fact it has great consequences for the non-philosophical practice of 'Philosophy III'. It becomes clear that the Laruellian privileging of science as that which has a 'transcendental pretension to know the real' (Laruelle 1989: 101) has to be abandoned. The 'precession of science over philosophy' (Laruelle 1989: 123) is lost with the separation of the real and the transcendental. Science and philosophy are now subject to the same equivalence in relation to the real and the same logic of determination-the-last-instance by the real.[20]

Again, though, this is not a relativism in any normal sense since the Laruelle of 'Philosophy III' maintains (as he does throughout all his thinking) his axiomatic understanding of the real as the unilateral causality or condition of all thought, that is to say, it continues to function as 'the sole real base' (Laruelle 1991: 193). He simply thinks and performs the affirmation of this unilateral causality (and the radical duality which it necessitates) differently. The key motif of 'Philosophy III' in this context becomes that of transcendental 'cloning'. The real can no longer be spoken of in terms of a transcendental because Laruelle has come to understand the transcendental itself as an operation of thought (of transcendence). He therefore takes the transcendental itself as that space or plane of thought which will function in a radical duality with the real (but unilaterally conditioned by it). If this is imagined topologically it becomes a layering of three planes:

the real (One/absolute autonomy) → **the transcendental** (clone/radical duality) ↔ **the transcendent** (philosophical dyad/mixing)

In 'Philosophy III', materials are extracted from philosophy (transcendence) by what Laruelle calls the 'force (of) thought', and they are then treated as equivalent *transcendentally* and on the plane of the transcendental and are thus 'placed back' into a radical duality in relation to the autonomous real. The 'force (of) thought' is a difficult and rather complex operation of Laruelle's non-philosophical thinking. It could best be defined as that effort or act of thought itself by which thought assumes the immanent real as its determination-in-the-last-instance; it is the effort by which thought assumes its identity with the real and maintains itself resolutely within a posture of immanence with regard to the real (Laruelle 1991: 72; 1996: 54, 99). The 'force (of) thought' is therefore the key operation which underpins or produces the performance of non-philosophical discourse.

According to this operation, philosophical materials are viewed transcendentally or as transcendentals but, since they are now held in a radical duality with the real, they are shorn of all transcendence and therefore take on the status of 'clones' of the real. Transcendental cloning therefore becomes the key operation of 'Philosophy III' and supersedes the operations of science proper to 'Philosophy II'. The transcendental is no longer the real itself but rather that plane of thought, radically separate from and in a duality with the real but 'deduced from the immanent real and adding nothing real to it [*déduite du Réel immanent et n'ajoutant à celui-ci rien de réel*]' (Laruelle 1996: 49).

The separation of the transcendental from the real, the resituation of science in relation to philosophy and the operation of transcendental cloning all emerge as lynchpins of 'Philosophy III', but do so solely in response to the demand for an ever more rigorous 'dualyzation' of non-philosophical thought in relation to the immanent One. Unsurprisingly, the attempt for ever greater rigour or radicality is continued in Laruelle's latest major work, *Philosophie non-standard*. The complex formulations in this work around the category of the 'generic' and the extraction of the conceptual apparatus of quantum mechanics can also be understood as a further development of his primary concern to perform non-philosophy in a way which follows through all the implications of the indivisibility and autonomy of radical immanence.[21] Yet, while it should now be clear that the persistent concern of non-philosophy is to maintain the 'radicality' of immanence in the performative dualyzation of philosophical material, it is perhaps less clear why this should be of such signal importance to Laruelle.

Democracy and invention

From the outset, it has been clear that his characterization of the philosophical decision as totalizing, hierarchical and even violent has given the central impetus to the demand for a rigorously non-philosophical practice. The demand of non-philosophy to rigorously separate philosophical materials from the operations of transcendence and its totalizing work of mixing and synthesis must be viewed in the context of a wider demand for a pluralizing democracy of thought production. Once the philosophical decision has been fully suspended in the dualyzation of non-philosophical practice, the hierarchical aspirations and conflictual attitude of philosophy are neutralized and a democratic production of thought forms becomes possible. Non-philosophy 'liberates an infinite, really universal, field of possibilities from all philosophical closure' and in so doing it represents an 'attempt to create . . . a *new democratic order of thought* that excludes conflict between philosophers and regional branches of knowledge' (Laruelle 1996: 11, 16). This act of liberation from philosophy's totalizing gesture and non-philosophy's affirmation of creative and inventive thought production is a constant from 'Philosophy II' through to the most recent work of 'Philosophy V'. This can be seen in, for example, Laruelle's call for the invention of 'new forms of expression, new practices, forms of writing, and new possibilities of this special way of thinking' in *Philosophie et non-philosophie* (Laruelle 1989: 127). It is also a repeated refrain in *Philosophie non-standard* which gives as its central ambition the development of a 'science of possible inventions [*science du pouvoir inventer*]' (Laruelle 2010a: 67–8) and vigorously calls for a 'struggle against all sorts of norms which limit the possible and paralyse invention' (Laruelle 2010a: 99).

As was indicated briefly in the Introduction (n. 8), Hallward's characterization of the field of contemporary French philosophy as a body of thought which privileges singularity and creativity and affirms an 'immediate and non-relational process of individuation', together with a 'radical refusal of mediation and representation' (Hallward 2003b: 9) could be very easily and appropriately applied to the Laruellian non-philosophy. Certainly, it is difficult to see how Laruelle's thinking can account for, or engage with, worldly relationality and questions of communal material existence when all these instances are arguably functions of the transcendence of worldly existence and consciousness, and of the specific material mediations which non-philosophy seeks to suspend or bracket. It is true that, as Ray Brassier has noted, Laruelle identifies the unobjectifiable immanence of the real with the 'ordinary man' or with the 'human' in person and therefore gives himself some leeway to engage with subjective or individuated existence. Yet this emphasis on 'man' and the 'human' is both rather arbitrary and, indeed, highly problematic insofar as it appears to contradict Laruelle's own axioms of radical immanence, as Ray Brassier convincingly argues (Brassier 2010: 127–8).

Rather than an engaged worldly philosophy, then, non-philosophy affirms itself far more as a thought of creativity and invention which will produce future worlds. It is a thought of the liberation of thought and of the democracy of knowledge. It is a discipline which is always orientated towards the future and to the futural production of new forms of thought. Yet Laruelle's thinking of radical immanence and of the One has arguably already achieved a great deal. The potential and importance of his ultra-realism and reversal of Kantianism have already been highlighted. Non-philosophy as ultra-realism arguably opens up new perspectives for the thinking of science and its relation to the real. Like so many of the figures discussed in this book, Laruelle has also endeavoured to liberate thought from the linguistic or textualist paradigm that has dominated so much structuralist, poststructuralist and difference philosophy in France since the 1960s. In beginning from the real and in treating the indivisibility of the real as its first axiom, non-philosophy 'liberates itself from contemporary textualism' (Laruelle 1991: 72–3). Text and language, for Laruelle, are only ever the occasional material that non-philosophy extracts in order then to dualyze and set back into the immanence of the real. Language, text, signifiers and signifieds, all become the simple material for non-philosophical dualyzation and its diverse inventions, rather than operating as a founding paradigm for, or outer limit of, thought.

Throughout his career, Laruelle has persistently identified his work as a heterodox and even heretical form of thought, one which will necessarily be misunderstood and rejected when viewed according to the norms philosophy sets for itself. The heterodox status of his writing, its complexity and the very challenge it presents to our received forms of reason perhaps account for the fact that he has been relatively unknown in the wider field of contemporary European philosophy to date. Yet this is a thinking with enormous transformative potential, both for the future of philosophy itself and for possible future non-philosophical inventions in diverse areas of knowledge. Whether non-philosophy will remain heterodox, heretical and marginal will depend very much on the success of the forms that it comes to invent and on its ability to create a multiplicity of new styles and techniques of thought. Its future will depend above all on its ability to create: 'forms of discourse and genres which are other than philosophy' (Laruelle 2010a: 16).

Conclusion: The Technique of Thought

All the thinkers discussed in this book have sought a renewal of philosophical thinking. They have sought to reinvigorate or reinvent the scope, claims and ambition of philosophy itself in the wake of (post-)structuralism, 'postmodernism' and deconstruction. In the case of Laruelle, such a renewal has come at the price of leaving the terrain of philosophy itself. His sustained attempt, under the sign of 'non-philosophy', to give the real 'the thought that it merits' suggests that there may be a precise and determinable relation between the method, practice or form in which thinking unfolds and the renewed status of the real that is thought. In *Philosophy and Non-Philosophy*, he underlines that the attempt to think the real as radical imma-nence, and therefore as an indivisible One, is the sole means to 'render justice to its specificity' (Laruelle 1989: 38). Such an affir-mation implies that the manner in which the real is thought may in some way in fact *dictate*, or at least strongly prescribe, the form which (non-)philosophical thought itself adopts. Such an insight informed the argument of the preceding chapter where the whole of Laruelle's non-philosophical enterprise was shown to rest on his claim that the discourse of philosophy 'does not reach the real' (Laruelle 1995: 177).

It could be argued, in fact, that all the thinkers discussed in this study seek to reinvent very specific styles, practices or *techniques* of thought in order to renew or transform philosophy. The specificity of each reinvention of philosophical technique can be seen as a response to the constraints imposed by the specificity of the real which each, in different ways, comes to think. However the real may be conceived (as unconditioned givenness in excess of being, as an excessive ontology of exposed bodies, as the opening of temporality in technics and so on), in each case thought adopts a method, practice or technique which seeks to do justice to the specificity of that conception. For example, one can see in Jean-Luc Marion's radicalization of phenomenology that the entire philosophy of givenness has as its condition of possibility the operation of the 'third reduction'. Only by extending the phenomenological method of reduction (beyond the reduction of objectness (Husserl) and Being (Heidegger)) can givenness be posed as unconditionally and absolutely given. Only on this basis can Marion then extend the field and scope of phenomenology in the way that he does and in turn elaborate his most significant and original insights, e.g. the irreducibility of phenomenal giving to any differential economy (*différance*), the existence of saturated phenomena, the auto-affection of the flesh and the 'gifted' as a rethought site of human consciousness and agency. The radicalization of phenomenology goes hand-in-hand with a radicalization of the protocols and procedures of phenomenology itself.

This relation between the transformation of philosophical technique and the renewed thinking of the real can be discerned more clearly when the various figures included in this study are compared with each other. Nancy's philosophy of trans-immanent sense might, for example, be compared with Laruelle's non-philosophy of the absolutely immanent One. In *The Sense of the World*, Nancy argues that 'Once the possibility of signifying truth is a thing of the past, another style is necessary'. Another style becomes necessary, he affirms, when 'sense exceeds significations' and therefore a specific praxis of thought imposes itself as an 'assumption of a responsibility for and to this excess' (Nancy 1993a: 37; 1997e: 19). Nancy's excessive bodily ontology, his thinking of shared existence and of the trans-immanence and infinity of sense must always performatively affirm sense itself as (infinitely) in excess of signification. This dictates the way he practises philosophical writing as a logic of exposure, as exscription, and as a thinking of, or at, the limit. Nancy is not concerned to place the transcendence of thought 'back into' immanence (as is Laruelle). Rather, he is concerned to demonstrate how the 'transcendence' of thought and world is produced *as such* in and through the exposure of infinite sense. This, then, is trans-immanence insofar as the materiality of an immanent real creates or presents a world *in* this exposure of sense *at* the limit of all signification (thus the 'trans' of 'trans-immanence' might mark the excessive, ungraspable instance of the infinite exposure of sense itself).

Laruelle, clearly, is less concerned by the event of exposure by which the 'transcendence' of thought and the world might be said to emerge than he is by the need to place this transcendence back into the immanence which is its ground and cause in the last instance. For Laruelle, the practice of thought adopted by Nancy, that of the exposure or ex-scription of sense at the limit, would concede too much to transcendence and the division of the real by the operations of the philosophical dyad. In return, Nancy might say that Laruelle's 'vision-in-One' and his non-philosophical practice come at the expense of not being able to think the instance of world itself, in its presentation, its exposure, sharing and lived embodied spacing. Certainly, the difference between the philosopher and the non-philosopher here is marked by their different conceptions of the real (as sense, as immanent One). Perhaps more decisively, though, this difference unfolds in and is most clearly marked by a divergence of the writing practices adopted by the philosophy of trans-immanence and the non-philosophy of the One respectively.

It might also be instructive to compare the philosophical practice of the two philosophers discussed here whose work has been so clearly marked by Althusser, namely Rancière and Badiou. As was argued in the Introduction, both these philosophers begin their careers with a break from Althusser and/or the structuralist-linguistic paradigm. Badiou's formulations about the necessity of mathematics as the sole discourse of ontology at times echo Laruelle's formulation of non-philosophy as the sole means of doing justice to the specificity of the real. Once Badiou has decided in favour of thinking being as inconsistent multiplicity (and therefore as an actual infinity in excess of any horizon of the one), then the mathematics of Cantorian set theory imposes itself exclusively and necessarily as the discourse of ontology. For all its apparent abstraction, if we take the immanent and material real to be inconsistent multiplicity, mathematics is the only way in which materiality can be approached or 'reached'. In order, then, to displace the categories of discourse and text, which Badiou denounced in the late 1970s as a form of 'idea-linguistery', he develops a mathematical paradigm which will supersede the structuralist-linguistic paradigm. This will allow for a renewed axiomatic and systematic thinking and, in turn, open the way for restored philosophical conceptions of truth, subjectivity, universality and so on. Once again, though, this renewal of philosophy is only made possible by the unique specificity of mathematical presentation which, as the only discourse adequate for the saying of being *as* being, comes to condition philosophy with its truths and with its axiomatic technique. Only in a realignment of philosophy with the techniques of mathematical presentation, then, can philosophy move beyond the impasses and aporias of finitude. For Badiou, in a move which is perhaps more polemical than it is philosophical, all those philosophies which adopt a more literary-philosophical or non-logico-mathematical technique are assimilated to sophistry, antiphilosophy or, more recently, the broad paradigm of 'democratic materialism'. Thus, it is on the basis of the technique adopted by thought that he draws lines of division and conflict within the field of contemporary philosophy and seeks to mark a decisive break with the past.

By contrast, Rancière's rejection of the Althusserian understanding of ideology leads him not to mathematics as the sole means of speaking the material immanence of the real, but rather to a reconception of the real as the ordering of a heterogeneous dimension of the sensible. Where Badiou subtracts or brackets sensible experience, Rancière realigns thought with a sustained attempt to re-articulate the register of the sensible, and to place the tangible and sensory at the very centre of his thinking. If, for Rancière, ideology 'does not simply exist in discourses, nor simply in systems, of images, of signs, etc.' (Rancière 1974: 271; 2011c: 151), then its critique or subversion cannot be effected in an Althusserian 'science' of ideas but must rather be pursued in a re-engagement with the contingent ordering, organization or distribution of the heterogeneous dimension of the sensible. From this flows the specificity of Rancière's engagements with history and with art or aesthetics, but also the specificity of his conceptual apparatus: 'the distribution of the sensible', 'politics', 'police', 'subjectivation' and so on. In opposition to Badiou, Rancière does not realign philosophy with the subtractive and the mathematical. This would be too abstract insofar is it would ignore the sensible and the tangible dimension of shared and above all *lived*, experience. Rather, the discourse of philosophy itself becomes a practice of writing which responds to the interruptive force of the heterogeneous and sensible real by always exceeding the restricted limits which might be prescribed by the discrete disciplines of philosophy, history, political thought, aesthetics and so on. The heterogeneous, sensible and material real demands a heterogeneous and resolutely material practice of writing rather than an ordering of writing according to the axiomatic technique of mathematics.

This notion of a *realignment* of philosophy or philosophical writing according to the demands made by specific reconceptions of the real is particularly useful when one comes to compare the work of Stiegler and Malabou. Malabou's practice of 'plastic reading', understood as a 'new structural approach' and as a 'metamorphosis of deconstructive reading' (Malabou 2005a: 97, 98; 2010b: 51, 52), is a philosophical technique which responds directly to her metamorphic and materialist ontology. Both the technique of reading and the ontology are ordered or determined by the very plasticity of being they attempt to think. Despite being very clearly marked by the influence and legacy of deconstruction, Malabou then comes to realign her philosophical thought, not with the paradigm of writing or text but with the empirical discoveries of contemporary neuroscience. Once again, the shift from the paradigm of writing or text dictates a realignment of philosophy, in this case, a realignment of philosophy with the natural sciences. However, this is in no way a return to a reductive biologism or naturalism. Rather, Malabou's alignment of her philosophical practice with neuroscience becomes a means by which her radically non-reductive thinking of plasticity can come to be thought in its embodied materiality. Oppositional concepts, for example, nature and nurture, accidents and essence, ideality and materiality, mind and body, are no less subjected to a rigorous deconstruction. However, this deconstruction now unfolds within the more fundamental conceptual framework of material plasticity and with reference to contemporary scientific discovery.

Likewise, Stiegler's thinking of technics and time is articulated upon a non-reductive realignment of philosophy with the investigations of scientific research. The findings of twentieth-century biological anthropology and discoveries concerning the early development of the human brain cortex, as well as tool use in early hominids, are key points of reference for Stiegler in his thinking of technical prosthetics and temporality. Malabou and Stiegler offer perhaps surprising innovations insofar as they both bring insights drawn from post-deconstructive and post-phenomenological contexts into direct relation and dialogue with insights drawn from biology. In each case, a break from deconstruction occurs in this realignment of philosophy with science and, in particular, a break from the specific articulations of writing, *différance* and the trace made in Derridean thought. Stiegler does not elaborate quite so explicitly about the practice, method or techniques of philosophical writing itself. It is arguable, however, that, like Malabou's plastic reading or, say, Nancy's writing or ex-scription of sense, Stiegler's thought unfolds as a material practice and as a specific instance of the dimension of technical prosthetics he is aiming to think within his philosophy as a whole. Both philosophical thought and writing are necessarily affirmed here as being a specific instance of the wider economy of technical prosthetics which, Stiegler argues, is the condition of all (temporal) human experience whatsoever.

What these comparisons of the seven philosophers discussed here might arguably be said to show is that the technique of thought which each adopts is necessarily a function or formation of the material real which each, in their different ways, seeks to think. Thought itself emerges here as a material practice which is related, as it were, by way of an immanent (or trans-immanent) cause to the very material dimension which comes to be thought. This notion of thought as a material practice or technique which is (in-the-last-instance, Laruelle would say) *determined* or *caused by* the very material immanence it seeks to circumscribe needs to be related to the question of the subject which has been returned to at various points throughout this study. It should be recalled that all the thinkers treated here have, albeit in very different ways, moved beyond the phenomenological and post-Kantian understanding of consciousness as *constitutive*. Marion's 'receiver' or 'gifted' is constituted by and in givenness (itself impersonal and beyond the economy of being, subject, constituted experience, etc.). Likewise, Nancy's self is constituted in its exposure, or access, to the infinite exteriority and excess of trans-immanent sense. Stiegler's self is constituted in its prosthetical-technical conditioning and Malabou's in its neuronal and cerebral plasticity. Similarly, both Rancière's and Badiou's differing conceptions of 'subjectivation' designate processes which are constituted in and by a material operation of interruption and inscription. By the same token, Laruelle identifies all thought and experience, and the force of philosophical thought in particular, as determined by the unobjectifiable and material immanence of the real. This reversal of constitutive consciousness into constituted selfhood or immanently caused or determined experience underpins the thoroughgoing and radical materialism which has been shown to be a central concern of all the thinkers treated here. Such a reversal of constitution, causation and determination also underpins the different ways in which each thinker seeks to return to and renew philosophical realism and to restore a concrete engagement with the shared material world.

What will have become abundantly clear, however, is that the material technique or practice of thought that each philosopher has come to adopt defines, to a large extent if not exclusively, the differences between them and the lines of opposition and conflict which define their relation to each other. On this basis, it could be said, following Stiegler, that there is a fundamental and material *technicity* of thought which the diverse techniques interrogated here articulate in diverse ways. Whether the real is positioned within the horizon of an ontology or quasi-ontology (as sense, technicity, plasticity or multiplicity) or whether it is positioned without regard to, or as an excess over, any horizon of being (as givenness, the sensible, the One), thought approaches or seeks to reach the real by way of a material practice, a technique which the real itself, in the specificity of its positioning, dictates or necessitates.

It might be concluded, then, that the break from the linguistic paradigm and the categories of discourse, text and writing has led these French philosophers to renew the practice and techniques of philosophy. This renewal perhaps finds its most significant expression in the realignment of philosophy with technological and scientific paradigms, anthropological, neuroscientific, mathematical or that of 'science' conceived in more general structural terms (Laruelle).[1] This book has sought to highlight the originality, importance and strength of the philosophical innovations that emerge within the work of each thinker treated here. It has also sought to indicate some of the potential limitations of their positions and to draw attention to the important differences between them. It has done so in order to highlight the specificity of the way in which the material practice of French philosophy has developed in the wake of post-structuralism, post-modernism and deconstruction.[2] On this basis, it can be argued that a transformation in philosophical practice or technique has occurred in response to the necessity of rethinking the real outside of the linguistic paradigm and in response to the necessity of repositioning of the real itself as *immanent to* the techniques or technicity of thought.

If it is possible to speak of the 'New French Philosophy', then this may be so only insofar as philosophy itself has sought to radically renew itself in the wake of the anti-foundationalism of post-structuralism, postmodernism and deconstruction. All these philosophies seek in various ways to move beyond the anti-foundationalist or deconstructive moment and do so in the name of what might be called the groundless or non-foundational ground of the real, conceived variably as givenness, sense, technicity, plasticity, the sensible, the multiple or the One. This variably configured real can perhaps be called a ground, but not in the sense of providing any solid foundation or bedrock to thought and knowledge. Rather, as Laruelle might put it, it is a matter of leaving the illusory ground of metaphysical foundations in favour of 'a real base – the only real base', that of the real itself. The question then is not exactly one of the philosophical determination of the real in the service of a foundational gesture. Rather, it becomes a question of how thought may best position itself up against, approach or 'reach' the real. It is a question of what renewed technique of thought might best accomplish this repositioning of, or approach to, the real. The task of thought which these philosophers take up, and the demand of thought to which they respond, is one of thinking material immanence and worldly, shared existence. They do so by way of techniques which affirm themselves as resolutely material. Only on this basis can philosophy renew itself and move beyond the closure of the metaphysics of the past to the opening of new forms in the future.

Notes

Introduction

1 On the question of the 'new' and its distinctness from questions of transformation, change, causality, determinism and emergence, see Dan Smith, 'The Conditions of the New' (Smith 2007: 1).
2 As Smith points out, Deleuze also traces this preoccupation back to Bergson's philosophy of creation (Smith 2007: 19, n. 2). One might also align this preoccupation with the assimilation of Nietzsche in France from the late nineteenth century onwards and with the question of the trans-valuation of values (see Douglas Smith 1996) or with the assimilation of Hegel and Hegelian dialectical thought (see Baugh 2003). Likewise the French reception of Heidegger from the mid-twentieth century onwards can be viewed as a preoccupation with the new in the context of the Heideggerian 'destruction' of ontotheology.
3 A contemporary shift towards a renewal of materialist thinking has also been the subject of *New Materialisms*; see Coole and Frost (2010).
4 For a more fully developed discussion of immanence and transcendence, see chapter 7 of this study.
5 Stiegler might be said more obviously to remain within a thinking of the 'quasi-transcendental', albeit in a different manner than Derrida; see Stiegler (2001b: 254).
6 It may be interesting to note that, in France the distinction between structuralism and post-structuralism has not had much currency with the differences between the two being viewed as different inflections within or of structuralism as a whole. This is not a distinction marked in Dosse's *History of Structuralism*; see both volumes of Dosse (1997).

7 At a specific moment of his career Deleuze specifically aligns his thought with structuralism; see for instance the essay published in French in 1972, 'How Do We Recognize Structuralism?' in Deleuze (2004a: 170–92).

8 Hallward's is a powerful argument which forcefully makes a demand upon the way we may read or engage with the tradition of twentieth-century French thought. In terms of the thinkers discussed in this book, it might best be applied to the non-philosophy of François Laruelle (chapter 7), or perhaps Marion's philosophy of givenness (chapter 1). However, it could be argued, approaching Hallward's argument from an entirely different perspective, that, despite its clear privileging of the singular, much French thought of the twentieth century has persistently engaged with the question of relationality, whether it be the question of self and other posed by existential phenomenology in the wake of Kojève's reading of Hegel (e.g. Sartre), the very same question posed in a post-phenomenological mode (e.g. Levinas), or the question of differential relations posed by structuralism. No doubt the asymmetrical relation (of non-relation) between self and other, or between the space of the same and that of alterity, is precisely the kind of (non-)relation that Hall-ward is criticizing in his demand for a more mediated 'alternative relationality'. Responding more directly to his specific framing of this question, one might also question whether the 'singular' in much French thought from the 1960s onwards is not always a *differential relation*, i.e. whether singularity is not always produced as a *relation* of difference with and between other singular instances. On this question as it is raised in Deleuzian thought, see Smith (2007: 11).

9 Many of these figures are included in the excellent 'Key Biographies in Brief' in Alan Schrift's *Twentieth-Century French Philosophy*; see Schrift (2006). For a broad account of twentieth-century French philosophy, see Gutting 2001; for Gutting's account of more recent French philosophy, see Gutting 2011.

10 Meillassoux is the author of one important work to date, *After Finitude* (see Meillassoux 2010). He is a former student and close colleague of Alain Badiou (chapter 6).

11 Again, Alain Schrift's book is excellent and most illuminating in this regard and the appendix 'Understanding French Academic Culture' is particularly instructive. By focusing on institutional relations and dynamics, Schrift's book marks a major step forward in the Anglo-American reception of French thought; see Schrift (2006: 188–208).

12 Althusser was a dominant intellectual figure in France and beyond throughout the 1960s; his thought will be discussed at greater length in chapter 5 and in relation to Rancière's early career.

13 In the context of this repeated rallying cry for a 'new materialism', it is worth noting in advance that the imperative of all these thinkers is to think materiality itself outside traditional conceptions of 'matter', whether conceived of as substance and as a relation of matter to form,

or in any distinction between matter and 'mind' or 'spirit'. In none of these thinkers will the material be re-conceptualized as ground or foundation.

14 For a full discussion of *Ego Sum* in Nancy's critique of the 'return' of the subject in the 1970s, see James (2006: 49–63).

15 In the 1970s, Marion does not so obviously engage in polemics against structuralism. He does, however, clearly mark his difference from Derrida and the thinking of *différance* in works such as *The Idol and Distance*. The motif of 'distance' he suggests does all the anti-metaphysical and anti-ontological work that *différance* can be said to do (Marion 1977: 286; 2001b: 232).

16 Laruelle, as is made clear in chapter 7, is directly concerned with questions of liberation and emancipation, but these are couched in less obviously political terms. Marion also approaches the question of the political more obliquely in the context of his thinking of the saturated phenomenon of the 'event'.

17 The 'new philosophers' of the 1970s have often been associated with a return to a more liberal Kantianism and a shift away from the Marxian non-conformist leftism of French thought rooted in the 1960s and in the immediate aftermath of May '68. For a persuasive critique of these philosophers, see *The Mediocracy: French Philosophy since the 1970s* (Lecourt 2002). See also Mark Lilla's anthology, *New French Thought: Political Philosophy* (Lilla 1994). The thought anthologized in Lilla's book has been described well by Eric Alliez as spanning the space 'between a liberal-conservative neo-Tocquevillian paradigm, an allegedly progressive ethics of communication and a republican philosophy of human rights' (Alliez 2010: 10).

18 Malabou's engagement with the finding of contemporary neuroscience is of particular interest in this respect.

Chapter 1 Jean-Luc Marion: Appearing and Givenness

1 *Dieu sans l'être* was translated in 1991 as *God without Being* (Marion 1982; 1991d).

2 See Gschwandtner (2007: xv).

3 Jean Beaufret was a key figure in the introduction and dissemination of Heidegger in France during the post-war period.

4 See, in particular, 'Comment ne pas parler. Dénégations' in Derrida (1987: 145–200).

5 See Janicaud et al. (2000). This volume contains a translation of the original work by Janicaud, *Le Tournant théologique de la phénomenologie française* (Janicaud 1990), together with a number of responses from those criticized in it including Marion himself.

6 See Marion (1977: 22, 30, 37; 2001b: 5, 12, 18). The blasphemy and even heresy of framing God within a horizon of being is asserted even

more strongly by Marion in his recent work, *In Excess*; see Marion (2001a: 181, 183; 2002a: 150, 152).

7 Marion makes a number of comments elsewhere on the alignment of the certainty of the Cartesian *cogito* with the non-negatability of 'donation'; see Marion (1997: 88–9; 2002c: 60; 2001a: 22; 2002a: 19). Specifically, Marion comments at length on the fact that 'donation' knows no negation: Marion (1997: 80–1; 2002c: 55).

8 The key point of reference here is, of course, Mauss's famous anthropological essay on gift-giving; see Mauss (2002). For a broader account of the way in which Mauss is taken up into the field of twentieth-century French philosophy, see Moore (2011).

9 For Derrida's identification of the tradition of metaphysics with the question of intuitionism, see Derrida (2000; 2006).

10 Janicaud, for instance, accuses Marion of, amongst other things, mistranslating Husserlian *Gegebenheit* (Janicaud 2005: 34–5). He also accuses Marion of mistranslating key Heideggerian terms such as *Ereignis,* see Janicaud (2005: 37–8).

11 In this context, Marion's conception can be closely related to the Kantian sublime as analysed in the *Critique of Judgment*. See Kant (2007: 61–79).

12 Marion remarks that the saturated phenomenon establishes the truth of phenomenality itself; see Marion (1997: 317; 2002c: 227).

13 Marion qualifies this in an essay printed in *The Visible and the Revealed*. It is not a question, he suggests, of doing away with a horizon or horizontality since that would, he concedes, bar any possibility of appearing at all. It is rather a matter of dispensing with the 'delimiting anteriority' of, or prior dependency upon, a horizon: see Marion (2005: 65; 2008b: 40).

14 See, for example, Marion (2001a: 155–95; 2002a: 128–62).

15 See Nancy (1991f).

Chapter 2   Jean-Luc Nancy: The Infinity of Sense

1 See Derrida (2000), Hutchens (2005) and James (2006).

2 See Alain Badiou, 'L'Offrande réservée', in Guibal and Martin (2004: 13–24). See also Critchley (1999: 239–53).

3 See Nancy (1981; 1983a; 1997d).

4 See James (2006: 91–7).

5 Derrida makes this point in relation to Nancy's use of the figure of touch; see Derrida (2006: 41).

6 See Nancy (1996a: 123; 2000c: 21).

7 See, for instance, Gutting (2001).

8 See James (2006: 49–63).

9 There are echoes here of Marion's thinking of the self and of the auto-affection of flesh as discussed in chapter 1.

10 Rancière's thinking of art as di▓▓▓scussed in chapter 5 is perhaps an exception to this.

11 See James (2006: 206–22▓▓).

12 For a more extended ▓▓ discussion of the phenomenological context framing Nancy u▓se of this term, see James (2007).

13 See, for insta▓▓ce, Robbe-Grillet (1989), Ricardou (1973) and Barthes (1974).

14 Some▓▓of Nancy's earlier work also explores the legacy of Christian ▓onotheism; see Nancy (1987; 1992a; 2008b).

1▓5 This recalls Jean-Luc Marion's understanding of the idolatrous God of metaphysics, as discussed in chapter 1.

16 Nancy, however, repeatedly affirms that his concern is not to restore or return to religion; see Nancy (2005a: 9, 104; 2008c: 1, 74).

17 See Alain Badiou, 'L'Offrande réservée', in Guibal and Martin (2004: 13–24).

18 There are strong echoes here of Georges Bataille's thinking of the sacred and of communication; see Bataille (1988).

Chapter 3 Bernard Stiegler: The Time of Technics

1 See in particular Gille (1986), Leroi-Gourhan (1993) and Simondon (1969).

2 See http://arsindustrialis.org/.

3 Stiegler refers to the most well-known accounts of this myth given by Aeschylus, Hesiod and Plato (Stiegler 1994: 30; 1998: 16). For Plato's recounting of the Epimetheus myth, see Plato, *Protagoras* 320d, 322a.

4 On this point, see Beardsworth (1998).

5 Derrida's reference in *Of Grammatology* to the thinking of technics elaborated by André Leroi-Gourhan is crucial here; see Derrida (1998: 84–7).

6 The influence of Husserl's *Crisis* on post-war French thought has arguably yet to be fully accounted for. Derrida's earliest work, of course, is a translation and commentary of 'On the Origin of Geometry' and published as an appendix to the *Crisis*. Also Foucault was heavily influenced by this major late Husserlian work. For a discussion of the influence of Husserl on Foucault more generally, see Hyder (2003).

7 Stiegler's arguments relating to the forgetting or suppression of technics within western thought appear then as a modification of the Heideggerian argument relating to the forgetting of being and modern technology as nihilism. See 'The Question Concerning Technology' in Heidegger (1993: 307–41).

8 See Leroi-Gourhan's account of the development of early hominids and the origins of *homo sapiens* in (Leroi-Gourhan 1993: 61–144).

9 For Derrida's account of the tra̶c̶e, see Derrida (1998: 27–73).
10 This neologism combines the terms 'epigenesis' (i.e. the modification of genetic information by environmental influences) and 'phylogenesis' (i.e. the evolutionary development of the species).
11 For a full account of Stiegler's relation to Derridean thought, see James (2010b).
12 On the question of urgency, see Bennington (2000).
13 For an introductory overview of Virilio's work, see James (2007).
14 See Simondon (1989).
15 Much of the argument of the second and third volumes of *Technics and Time* draws on Husserl's account of time consciousness as elaborated in *On the Phenomenology of the Internal Consciousness of Time*; see Husserl (1991).
16 Stiegler's analyses here also appear indebted to the thinking of libidinal economy such as it is developed by Klossowski and Lyotard of the late 1960s and early 1970s. See Klossowski (2005) and Lyotard (2004).
17 This also echoes Rancière's thinking of 'sensible community' discussed in chapter 5.

Chapter 4   Catherine Malabou: The Destiny of Form

1 For Aristotle's discussions of matter and form, see Aristotle, *Physics* I.2; for his discussion of the relation of substance to form, see Aristotle, *Metaphysics* 7: 7–9.
2 See Baugh (2003: 119, 99); Sartre (1969: 243–5).
3 This emphasis on a time of anticipation and futurity which is without identity recalls Derrida's thinking of the messianic in *Spectres of Marx*; see Derrida (1994).
4 See Martinon (2007: 43–61). As Martinon underlines, translation itself is a plastic process in which one form gives way to another.
5 Once again, one might find a resonance here with other thinkers treated in this study. Here the subject is not constitutive but, as with Marion's 'gifted', is exposed to something which arrives or is given in excess of the constitutive horizons of phenomenological consciousness.
6 These distinctions most obviously refer back to Thomist philosophy which describes human being as a substance doubly determined, primarily by essence (*essentia*), and secondarily by *accidents*. The latter are secondary because they are contingent and can change without affecting essence; the former is primary because it is necessary to the being of human *as* human, i.e. as a substance different from other non-human substances which it can only know via their accidents. For a full account of the Thomist theory of accidents and essence, see Gilson (1992: 22–4).

7 Malabou also describes this as a 'mutual giving of form between the empirical and the noetic' (Malabou 1996a: 68; 2005b: 45). As will become clear, this has crucial implications for the distinction between nature and artifice, or the natural and the cultural, particularly in relation to Malabou's later engagements with psychoanalysis, neuroscience and genetics.
8 See Heidegger (1998: 97–135, 136–54).
9 See, for instance, Laplanche and Pontalis (2011).
10 This will be discussed further at the end of this chapter.
11 Malabou's thinking here could be opposed to the thesis relating to male and female brains developed by Simon Baron Cohen in *The Essential Difference* (Baron Cohen 2004).
12 See Damasio (2006), LeDoux (2003) and Changeux (1997).
13 See Jeannerod (2002: 18–22).
14 For Freud's analysis of Judge Daniel Schreber, see Freud (2003). For an in-depth account of the significance of the Schreber case for Freud, see Chabot (1982).
15 Malabou refers directly to Damasio's work (Malabou 2007: 78); see Damasio (1999).

Chapter 5   Jacques Rancière: The Space of Equality

1 See *For Marx*, Althusser (2005).
2 For a more extended biographical sketch, see Deranty (2010: 1–13).
3 Mark Robson makes this point very well; see Robson (2005: 5).
4 See May's discussion of Rancière in relation to the political thought of Nozick and Rawls, see May (2008: 6–35).
5 As May points out, Rancière's understanding of disagreement is indebted to Aristotle's conception of speech; see Deranty (2010: 73).
6 Famously, in the essay 'Ideology and Ideological State Apparatuses', Althusser describes ideology as an imaginary relation of the subject to the world: 'Ideology represents the imaginary relationship of individuals to their real conditions of existence' (in Sharma and Gupta 2006: 100).
7 On this point, see Althusser's essay, 'Theory, Theoretical Practice and Theoretical Formation of Theoretical Practice', in Elliott (1990).
8 In the opening pages of Althusser's lesson, Rancière remarks pointedly that: 'Althusserism died on the barricades of May with a good number of other ideas of the past' (Rancière 1974: 10; 2011c: xx).
9 See, for example, *The Nights of Labour* (Rancière 1981; 1989), *The Philosopher and his Poor* (Rancière 1983; 2004c) and *Esthétiques du peuple* (Rancière 1985).
10 See Rancière (1987). Oliver Davis gives an important commentary on the significance of Jacottet for Rancière; see Davis (2010: 25–35).

11 There is arguably a residue of the Althusserian desire for demystification in Rancière's attempt to give a fundamental and more 'real' account of what politics is in its pure form.
12 Rancière's understanding of disagreement can be seen as a refutation of Lyotard's argument relating to the 'differend' in his book of that name. See Lyotard (1988).
13 Rancière opposes Habermas's affirmation of the possibility and necessity of rational consensus in the social sphere; see Habermas (1984). Rancière's understanding of politics and political agency can also be directly opposed to the liberal political theory of leading figures such as David Miller; see Miller (2000).
14 'Politics in its specificity is rare. It is always local and occasional' (Rancière 1995a: 188; 1998d: 139).
15 Rancière makes it very clear that not all police orders are the same and that some police orders may be better than others (Rancière 1995a: 54; 1998d: 30).
16 Rancière's relation to anarchism has been discussed at length by Todd May; see May (2008: 82–110, 99).

Chapter 6   Alain Badiou: The Science of the Real

1 On this trajectory of French thought, see Gutting (2001: 40–8, 227–8, 377–8) and Schrift (2006: 10–12, 36–9).
2 Category theory is a branch of contemporary mathematics which is concerned with structures, with systems and interrelations of structures. It can be seen as an alternative to set theory as a foundation for mathematics.
3 For full-length and wider reaching introductions to Badiou's work, see in particular Hallward (2003a) and Feltham (2008).
4 On the importance of Badiou's political engagements to the development of his philosophy, see Hallward (2003a: 29–30).
5 On this question of ontological decision again, see Hallward (2003a, 76).
6 For a fuller discussion of inconsistent multiplicity as thought by Badiou from Cantor, see Depoortere (2009: 63–6).
7 On the ontologization of number within post-Cantorian mathematics, see Badiou (1990: 18–19; 2008e: 8–9).
8 For a useful summary account of the development of transfinite set theory, see Hallward (2003a: 323–48).
9 This formalization of ontological void in the notation of the empty set (∅) resonates strongly with the Levinassian thinking of the 'il y a', i.e. that which remains in the absence of all things as a 'plenitude of emptiness [*plénitude du vide*]' (Levinas 1983: 26). By the same token, then, it might also recall the Blanchottian *dehors*, or diverse other ways that French thought prior to Badiou has sought to think an excess over being.

10 Badiou ascribes a greater homogeneity and stability to the multiples of the natural world which, he suggests, lacks the internal contradictions of human historical situations; see Badiou (1988: 147; 2005b: 128).

11 The notion of 'state' here might be usefully compared with that of 'police order' discussed in relation to Rancière in chapter 5.

12 In this respect, Badiou's thought is similar to the logic of undecidability and incalculability developed by Derrida in texts such as *Spectres of Marx* (Derrida 1994). Badiou says as much himself in a footnote to *Logics of Worlds* (Badiou 2006a: 570; 2009c: 545).

13 See also Badiou (1988: 23–4; 2005b: 16–17).

14 Again, it is Mullarkey who has underlined the extent to which the works which follow *Being and Event*, such as *Conditions* (Badiou 1992a; 2008c), *Metapolitics* (Badiou 1998a; 2005e) and *Handbook of Inaesthetics* (Badiou 1998c; 2005c) are all devoted to the philosophical subtraction of truths from the generic conditions of philosophy (Mullarkey 2006: 132–3).

15 Badiou is very specific on this point: 'the linguistic, relativist, and neo-sceptical parenthesis of contemporary academic philosophy – a philosophy which is at bottom the sophisticated handmaiden of democratic materialism' (Badiou 2006a: 15; 2009c: 7).

16 See Badiou in Guibal and Martin (2004: 13–24); on the question of 'actual' infinity in Badiou and Nancy, see also James in Alexandrova, Devisch et al. (2011). It is also arguable that this questionable and reductive forcing of diverse philosophical positions into an overly homogenized paradigm can be discerned in the work of Badiou's students, most notably in the thesis relating to Kantianism and 'co-relationalism' advanced by Quentin Meillassoux in *After Finitude* (2010).

17 In early works such as *Theory of the Subject*, Badiou makes this very clear: 'it is materialism that we must found anew with the renovated arsenal of our mental powers' (Badiou 1982: 198; 2009e: 182).

18 Badiou (2006a, 128; 2009c: 110).

19 Hallward argues that the ontology of *Being and Event* lacks a proper account of relationality; *Logics of Worlds* clearly responds to this potential problem; see Hallward (2003a: xxxiii).

20 Some of Badiou's commentators have commented critically on the shift, in his later work, which arguably makes concessions to the thinking of finitude. See, for example, Feltham on Badiou's thinking of the conditioning of philosophy (Feltham 2008: 127–8).

21 Badiou takes pains to differentiate his own conception of the subject from other more traditional conceptions at a number of points throughout *Logics of Worlds*. He emphasizes, for instance, that his subject is not a (phenomenological) subject of conscious experience, nor a (neo-Kantian) moral or ethical subject, nor still an (Althusserian) ideological subject (Badiou 2006a: 55–6; 2009c: 48). Later, in *Logics of Worlds*, he also underlines the extent to which, according

to the logic of dialectical materialism: 'consciousness is at best a distant effect of real assemblages' (Badiou 2006a: 185; 2009c: 173–4).

22 Badiou's anti-Kantian thinking has inspired the work of younger philosophers who have aligned themselves with the term 'speculative realism' or 'speculative materialism'; see Meillassoux (2010) and Brassier (2010).

23 The notion of antagonistic contradiction or splitting into two of any given situation is a constant of Badiou's thought from *Theory of the Subject* to *The Logics of Worlds*. See Badiou (1982: 32; 2009e:14) and Badiou (2006a: 459; 2009c: 448).

Chapter 7   François Laruelle: Beginning with the One

1 For a discussion of Nancy and Lacoue-Labarthe's work during this period, see James (2006: 13–26).

2 Choplin's persuasively argues that there is no decisive break between Philosophy II and III; see Choplin (2007: 115).

3 Nancy remarks on the difficult readability of Laruelle's work in an interview published at the end of *Le Déclin de l'écriture*; see Laruelle (1977b: 245–6).

4 Laruelle sometimes but not always capitalizes the term in a way that directly recalls its Lacanian usage. For consistency, it is not capitalized here except in citation where Laruelle himself has done so.

5 Laruelle consistently associates transcendence with the determination of the real by concepts and therefore as a process of negation, negativity and splitting ('scission'); in this respect, he is clearly influenced by the Hegelian account of determination.

6 There are also influences of other philosophies of immanence, such as the thought of Spinoza, Bergson and Henry.

7 See, in particular, Deleuze (2004b: 41–51).

8 Michel Henry's account of radical immanence in works such as *The Essence of Manifestation* appears to be decisive for Laruelle; formulations such as 'Transcendence rests upon immanence' appear close to Laruelle's; see Henry (1973: 41).

9 See Heidegger, 'The Question Concerning Technology' (Heidegger 1993: 307–41).

10 To this extent, Laruelle echoes Badiou's understanding of the beginning of philosophy in the identity between One and Being posed by Parmenides; Badiou writes in *Being and Event*: 'The reciprocity of the one and being is certainly the inaugural axiom of philosophy' (Badiou 1988: 31; 2005b: 23).

11 In this respect, whilst Laruelle's gesture is structuralist, the structure he uncovers, that of the mixed, is close to Heidegger's characterization of metaphysics as ontotheology.

12 Yet in *Philosophies of Difference* he does talk of an attempted 'destruction' of the 'Greco-Occidental style'; see Laruelle (1986: 11; 2010c: xviii).

13 See the discussion of Althusser in chapter 5.

14 The importance placed by Laruelle on axiomatic thinking clearly recalls Badiou's thinking of axiomatics derived from set theory; see chapter 6.

15 Natural science is given a privileged position in *En tant qu'un* insofar as it is not determined in its content by language or the concepts of language; see Laruelle (1991: 202).

16 See Kant, *Critique of Pure Reason* B: xvi.

17 Ray Brassier rightly notes that Laruelle's logic of determination in the last instance is the key to his untying of the post-Kantian philosophical legacy; see Brassier (2010: 139).

18 As indicated in note 15 above, Laruelle accords a great privilege to natural science in *En tant qu'un*, writing that: 'there is more *real and really universal* thought in, say, Riemann and Einstein than there is in Hegel and Heidegger' (Laruelle 1991: 67).

19 On this point, see Choplin (2007: 115, n. 38).

20 Arguably in Philosophy V and in particular *Philosophie non-standard* (Laruelle 2010a), science regains the prominent and privileged position it enjoyed in Philosophy II.

21 *Philosophie non-standard* draws on the concepts and language of quantum mechanics. In effect, the conceptual frame of quantum physics is 'extracted' from its context of empirical science and redeployed in a different discursive/performative context.

Conclusion: The Technique of Thought

1 Nancy's thinking of technicity and eco-technics also has the potential to be thought in these terms (see James 2006: 251, n. 29), as has his thinking of 'sense' when approached in relation to questions of the natural world.

2 A more developed engagement with the question of the 'technique of thought' and with the lines of conflict and opposition which structure this field will be the task of a subsequent work, *The Technique of Thought: Immanence and Technicity in Recent French Philosophy* (forthcoming).

Bibliography

Jean-Luc Marion

Principal works

(1970) *Avec ou sans Dieu*. Paris: Beauchesne.
(1975) *Sur l'ontologie grise de Descartes*. Paris: J. Vrin.
(1977) *L'Idole et la distance*. Paris: B. Grasset.
(1981) *Sur la théologie blanche de Descartes*. Paris: Presses universitaires de France.
(1982) *Dieu sans l'être*. Paris: Fayard.
(1986a) *Sur le prisme métaphysique de Descartes*. Paris: Presses universitaires de France.
(1986b) *Prolégomènes à la charité*. Paris: Éd. de la Différence.
(1989) *Réduction et donation*. Paris: Presses universitaires de France.
(1991a) *Questions cartésiennes*. Paris: Presses universitaires de France.
(1991b) *Dieu sans l'être*. Paris: Presses universitaires de France (new edn).
(1991c) *La Croisée du visible*. Paris: Presses universitaires de France.
(1996) *Questions cartésiennes II*. Paris: Presses universitaires de France.
(1997) *Étant donné: essai d'une phénoménologie de la donation*. Paris: Presses universitaires de France.
(2001a) *De surcroît: étude sur les phénomènes saturés*. Paris: Presses universitaires de France.
(2003) *Le Phénomène érotique*. Paris: Grasset.
(2005) *Le Visible et le révélé*. Paris: les Éditions du Cerf.
(2008a) *Au lieu de soi: l'approche de saint Augustin*. Paris: Presses universitaires de France.
(2009) *Certitudes négatives*. Paris: Grasset.
(2010) *Le Croire pour le voir*. Paris: Parole et silence.

Works in translation

(1991d) *God Without Being.* Trans. T. A. Carlson. Chicago: Chicago University Press.
(1998) *Reduction and Givenness: Investigations of Husserl, Heidegger and Phenomenology.* Trans. T. A. Carlson. Evanston: Northwestern University Press.
(1999a) *Cartesian Questions: Method and Metaphysics.* Foreword by D. Garber. Chicago: Chicago University Press.
(1999b) *On Descartes' Metaphysical Prism.* Trans. J. L. Kosky. Chicago: Chicago University Press.
(2001b) *The Idol and Distance.* Trans. T. A. Carlson. New York: Fordham University Press.
(2002a) *In Excess: Studies in Saturated Phenomena.* Trans. R. Horner and V. Berraud. New York: Fordham University Press.
(2002b) *Prolegomena to Charity.* Trans. S. E. Lewis. New York: Fordham University Press.
(2002c) *Being Given: Towards a Phenomenology of Givenness.* Trans. J. L. Kosky. Stanford: Stanford University Press.
(2004) *The Crossing of the Visible.* Trans. J. K. A. Smith. Stanford: Stanford University Press.
(2007a) *The Erotic Phenomenon.* Trans. S. E. Lewis. Chicago: Chicago University Press.
(2007b) *On the Ego and on God: Further Cartesian Questions.* Trans. C. M. Gschwandtner. New York: Fordham University Press.
(2008b) *The Visible and the Revealed.* Trans. C. M. Gschwandtner et al. New York: Fordham University Press.

Selected secondary works

Caputo, J. D. and Scanlon, M. J. (eds) (2007) *Transcendence and Beyond: A Postmodern Inquiry.* Bloomington: Indiana University Press.
Gschwandtner, C. M. (2007) *Reading Jean-Luc Marion: Exceeding Metaphysics.* Bloomington: Indiana University Press.
Hart, K. (ed.) (2007) *Counter-Experiences: Reading Jean-Luc Marion.* Notre Dame: University of Notre Dame Press.
Horner, R. (2001) *Rethinking God as Gift: Marion, Derrida, and the Limits of Phenomenology.* New York: Fordham University Press.
Horner, R. (2005) *Jean-Luc Marion: A Theo-logical Introduction.* Aldershot: Ashgate.
Kessler M. and Sheppard, C. (2003) *Mystics: Presence and Aporia.* Chicago: University of Chicago Press.
Leask, I. and Cassidy, E. (eds) (2005) *Givenness and God: Questions of Jean-Luc Marion.* New York: Fordham University Press.

Mackinlay, S. (2010) *Interpreting Excess: Jean-Luc Marion, Saturated Phenomena and Hermeneutics*. New York: Fordham University Press.

Jean-Luc Nancy

Principal works

(1972) *Le Titre de la lettre*. Paris: Galilée.
(1973) *Le Remarque spéculatif*. Paris: Galilée.
(1976) *Logodaedalus: Le Discours de la syncope*. Paris: Aubier-Flammarion.
(1978) *L'Absolu littéraire*. With P. Lacoue-Labarthe. Paris: Seuil.
(1979) *Ego Sum*. Paris: Flammarion.
(1981) *Rejouer le politique*. With P. Lacoue-Labarthe. Paris: Gallimard.
(1982) *Le Partage des voix*. Paris: Galilée.
(1983a) *Le Retrait du politique*. With P. Lacoue-Labarthe. Paris: Galilée.
(1983b) *L'impératif catégorique*. Paris: Flammarion.
(1986a) *L'Oubli de la philosophie*. Paris: Galilée.
(1986b) *La Communauté désœuvrée*. Paris: Christian Bourgois.
(1987) *Des Lieux divins*. Mauvezin: Trans-Europ-Repress.
(1988a) *L'Expérience de la liberté*. Paris: Galilée.
(1990a) *Une Pensée finie*. Paris: Galilée.
(1991a) *Le Poids d'une pensée*. Grenoble: Presses universitaires de Grenoble.
(1991b) *La Comparution*. With J. Christoph-Bailly. Paris: Christian Bourgois.
(1991c) *Le Myth nazi*. With P. Lacoue-Labarthe. La Tour d'Aigue: De l'Aube.
(1991d) *Le Poids d'une pensée*. Grenoble: Presses universitaires de Grenoble.
(1992a) *Corpus*. Paris: Métaillé.
(1993a) *Le Sens du monde*. Paris: Galilée.
(1994) *Les Muses*. Paris: Galilée.
(1996a) *Être singulier pluriel*. Paris: Galilée.
(1997a) *Hegel: L'Inquiétude du négatif*. Paris: Hachette.
(1998) La Déconstruction du christianisme, *Études Philosophiques* 4: 503–19.
(2000a) *Le Regard du portrait*. Paris: Galilée.
(2000b) *L'Intrus*. Paris: Galilée.
(2001a) *La Pensée dérobée*. Paris: Galilée.
(2001b) *La Communauté affrontée*. Paris: Galilée.
(2001c) *L'Évidence du film: Abbas Kiarostami*. Brussels: Yves Gevaert
(2001d) *L'"Il y a" du rapport sexuel*. Paris: Galilée.
(2001e) *Visitation (de la peinture chrétienne)*. Paris: Galilée.
(2002a) *La Création du monde ou la mondialisation*. Paris: Galilée.

(2002b) *À l'écoute*. Paris: Galilée.
(2003a) *Noli me tangere*. Paris: Bayard.
(2003b) *Au fond des images*. Paris: Galilée.
(2005a) *La Déclosion. Déconstruction du christianisme 1*. Paris: Galilée.
(2007a) *Tombe de sommeil*. Paris: Galilée.
(2007b) *Juste impossible*. Paris: Bayard.
(2008a) *La Vérité de la démocratie*. Paris: Galilée.
(2009a) *Le Plaisir au dessin*. Paris: Galilée.
(2009b) *Dieu, l'Amour, la Justice, la Beauté*. Paris: Bayard.
(2010a) *Identité. Fragments, franchises*. Paris: Galilée.
(2010b) *L'Adoration. Déconstruction du Christianisme 2*. Paris: Galilée.

Works in English translation

(1988b) *The Literary Absolute: The Theory of Literature in German Romanticism*. With P. Lacoue-Labarthe. Trans. Philip Barnard and Cheryl Lester. Albany: State University of New York Press.
(1990b) Sharing Voices. Trans. G. L. Ormiston, in G. L. Ormiston and A. D. Schrift (eds), *Transforming the Hermeneutic Context: From Nietzsche to Nancy*. Albany: State University of New York Press, pp. 211–60.
(1991e) *The Inoperative Community*. Ed. P. Connor. Trans. P. Connor et al. Minneapolis: University of Minnesota Press.
(1991f) *Who Comes after the Subject?* Ed. J.-L. Nancy et al. London: Routledge.
(1992b) *The Compearance*. Trans. Tracy B. Strong. Newbury Park: Sage.
(1992c) *The Title of the Letter: A Reading of Lacan*. With P. Lacoue-Labarthe. Trans. F. R. and D. Pettigrew. Albany: State University of New York Press.
(1993b) *The Birth to Presence*. Trans. B. Holmes et al. Stanford: Stanford University Press.
(1993c) *The Experience of Freedom*. Trans. B. McDonald. Stanford: Stanford University Press.
(1996b) *The Muses*. Trans. P. Kamuf. Stanford: Stanford University Press.
(1997b) *The Forgetting of Philosophy*. In *The Gravity of Thought*. Trans. F. Raffoul and G. Recco. Atlantic Highlands: Humanities Press.
(1997c) The Gravity of Thought, in *The Gravity of Thought*. Trans. F. Raffoul and G. Recco. Atlantic Highlands: Humanities Press.
(1997d) *Retreating the Political*. With P. Lacoue-Labarthe. Ed. Simon Sparks. Trans. C. Surprenant et al. London: Routledge.
(1997e) *The Sense of the World*. Trans. J. S. Librett. Minneapolis: University of Minnesota Press.
(2000c) *Being Singular Plural*. Trans. A. E. O'Byrne and R. D. Richardson. Stanford: Stanford University Press.

(2001f) *The Speculative Remark.* Trans. C. Surprenant. Stanford: Stanford University Press.

(2002c) *Hegel: The Restlessness of the Negative.* Trans. J. Smith and S. Miller. Minneapolis: University of Minnesota Press.

(2002d) *L'Intrus.* Trans. S. Hanson. East Lansing: Michigan State University Press.

(2003c) *A Finite Thinking.* Trans. S. Sparks. Stanford: Stanford University Press.

(2005b) *The Ground of the Image.* Trans. J. Fort. New York: Fordham University Press.

(2006) *Multiple Arts: The Muses II.* Trans. S. Sparks et al. Stanford: Stanford University Press.

(2007c) *The Creation of the World, or, Globalization.* Trans. F. Raffoul et al. Albany: State University of New York Press.

(2007d) *Listening.* Trans. C. Mandell. New York: Fordham University Press.

(2008b) *Corpus.* Trans. R. Rand. New York: Fordham University Press.

(2008c) *Dis-enclosure: The Deconstruction of Christianity.* Trans. B. Bergo et al. New York: Fordham University Press.

(2008d) *Noli me tangere: On the Raising of the Body.* Trans. S. Clift et al. New York: Fordham University Press.

(2008e) *The Discourse of the Syncope: Logodaedalus.* Trans. S. Anton. Stanford, Stanford University Press.

(2008f) *Philosophical Chronicles.* Trans. F. Manjali. New York: Fordham University Press.

(2009c) *The Fall of Sleep.* Trans. C. Mandell. New York: Fordham University Press.

(2009d) *On the Commerce of Thinking.* Trans. D. Wills. New York: Fordham University Press.

(2010c) *The Truth of Democracy.* Trans. P.-A. Brault and M. Naas. New York: Fordham University Press.

Selected secondary works

Alexandrova, A., Devisch, I. et al. (eds) (2011) *Re-treating Religion: Deconstructing Christianity with Jean-Luc Nancy.* New York: Fordham University Press.

Armstrong, P. (2009) *Reticulations: Jean-Luc Nancy and the Networks of the Political.* Minneapolis: University of Minnesota Press.

Derrida, J. (2000) *Le Toucher, Jean-Luc Nancy.* Paris: Galilée.

Derrida, J. (2006) *On Touching.* Trans. C. Izarry. Stanford: Stanford University Press.

Guibal, F. and Martin, J.-C. (2004) *Le Sens en tous sens: autour des travaux de Jean-Luc Nancy.* Paris: Galilée.

Heikkilä, M. (2008) *At the Limits of Presentation: Coming-into-Presence and its Aesthetic Relevance in Jean-Luc Nancy's Philosophy*. Frankfurt: Peter Lang.

Hutchens, B. (2005) *Jean-Luc Nancy and the Future of Philosophy*. Chesham: Acumen.

James, I. (2002) The Persistence of the Subject: Jean-Luc Nancy, *Paragraph* 25(1): 125–41.

James, I. (2005a) On Interrupted Myth, *Journal of Cultural Research* 9(4): 331–49.

James, I. (2005b) Art, Technics, Special issue *Thought's Exposure: Critical Essays on Jean-Luc Nancy*, *Oxford Literary Review* 27: 83–102.

James, I. (2006) *The Fragmentary Demand: An Introduction to the Philosophy of Jean-Luc Nancy*. Stanford: Stanford University Press.

James, I. (2007) The Evidence of the Image: Nancy and Kiarostami, *L'Esprit Créateur* 47(3): 68–79.

James, I. (2010a) Naming the Nothing: Nancy and Blanchot on Community, in *The Politics of Nothing: Sovereignty and Modernity*. Special issue of *Culture, Theory, Critique* 51(2): 171–87.

May, T. (1997) *Reconsidering Difference: Nancy, Derrida, Levinas, Deleuze*. University Park: Pennsylvania State University Press.

Ormiston, G. L. and Schrift A. D. (1990) *Transforming the Hermeneutic Context: From Nietzsche to Nancy*. New York: New York State University Press.

Sheppard, D. and Sparks, S. (eds) (1997) *On Jean-Luc Nancy: The Sense of Philosophy*. Stanford: Stanford University Press.

Watkin, C. (2009) *Phenomenology or Deconstruction: The Question of Ontology in Maurice Merleau-Ponty, Paul Ricoeur and Jean-Luc Nancy*. Edinburgh: Edinburgh University Press.

Bernard Stiegler

Principal works

(1994) *La Technique et le temps 1. La Faute d'Épiméthée*. Paris: Galilée.

(1995) *Echographies de la télévision*. With Jacques Derrida. Paris: Galiée.

(1996) *La Technique et le temps 2. La Désorientation*. Paris: Galiliée.

(2001a) *La Technique et le temps 3. Le Temps du cinéma et la question du mal-être*. Paris: Galilée.

(2003a) *Passer à l'acte*. Paris: Galilée.

(2003b) *Aimer, s'aimer, nous aimer*. Paris: Galilée.

(2004a) *De la misère symbolique 1. L'époque hyperindustrielle*. Paris: Galilée.

(2004b) *Mécréance et discrédit 1. La décadence des démocraties industrielles*. Paris: Galiée.

(2005a) *De la misère symbolique 2: La Catastrophè du sensible*. Paris: Galilée.

(2005b) *Constituer l'Europe 1.* Paris: Galilée.
(2005c) *Constituer l'Europe 2.* Paris: Galilée.
(2006a) *Mécréance et discrédit 2: Les sociétés incontrôlables d'individus désaffectés.* Paris: Galilée.
(2006b) *Mécréance et discrédit 3. L'esprit perdu du capitalisme.* Paris: Galilée.
(2006c) *La Télécratie contre la démocratie.* Paris: Flammarion.
(2006d) *Réenchanter le monde.* With G. Collins et al. Paris: Flammarion
(2006e) *De la démocratie participative.* With M. Crépon et al. Paris: Flammarion.
(2008) *Prendre soin.* Paris: Flammarion.
(2009a) *Pour une nouvelle critique de l'économie politique.* Paris: Galilée.
(2009b) *Pour en finir avec la mécroissance.* With A. Giffard et al. Paris: Flammarion.
(2010a) *Ce qui fait que la vie vaut la peine d'être vécue.* Paris: Flammarion.

Works in translation

(1998) *Technics and Time 1: The Fault of Epimetheus.* Trans. Richard Beardsworth and George Collins. Stanford: Stanford University Press.
(2001b) Derrida and Technology, in T. Cohen (ed.), *Jacques Derrida and the Humanities.* Cambridge: Cambridge University Press, pp. 238–70.
(2002) *Echographies of Television.* Trans. J. Bajorek. Cambridge: Polity.
(2009c) *Technics and Time 2: Disorientation.* Trans. S. Barker. Stanford: Stanford University Press.
(2009d) *Acting Out.* Trans. D. Barison et al. Stanford: Stanford University Press.
(2010b) *For a New Critique of Political Economy.* Trans. D. Ross. Cambridge: Polity.
(2010c) *Taking Care of Youth and the Generations.* Trans. S. Barker. Stanford: Stanford University Press.
(2011) *Technics and Time 3: Cinematic Time and the Question of Malaise.* Trans. S. Barker. Stanford: Stanford University Press.

Selected secondary works

Beardsworth, R. (1998) Thinking Technicity. *Cultural Values* 2(1): 70–86.
Bennington, G. (2000) Emergencies, in *Interrupting Derrida.* London: Routledge, pp. 162–79.

James, I. (2010b) Bernard Stiegler and the Time of Technics, *Cultural Politics* 6(2) (March): 207–28.

Roberts, B. (2005). Stiegler Reading Derrida: The Prosthesis of Deconstruction in Technics, *Postmodern Culture* 16(1).

Catherine Malabou

Principal works

(1996a) *L'Avenir de Hegel: plasticité, temporalité, dialectique*. Paris: J. Vrin.

(1996b) *Le Temps: textes expliqués, sujets analysés*. Paris: Hatier.

(1999) *Jacques Derrida: La contre-allée*. With Jacques Derrida. Paris: Quinzaine Littéraire.

(2000) *Plasticité*. Paris: L. Scheer.

(2004a) *Le Change Heidegger: du fantastique en philosophie*. Paris: L. Scheer.

(2004b) *Que faire de notre cerveau?* Paris: Bayard.

(2005a) *La Plasticité au soir de l'écriture: dialectique, destruction, déconstruction*. Paris: L. Scheer.

(2007) *Les Nouveaux blessés: de Freud à la neurologie, penser les traumatismes contemporains*. Paris: Bayard.

(2009a) *Ontologie de l'accident: essai sur la plasticité destructrice*. Paris: L. Scheer.

(2009b) *La Chambre du milieu: de Hegel aux neurosciences*. Paris: Hermann.

(2009c) *Changer de différence: Le féminin et la question philosophique*. Paris: Galilée.

(2009d) *Espèces d'accident*. Paris: L. Scheer.

(2009e) *La Grande exclusion: l'urgence sociale, symptômes et thérapeutique*. With Xavier Emmanuelli. Montrouge: Bayard.

(2010a)*Tu seras mon corps pour moi*. With Judith Butler. Paris: Bayard.

Works in translation

(2004c) *Counterpath: Traveling with Jacques Derrida*. Trans. David Wills. Stanford: Stanford University Press.

(2005b) *The Future of Hegel: Plasticity, Temporality, and Dialectic*. Trans. L. During. London: Routledge.

(2008) *What Should We Do with Our Brain?* Trans. S. Rand. New York: Fordham University Press.
(2010b) *Plasticity at the Dusk of Writing*. Trans. C. Shread. New York: Columbia.

Selected secondary works

Martinon, J.-P. (2007) *On Futurity: Malabou, Nancy and Derrida*. Basingstoke: Palgrave Macmillan.

Jacques Rancière

Principal works

(1974) *La Leçon d'Althusser*. Paris: Gallimard.
(1981) *La Nuit des prolétaires: archives du rêve ouvrier*. Paris: Fayard.
(1983) *Le Philosophe et ses pauvres*. Paris: Fayard (first edn).
(1984) *L'Empire sociologue*. Paris: La Découverte.
(1985) *Esthétiques du peuple*. Paris: La Découvert/P. U. Vincennes.
(1987) *Le Maître ignorant: cinq leçons sur l'émancipation intellectuelle*. Paris: Fayard.
1990) *Courts voyages au pays du peuple*. Paris: Seuil.
(1992) *Les Noms de l'histoire: essai du poétique du savoir*. Paris: Seuil.
(1995a) *La Mésentente: politique et philosophie*. Paris: Galilée.
(1996) *Mallarmé: la politique de la sirène*. Paris: Hachette.
(1998a) *Aux bords du politique*. Paris: La Fabrique.
(1998b) *La Chair des mots: politiques de l'écriture*. Paris: Galilée.
(1998c) *La Parole muette: essai sur les contradictions de la littérature*. Paris: Hachette.
(2000) *La Partage du sensible: esthétique et politique*. Paris: La Fabrique.
(2001a) *L'Inconscient esthétique*. Paris: Galilée.
(2001b) *La Fable cinématographique*. Paris: Seuil.
(2003a) *Le Destin de images*. Paris: La Fabrique.
(2003b) *Les Scènes du peuple*. Lyon: Horslieu.
(2004a) *La Malaise dans l'esthétique*. Paris: Galilée.
(2005a) *La Haine de la démocratie*. Paris: La Fabrique.
(2005b) *Chroniques des temps consensuels*. Paris: Seuil.
(2007a) *Le Philosophe et ses pauvres*. Paris: Flammarion (second edn).
(2007b) *Politique de la littérature*. Paris: Galilée.
(2008) *Le Spectateur émancipé*. Paris: La Fabrique.
(2009a) *Moments politiques: interventions 1977–2009*. Paris: La Fabrique.

Works in translation

(1989) *The Nights of Labour: The Workers' Dream in Nineteenth-Century France*. Philadelphia: Temple University Press.

(1991) *The Ignorant Schoolmaster*. Trans. K. Ross. Stanford: Stanford University Press.

(1994) *The Names of History: On the Poetics of Knowledge*. Trans. H. Melehy. Minneapolis: University of Minnesota Press.

(1995b) *On the Shores of Politics*. Trans. L. Heron. London: Verso.

(1998d) *Disagreement: Politics and Philosophy*. Trans. J. Rose. Minneapolis: University of Minnesota Press.

(2003c) *Short Voyages to the Land of the People*. Trans. J. B. Swenson. Stanford: Stanford University Press.

(2004b) *The Flesh of Words*. Trans. C. Mandell. Stanford: Stanford University Press.

(2004c) *The Philosopher and his Poor*. Trans. J. Drury et al. Durham, NC: Duke University Press.

(2004d) *The Politics of Aesthetics: The Distribution of the Sensible*. Trans. G. Rockhill. London: Continuum.

(2006a) *Film Fables*. Trans. E. Battista. Oxford: Berg.

(2006b) *Hatred of Democracy*. London: Verso.

(2007c) *The Future of the Image*. Trans. G. Elliott. London: Verso.

(2009b) *The Aesthetic Unconscious*. Trans. D. Keats and J. Swenson. Cambridge: Polity.

(2009c) *Aesthetics and its Discontents*. Trans. S. Corcoran. Cambridge: Polity.

(2009d) *Dissensus: Politics and Aesthetics*. Trans. S. Corcoran. London: Continuum.

(2009e) *The Emancipated Spectator*. London: Verso.

(2010) *Chronicles of Consensual Times*. Trans. S. Corcoran. London: Continuum.

(2011a) *Mallarmé: The Politics of the Siren*. Trans. S. Corcoran. London: Continuum.

(2011b) *The Politics of Literature*. Trans. J. Rose. Cambridge: Polity.

(2011c) *Althusser's Lesson*. Trans. E. Battista. London: Continuum.

Selected secondary works

Bingham, C. W. (2010) *Jacques Rancière: Education, Truth, Emancipation*. London: Continuum.

Davis, O. (2010) *Jacques Rancière*. Cambridge: Polity.

Deranty, J.-P. (ed.) (2010) *Jacques Rancière: Key Concepts*. Durham: Acumen.

Hewlett, N. (2007) *Badiou, Balibar, Rancière: Rethinking Equality*. London: Continuum.

May, T. (2008) *The Political Thought of Jacques Rancière*. Edinburgh: Edinburgh University Press.

May, T. (2010) *Contemporary Political Movements and the Thought of Jacques Rancière*. Edinburgh: Edinburgh University Press.

Nordmann, C. (2007) *Bourdieu, Rancière: La politique entre sociologie et philosophie*. Paris: Éditions Amsterdam.

Robson, M. (ed.) (2005) *Jacques Rancière: Aesthetics, Politics, Philosophy*. Edinburgh: Edinburgh University Press.

Rockhill, G. and Watts, P. (eds) (2009) *Jacques Rancière: History, Politics, Aesthetics*. Durham, NC: Duke University Press.

Ruby, C. (2009) *L'Interruption: Jacques Rancière et la politique*. Paris: La Fabrique.

Stamp, R. and Bowman, P. (2011) *Reading Rancière*. London: Continuum.

Alain Badiou

Principal works

(1969) *Le Concept de modèle: introduction à une épistemologie matérialiste*. Paris: Maspero.

(1975) *Théorie de la contradiction*. Paris: Maspero.

(1976) *Le Mouvement ouvrier révolutionnaire contre le syndicalisme*. Paris: Éditions Potemkine.

(1978) *La Contestation dans le P. C. F*. Paris: Éditions Potemkine.

(1980) *Jean-Paul Sartre*. Paris: Éditions Potemkine.

(1982) *Théorie du sujet*. Paris: Seuil.

(1985) *Peut-on penser la politique*. Paris: Seuil.

(1988) *L'Être et l'événement*. Paris: Seuil.

(1989a) *Manifeste pour la philosophie*. Paris: Seuil.

(1989b) *Samuel Beckett: l'écriture du générique et l'amour*. Paris: Le Perroquet.

(1990) *Le Nombre et les nombres*. Paris: Seuil.

(1991) *D'Un désastre obscur*. Paris: Éditions de l'Aube.

(1992a) *Conditions*. Paris: Seuil.

(1992b) *Casser en deux l'histoire du monde?* Paris: Le Perroquet.

(1993) *L'Éthique*. Paris: Hatier.

(1995) *Beckett: l'increvable désir*. Paris: Hachette.

(1997a) *Saint Paul: la fondation de l'universalisme*. Paris: Presses universitaires de France.

(1997b) *Deleuze: 'la clameur de l'être'*. Paris: Hachette.

(1998a) *Abrégé de métapolitique*. Paris: Seuil.

(1998b) *Court traité d'ontologie transitoire*. Paris: Seuil.

(1998c) *Petit manuel d'inesthétique*. Paris: Seuil.

(2002) *La Révolution culturelle: La dernière révolution?* Paris: Le Clavier.

(2003a) *Circonstances 1. Kosovo, 11 septembre, Chirac-Le Pen*. Paris: L. Scheer.

(2004a) *Circonstances 2. Irak, foulard, Allemagne-France.* Paris: L. Scheer.
(2005a) *Circonstances 3. Portées du mot 'juif'.* Paris: L. Scheer.
(2006a) *Logiques des mondes: L'être et l'événement 2.* Paris: Seuil.
(2007a) *Circonstances 4. De quoi Sarkozy est-il le nom ?* Paris: Nouvelles Éditions Lignes.
(2008a) *Second manifeste pour la philosophie.* Paris: Fayard.
(2008b) *Petit panthéon portative.* Paris: La Fabrique.
(2009a) *L'Hypothèse communiste.* Paris: Nouvelles Éditions Lignes.
(2009b) *L'Antiphilosophie de Wittgenstein.* Caen: Nous.
(2010a) *Le Fini et l'infini.* Paris: Bayard.
(2010b) *Cinéma.* Paris: Nova.

Works in translation

(1999) *Manifesto for Philosophy.* Trans. N. Madarasz. Albany: State University of New York.
(2000) *Deleuze: 'The Clamor of Being'.* Trans. L. Burchill. Minneapolis: University of Minnesota Press.
(2001) *Ethics: An Essay on the Understanding of Evil.* Trans. P. Hallward. London: Verso.
(2003b) *On Beckett.* Trans. N. Power and A. Toscano. Manchester: Clinamen.
(2003c) *Saint Paul: The Foundation of Universalism.* Trans. R. Brassier. Stanford: Stanford University Press.
(2004b) *Theoretical Writings.* Trans. R. Brassier and A. Toscano. London: Continuum.
(2005b) *Being and Event.* Trans. Oliver Feltham. London: Continuum.
(2005c) *Handbook of Inaesthetics.* Trans. A. Toscano. Stanford: Stanford University Press.
(2005d) *Infinite Thought: Truth and the Return to Philosophy.* London: Continuum.
(2005e) *Metapolitics.* Trans. J. Barker. London: Verso.
(2006b) *Briefings on Existence.* Trans. N. Madarasz. Albany: State University of New York.
(2007b) *The Century.* Trans. A. Toscano. Cambridge: Polity.
(2007c) *The Concept of Model.* Trans. Z. L. Fraser and T. Tho. Melbourne: re.press.
(2008c) *Conditions.* Trans. S. Corcoran. London: Continuum.
(2008d) *The Meaning of Sarkozy.* Trans. D. Fernbach. London: Verso.
(2008e) *Number and Numbers.* Trans. R. Mackay. Cambridge: Polity.
(2009c) *Logic of Worlds: Being and Event 2.* Trans. A. Toscano. London: Continuum.
(2009d) *Pocket Pantheon: Figures of Postwar Philosophy.* Trans. David Macey. London: Verso.
(2009e) *Theory of the Subject.* Trans. B. Bosteels. London: Continuum.
(2010c) *The Communist Hypothesis.* Trans. David Macey. London: Verso.

Selected secondary works

Ashton, P. et al. (2006) *The Praxis of Alain Badiou*. Melbourne: re.press.

Barker, J. (2002) *Alain Badiou: A Critical Introduction*. London: Pluto.

Bartlett, A. J. and Clemens, J. (eds) (2010) *Alain Badiou: Key Concepts*. Durham: Acumen.

Bosteels, B. (2009) *Alain Badiou, une trajectoire polémique*. Paris: La Fabrique.

Calgagno, A. (2007) *Badiou and Derrida: Politics, Events and their Time*. London: Continuum.

Callinicos, A. (2006) *The Resources of Critique*. Cambridge: Polity.

Depoortere, F. (2009) *Badiou and Theology*. London: Continuum.

Feltham, O. (2008) *Alain Badiou: Live Theory*. London: Continuum.

Gibson, A. (2006) *Badiou and Beckett: The Pathos of Intermittency*. Oxford: Oxford University Press.

Hallward, P. (2003a) *Badiou: A Subject to Truth*. Minneapolis: University of Minnesota Press.

Hallward, P. (ed.) (2004) *Think Again: Alain Badiou and the Future of Philosophy*. London: Continuum.

Hewlitt, N. (2007) *Badiou, Balibar, Rancière: Rethinking Emancipation*. London: Continuum.

Johnston, A. (2009) *Badiou, Žižek, and Political Transformations: The Cadence of Change*. Evanston: Northwestern University Press.

Kacem, M. B. (2011) *Après Badiou*. Paris: Grasset.

Leclerc, J.-J. (2010) *Badiou and Deleuze Read Literature*. Edinburgh: Edinburgh University Press.

Miller, A. (2008) *Badiou, Marion and St Paul*. London: Continuum.

Mullarkey, J. (2006) *Post-Continental Philosophy: An Outline*. London: Continuum.

Norris, C. (2009) *Badiou's 'Being and Event': A Reader's Guide*. London: Continuum.

Pluth, E. (2010) *Badiou: A Philosophy of the New*. Cambridge: Polity.

Riera, G. (2005) *Alain Badiou: Philosophy and its Conditions*. Albany: State University of New York Press.

François Laruelle

Principal works

(1972) *Phénomène et différence. Essai sur l'ontologie de Ravaisson*. Paris: Éditions Klincksieck.

(1976) *Machines textuelles: déconstruction et libido d'écriture*. Paris: Éditions du Seuil.

(1977a) *Nietzsche contre Heidegger: thèses pour une politique nietzschéenne*. Paris: Payot.

(1977b) *Le Déclin de l'écriture*. Paris: Aubier-Flammarion.
(1978) *Au-delà du principe de pouvoir*. Paris: Payot.
(1981) *Le Principe de minorité*. Paris: Aubier.
(1985) *Une biographie de l'homme ordinaire. Des autorités et des minorités*. Paris: Aubier.
(1986) *Les Philosophies de la différence: introduction critique*. Paris: Presses universitaires de France.
(1989) *Philosophie et non-philosophie*. Liège: Pierre Mardaga.
(1991) *En tant qu'un*. Paris: Aubier.
(1992) *Théorie des identités*. Paris: Presses universitaires de France.
(1995) *Théorie des Étrangers*. Paris: Kimé.
(1996) *Principes de la non-philosophie*. Paris: Presses universitaires de France.
(1998a) *Discipline hérétique – esthétique psychanalyse religion*. Paris: Kimé.
(1998b) *Dictionnaire de la non-philosophie*. Paris: Kimé.
(2000) *Introduction au non-marxisme*. Paris: Presses universitaires de France.
(2002) *Le Christ futur*. Paris: Maisonneuve et Larose.
(2004) *La lutte et l'utopie à la fin des temps philosophiques*. Paris: Kimé.
(2005) *Homo ex machina*. Paris: L'Harmattan.
(2007a) *Mystique non-philosophique à l'usage des contemporains*. Paris: L'Harmattan.
(2007b) *Fabriques de l'insécurité*. Paris: L'Harmattan.
(2008) *Introduction aux sciences génériques*. Paris: Pétra.
(2010a) *Philosophie non-standard*. Paris: Kimé.

Works in translation

(2010b) *Future Christ*. Trans. A. P. Smith. London: Continuum.
(2010c) *Philosophies of Difference*. Trans. R. Gangle. London: Continuum.

Selected secondary works

Brassier, R. (2003) Axiomatic Heresy: The Non-Philosophy of Francois Laruelle, *Radical Philosophy* 121: 24–35.
Brassier, R. (2010) *Nihil Unbound: Enlightenment and Extinction*. Basingstoke: Palgrave Macmillan.
Bufalo, E. del (2003) *Deleuze et Laruelle: de la schizo-analyse à la non-philosophie*. Paris: Kimé.
Choplin, H. (1997) *De la phénoménologie à la non-philosophie: Levinas et Laruelle*. Paris: Kimé.
Choplin, H. (2000) *La Non-philosophie de François Laruelle*. Paris: Kimé.

Choplin, H. (2007) *L'espace de la pensée française contemporaine: à partir de Levinas et de Laruelle*. Paris: L'Harmattan.

Mollet, E. (2003) *Bourdieu et Laruelle: sociologie réflexive et non-philosophie*. Paris: Éd. Pétra.

Moulinier, D. (1998) *De la psychanalyse à la non-philosophie: Lacan et Laruelle*. Paris: Kimé.

Mullarkey, J. (2006) *Post-Continental Philosophy: An Outline*. London: Continuum.

Rannou, J.-L. (2005) *La Non-philosophie, simplement: une introduction synthétique*. Paris: L'Harmattan.

Other works cited

Alliez, E. (2010) What is – or What is Not – French Philosophy Today? *Radical Philosophy* 161: 9–17.

Althusser, L. (1996 [1965]) *Lire le Capital*. Paris: Presses universitaires de France.

Althusser, L. (2005) *For Marx*. Trans. B. Brewster. London: Verso.

Baron Cohen, S. (2004) *The Essential Difference*. New York: Basic Books.

Barthes, R. (1974) *S/Z*. Trans. R. Miller. New York: Farrar, Straus and Giroux.

Bataille, G. (1988) *Inner Experience*. Trans. L. A. Boldt. New York: State University of New York Press.

Baugh, B. (2003) *French Hegel*. London: Routledge.

Blanchot, M. (1993) *The Infinite Conversation*. Trans. S. Hanson. Minneapolis: University of Minnesota Press.

Changeux, J.-P. (1997) *Neuronal Man: The Biology of the Mind*. Princeton: Princeton University Press.

Chabot, C. B. (1982) *Freud on Schreber: Psychoanalytic Theory and the Critical Act*. Boston: University of Massachusetts Press.

Coole, D. and Frost, S. (eds) (2010) *New Materialisms: Ontology, Agency, Politics*. Durham, NC: Duke University Press.

Critchley, S. (1999) *Ethics, Politics, Subjectivity*. London: Verso.

Damasio, A. (1999) *The Feeling of What Happens: Body and Emotion in the Making of Consciousness*. San Diego: Harcourt Brace.

Damasio, A. (2006) *Descartes' Error*. London: Vintage.

Deleuze, G. (1990) Post-scriptum sur les sociétés de contrôle, *L'Autre journal* 1(49).

Deleuze, G. (2004a) *Desert Islands and Other Texts*. Trans. M. Taormina. New York: Semiotext(e).

Deleuze, G. (2004b) *Difference and Repetition*. Trans. Paul Patton. London: Continuum.

Deleuze, G. (2006) *The Fold: Leibniz and the Baroque*. Trans. Tom Conley. London: Continuum.

Derrida, J. (1976) *Of Grammatology*. Trans. G. C. Spivak. Baltimore: Johns Hopkins University Press.

Derrida, J. (1987) *Psyché. Inventions de l'autre II*. Paris: Galilée.

Derrida, J. (1991) *Donner le temps I*. Paris: Galilée.

Derrida, J. (1992) *Given Time I*. Trans. P. Kamuf. Chicago: Chicago University Press.

Derrida, J. (1994) *Spectres of Marx*. Trans. P. Kamuf. London: Routledge.

Derrida, J. (1996) *Speech and Phenomena*. Trans. D. B. Allison and N. Garver. Evanston: Northwestern University Press.

Derrida, J. (1998) *Of Grammatology*. Trans. G. C. Spivak. Baltimore: Johns Hopkins University Press.

Derrida, J. (2000) *Jean-Luc Nancy, Le Toucher*. Paris: Galilée.

Derrida, J. (2006) *On Touching – Jean-Luc Nancy*. Trans. C. Irizarry. Stanford: Stanford University Press.

Dosse, F. (1997) *History of Structuralism*. 2 vols. Trans. D. Glassman. Minneapolis: University of Minnesota Press.

Elliott, G. (ed.) (1990) *Philosophy and the Spontaneous Philosophy of the Scientists*. London: Verso.

ffrench, P. (1995) *The Time of Theory: A History of Tel Quel* (1960–1983). Oxford: Clarendon Press.

Foucault, M. (2002) *The Order of Things*. London: Routledge.

Foucault, M. (2010) *The Birth of Biopolitics: Lectures at the Collège de France, 1978–1979*. London: Picador.

Freud, S. (2003) *The Schreber Case*. Trans. A. Webber. Harmondsworth: Penguin.

Gazzaniga, M. S. (ed.) (2004) *The Cognitive Neurosciences*. Cambridge MA: MIT Press.

Gille, B. (1986) *History of Techniques*. Trans. P. Southgate and T. Williamson. New York: Gordon and Breach.

Gilson, E. (1992) *Le Thomisme*. Paris: Presses universitaires de France.

Gschwandtner, C. M. (2007) *Reading Jean-Luc Marion*. Bloomington: Indiana University Press.

Gutting, G. (2001) *French Philosophy in the Twentieth Century*. Cambridge: Cambridge University Press.

Gutting, G. (2011) *Thinking the Impossible: French Philosophy since 1960*. Oxford: Oxford University Press.

Habermas, J. (1984) *The Theory of Communicative Action*. Trans. T. McCarthy. Portsmouth: Heinemann.

Hallward, P. (2003b) The One and the Other: French Philosophy Today. *Angelaki* 8(2): 1–32.

Heidegger, M. (1993) *Basic Writings*. Ed. D. F. Krell. London: Routledge.

Heidegger, M. (1998) *Pathmarks*. Trans. W. McNeill. Cambridge: Cambridge University Press.

Henry, M. (1973) *The Essence of Manifestation*. Trans. G. Etzkorn. The Hague: Nijhoff.

Henry, M. (2009) *Seeing the Invisible*. Trans. S. Davidson. London: Continuum.

Husserl, E. (1970) *The Crisis of European Sciences and Transcendental Phenomenology*. Trans. D. Carr. Evanston: Northwestern University Press.

Husserl, E. (1991) *On the Phenomenology of the Consciousness of Internal Time*. Trans. J. B. Brough. Dordrecht: Kluwer.

Husserl, E. (1999) *Cartesian Meditations*. Trans. Dorion Cairns. Dordrecht: Kluwer.

Hyder, D. (2003) Foucault, Cavaillès, and Husserl on the Historical Epistemology of the Sciences. *Perspectives on Science* 11(1): 107–29.

Janicaud, D. (1990) *Le Tournant théologique de la phenomenologie française*. Paris: Éditions de l'Éclat.

Janicaud, D. (2005) *Phenomenology 'Wide Open': After the French Debate*. Trans. C. N. Cabral. New York: Fordham University Press.

Janicaud, D. et al. (2000) *Phenomenology and the 'Theological Turn': The French Debate*. New York: Fordham University Press.

Jeannerod, M. (2002) *La Nature de l'esprit*. Paris: Odile Jacob.

Kant, E. (2007) *The Critique of Judgment*. New York: Cosimo.

Klossowski, P. (2005) *Nietzsche and the Vicious Circle*. Trans. D. W. Smith. London: Continuum.

Lacan, J. (1988) *The Seminar of Jacques Lacan: Book 1*. Trans. J. Forrester. Cambridge: Cambridge University Press.

Lacan, J. (2011) *Le Séminaire livre XIX . . . ou pire*. Ed. Jacques-Alain Miller. Paris: Seuil.

Laplanche, J. and Pontalis, J.-B. (2011) *Fantasme originaire, fantasmes des origines, origines du fantasme*. Paris: Hachette.

Lecourt, D. (2002) *The Mediocracy: French Philosophy since the 1970s*. London: Verso.

LeDoux, J. (2003) *Synaptic Self: How our Brains Become Who We Are*. Harmondsworth: Penguin.

Leroi-Gourhan, A. (1993) *Gesture and Speech*. Trans. A. B. Berger. Cambridge, MA: MIT Press.

Levinas, E. (1983) *Le Temps et l'autre*. Paris: Presses universitaires de France.

Lilla, M. (1994) *New French Thought: Political Philosophy*. Princeton: Princeton University Press.

Lyotard, J.-F. (1988) *The Differend*. Trans. G. v.d. Abeele. Manchester: Manchester University Press.

Lyotard, J.-F. (2004) *Libidinal Economy*. Trans. I. H. Grant. London: Continuum.

Malpas, S. (2003) *Jean-François Lyotard*. London: Routledge.

Mauss, M. (2002) *The Gift*. Trans. W. D. Halls. London: Routledge.

Meillassoux, Q. (2010) *After Finitude: An Essay on the Necessity of Contingency*. London: Continuum.

Merleau-Ponty, M. (1968) *The Visible and the Invisible*. Evanston: Northwestern University Press.

Merleau-Ponty, M. (2002) *The Phenomenology of Perception*. London: Routledge.

Miller, D. (2000) *Citizenship and National Identity*. Cambridge: Polity.

Moore, G. (2011) *The Politics of the Gift: Exchanges in Poststructuralism*. Edinburgh: Edinburgh University Press.

Nietzsche, F. (1974) *The Gay Science*. Trans. W. Kaufman. London: Vintage.

Nietzsche, F. (1990) *Twilight of the Idols*. Trans. R. J. Hollingdale. Harmondsworth: Penguin.

Ricardou, J. (1973) *Le Nouveau Roman*. Paris: U.G.E.

Ricoeur, P. (1992) *History and Truth*. Evanston: Northwestern University Press.

Ricoeur, P. (2006) *Memory, History and Forgetting*. Trans. K. Blamey and D. Pellauer. Chicago: Chicago University Press.

Robbe-Grillet, A. (1989) *For a New Novel*. Trans. R. Howard. Evanston: Northwestern University Press.

Sartre, J.-P. (1969) *Being and Nothingness*. Trans. H. E. Barnes. London: Routledge.

Sharma, A. and Gupta, A. (2006) *The Anthropology of the State: A Reader*. Oxford: Blackwell.

Schrift, A. (2006) *Twentieth-Century French Philosophy*. Oxford: Blackwell.

Simondon, G. (1969) *Du mode d'existence des objets techniques*. Paris: Aubier.

Simondon, G. (1989) *L'Individuation psychique et collective*. Paris: Aubier.

Smith, D. (1996) *Transvaluations: Nietzsche in France 1872–1972*. Oxford: Clarendon Press.

Smith, D. (2007) The Conditions of the New. *Deleuze Studies* 1(1): 1–21.

Index